the **Food Lover's Companion** to the

NAPA

VALLEY

the Food Lover's Companion to the
NAPA
VALLEY

Where to Eat, Cook, and Shop in the Wine Country, Plus 50 Irresistible Recipes

BY LORI LYN NARLOCK

Foreword by Thomas Keller
Photographs by Michael Carabetta

CHRONICLE BOOKS
SAN FRANCISCO

DEDICATION To two extraordinary women: Laura, who has given me the gift of her friendship and all the riches that has included, and my sister Lisa, who provided a roof over my head when I first moved home and started me on a journey that resulted in this book.

Library of Congress Cataloging-in-Publication Data:

Narlock, Lori Lyn, 1962–
    The Food Lover's Companion to the Napa Valley : Where to Eat, Cook, and
Shop in the Wine Country, plus 50 Irresistible Recipes / by Lori Lyn Narlock ;
photographs by Michael Carabetta.
        p. cm.
    ISBN 0-8118-3619-3
    1. Food—Guidebooks. 2. Grocery trade—California—Napa
Valley—Guidebooks. 3. Restaurants—California—Napa
Valley—Guidebooks. 4. Cookery, American—California style. I. Title.
    TX354.5 .N37 2003
    641.3'1'02579419—dc21
                                2002010088

Manufactured in the United States of America.

Design by Annabelle Gould

Distributed in Canada by Raincoast Books
9050 Shaughnessy Street
Vancouver, BC V6P 6E5

10 9 8 7 6 5 4 3 2 1

Chronicle Books LLC
85 Second Street
San Francisco, California 94105

www.chroniclebooks.com

ACKNOWLEDGMENTS

First and foremost, I want to thank all of the creative, hardworking individuals who make Napa Valley the culinary delight that it is. I hope that I have done you justice in these pages.

A project of this scope would not have been possible without the help of many, many friends and colleagues. I'd like to begin by thanking my agent, Lisa Ekus, who said yes when the book was merely a sentence.

Chronicle Books is an amazing collection of talented individuals who produce especially beautiful books. I'd like to thank everyone who works there for their efforts, especially Bill LeBlond for giving this book the green light, Amy Treadwell for her infinite patience, and Michael Carabetta, whose wit and artist's eye made running around the Valley to shoot photos more fun than should be allowed.

I want to thank Monty Sander, who opened all kinds of doors for me in Napa and then pushed me through each one. He and his marvelous sidekick, Tom Fuller, have been phenomenal sources of information and inspiration.

I am extremely grateful to Thomas Keller for perfectly expressing what it is that makes the Napa Valley such a special place.

The chefs of Napa Valley are unsurpassable. Every day they step behind their stoves and transform raw ingredients into masterful meals. I especially owe thanks to those who contributed recipes to this book and who shared information and food with me.

Thank you to Lin Weber for writing her books on Napa history, *Old Napa Valley* and *Roots of the Present*. They were wonderful to read and an infinite source of information.

Along the way I had two wonderful friends help me with the busy work, Misty Johnston and Lauren Midgley. Their efforts were invaluable.

Numerous friends and colleagues endured my incessant requests for their opinions and ideas. I'd like especially to thank Brian and Kristina Streeter, Jamie Purviance, Ira Zuckerman, Anne Moses, John Bauccio, Sheila Franks, and Hilary Wolf.

I must also express my gratitude to Carol Cerreta, Shelby and Phil Mauldin, Caroline and Timmy Leigh-Wood, and Nicole Mauldin, who without reservation taste-tested every recipe in the book.

My deepest heartfelt thanks to my brother-in-law, Ed, and my friend Artie for the contributions they made to my life while I wrote this book.

And last but not least, I owe a debt of gratitude for all of the food professionals of Napa Valley, from the visionaries to the servers, who make it a pleasure to take a place at the table.

CONTENTS

FOREWORD

by Thomas Keller, The French Laundry

People often shyly ask me what I like to eat or what I think is a great meal. They seem to think that just because I cook the way I do at the French Laundry, my expectation of everywhere else I eat should be the same. Many are taken aback when I say that, just like everybody else, I enjoy eating simple food. To me, wonderful lentil soup with warm crusty bread, for instance, is an ideal choice on a cold rainy evening. Although the idea of eating truffles and foie gras every night might appeal to some, that's not being realistic—just as I don't expect a battery of thirty cooks preparing my dinner day in and day out.

What comprises a great meal? What is that fleeting je-ne-sais-quoi that elevates a good supper to a great one? It's a little bit of everything—but primarily I think it has something to do with timing. A hot dog can be the best hot dog you've ever had when you're eating it with your best friend you haven't seen in ages at a 49ers game and they're winning over Green Bay 21 to 3.

I am reminded of the fantastic meals that we had at my friend Bob Long's place while planning the opening of the French Laundry. Some nights I would be cooking; on others, dinner was the result of everyone's joint efforts. All the same, they were all wonderful and memorable feasts. We had it easier than most—surrounding us was local produce so fresh it made you want to weep. There was perfect company (everyone eagerly anticipating the inception of the restaurant), gorgeous food, and this stunning valley providing the backdrop for the evening. You could almost feel an electrical charge crackling in the air—moments frozen in my memory forever.

I can never get over how beautiful the Napa Valley is. Each season there is always a little something that surprises, that keeps you guessing, and that makes you fall in love with it all over again. I think that's what gives the French Laundry its aura. Aside from its historic past, the various people who owned and managed it gave it its personality; its location has somehow made it complete.

Napa Valley is like no other place on earth. This narrow stretch of fertile land has become the source of some of the world's greatest wines and home to some of the best restaurants in the world: a place people travel to from far and wide for the sole purpose of eating and drinking. Whether they are serious gourmands, oenophiles, or just curious, the profile is the same: They come for the food and wine.

That's why Lori's book is so important. It is about the very best in Napa. This exceptionally well-researched book provides inside information on where to go for the best of anything. It is not just for first-time visitors to the area, but for those of us who have made the Napa Valley our home. It will be especially helpful for those days when you want to hang out with close friends and you crave a different scene but can't think of a place to go. Or when you have family visiting for the first time and you're racking your brain over where to take them. Never again. With this book as a guide, there's always somewhere special just around the corner.

Bon appétit.

INTRODUCTION

Napa Valley has been described as "heaven on earth" by Francis Coppola, "surreal" by New York's food maven Arthur Schwartz, and "Disneyland for wine lovers" by the *Los Angeles Times*. I call it home.

I cook, shop, and eat in the Napa Valley every day. And not a day goes by that I don't feel grateful to live within such unabashed beauty and abundance. I grew up in the wine country, long before it was fashionable, when it was still mostly dairy farms and the wine industry was in its infancy. I moved away to experience urban life and returned for what was supposed to be a summer. That was many years ago.

The first day I was home I fell in love with the blue, blue skies, the verdant vineyards, and the smell of sun-warmed earth. I became enamored with the bountiful food and wine. I reveled in the company of others who appreciated it as much as I did. I couldn't believe my good fortune. And nothing made me happier than sharing it.

Friends and friends of friends came to me for recommendations when they were planning a visit. I was always pleased to suggest a restaurant, point out some must-sees, and create an itinerary. This book was conceived from those references.

I embarked on this project with the goal of sharing the best of Napa Valley with everyone. I wanted to enrich visitors' experience and create a handy reference for locals. In the process I developed a greater appreciation for this glorious place and the people who have shaped it.

When I began working on this book, one of the first people I spoke with was Victoria Gott, who owns Palisades Market in Calistoga with her sons, Joel and Duncan. During the course of our conversation she confided that her foot size has grown from an 8½ to a 10 due to the long hours spent on her feet tending to her business. That tiny confession stuck with me, and as I met and spoke with more people, its impression grew stronger.

Napa Valley's success as a food destination is due almost entirely to hardworking, incredibly creative, and dynamic individuals who are tireless in their efforts. True, Napa is blessed with extraordinary natural resources and a stellar location. But these raw materials would be for naught if it weren't for people like Victoria Gott, Thomas Keller, Don Watson, Donna Scala, and Bradley Kantor, to name a few, who devote their lives to creating unforgettable food.

How It All Came to Be

Powerful volcanoes and seismic activity are responsible for creating the alluvial plain that today is Napa Valley. One historical account mentions that ancient hunters found their way to this fertile land as early as twelve thousand years ago. They came to hunt giant lions, sloths, mammoths, bears, and wolves.

This image is quite a contrast to the lush vineyards, prolific wineries, and genteel vintners that have brought Napa Valley its more recent notoriety. Over the course of the last two–hundred–plus years, the fits and starts of such wine growing and production have defined Napa Valley's history.

The Wappos, the Valley's earliest residents, existed in the paradise that Napa Valley was in the early 1800s. The streams were crowded with steelhead salmon, trout, and freshwater eels. An abundance of deer, antelope, and elk lived on the land. And the earth was an unlimited source of edible goods, including acorns and buckeyes.

It was this Eden that José Altimira, a Franciscan father building California missions, rode into in 1823, forever changing the course of the Valley's future. His pronouncement that the fertile soil was ideal for raising livestock and growing vineyards initiated the demise of the Wappos and the birth of Napa Valley agriculture.

The land was quickly divided into land grants that were given to Spanish and Mexican nationals, who started cattle ranches. Nearly as quickly as cattle supplanted the indigenous animals in the Valley, and wine grapes were planted where wild grasses once grew.

George Yount, a native of North Carolina, was the first American settler to be given a land grant. He planted fruit trees, grain crops, and grapes, from which he is rumored to have made wine. The land he owned is now the site of some of the Valley's most revered cabernet sauvignon vineyards.

A shipwrecked Englishman, Edward Bale, also found his way here and married one of General Mariano Vallejo's nieces to obtain a land grant.

He built the Bale Grist Mill, an integral business and an important social gathering spot for much of the mid-1880s.

When the Bear Flag Rebellion, an overthrow of the Mexican government, occurred in 1846, the cattle ranches were taken over by new settlers and broken into smaller ranches, most of which were converted to crops. Within a couple of years, settlers had planted more than 150,000 walnut, apple, and peach trees in addition to an assortment of vegetables and grains. And when the Gold Rush hit, they sold their crops at a handsome profit to cash-rich miners.

One farm established around that time, the Trubody Ranch south of Yountville, still exists. The Trubodys planted thirty-five acres of blackberries and sold them at a nice price, according to current owners Jeff and Mary Page. Jeff's grandmother was the housekeeper for the Trubodys, and he grew up on the property. He and Mary purchased the ranch and live in the Trubody's original farmhouse.

Another remnant of that time is the rows of eucalyptus trees planted throughout the Valley as windbreaks to protect precious crops. Those planted by John Trubody, the ranch founder, are still on Highway 29 in the center divide.

About the same time, English settler John Patchett bought a parcel of land that had been the second land grant. He planted a vineyard and hired California's first wine maker, Charles Krug, who had been making wine in Sonoma. Krug then married the daughter of Edward Bale and received a dowry of five-hundred-plus acres on which he built his own winery and cellar, in the same location where they are today, north of St. Helena.

The 1850s were a time of rapid growth for wineries. More Europeans moved to Napa Valley to seek their fortunes as vintners. Far Niente, Greystone, Inglenook, and Trefethen were built (and designed by the same architect, Hamden McIntyre). Gustave Niebaum opened the Valley's first sample room at Inglenook, a sign of things to come.

By the mid-1880s, phylloxera wiped out the fledgling industry. Prune and walnut orchards replaced vineyards. The earlier established wine industry helped turn prunes into a prosperous business by using the same market channels that had developed for selling and shipping wine. The prunes were dried because they traveled better. As a result, fruit drying became a popular business also.

At the turn of the century, poultry and dairy farming began to take hold. Ambrosia Dairy, a business that would last for more than half a century, was established. Oakville, where some of the world's most expensive cabernet sauvignon grapes are grown today, was also used for dairy farms. More than 500,000 fruit, nut, and olive trees were growing in the Valley, as well as wheat, one of the most prolific crops, which by 1909 made up 10 percent of all wheat grown in the United States.

In 1902, when it was discovered that native St. George rootstock vines were phylloxera free and could be grafted with *Vitis vinifera* cuttings, the vineyards were replanted and the wine industry was revived.

It didn't last long. Nearly as soon as vintners started making wine, Prohibition was enacted and wine making came to a standstill. Grapes, which were still grown for sacramental wines, illegal alcoholic beverages, and as table fruit, began to suffer declining prices and prunes became a major crop again.

After Prohibition was repealed and World War II ended, the vineyards were rejuvenated. Within two decades, the valley was experiencing a Renaissance. People from all over the country, including the Davies, the Winiarskis, and the Barretts, moved to Napa Valley to join the families already here, like the Mondavis, the Martinis, and the Heitzes, to create an exciting new industry. Wineries were constructed and vineyards were planted. And in 1976 the wine world was changed forever when a famous French competition proclaimed Stags' Leap Wine Cellars and Chateau Montelena winners alongside French wines in a blind tasting.

A year later, Domaine Chandon opened the doors to their restaurant. After a rocky start as a buffet, the restaurant went upscale, bringing with it a new focus on fine dining. That same year, Don and Sally Schmitt established the French Laundry. Within ten years, Mustards, Auberge du Soleil, and Meadowood opened and California cuisine emerged.

Napa's first cooking school, Cuisine Renaissance, was established around the same time and began bringing in some of the world's most acclaimed food authorities, including Marcella Hazan, Diana Kennedy, and Biba Caggiano, to teach classes. Wineries also began shining a spotlight on food; Trefethen, Mondavi, Beringer, and other wineries began cooking classes to celebrate the marriage of food and wine.

In the ensuing thirty years, Napa Valley has become a wine and food destination. Ironically, it has also come full circle, from the Wappos' diet of indigenous foods to an august cuisine built on a foundation of seasonal local foods.

The Seasons

Napa Valley is often compared to Provence and Tuscany. It does share some of the same traits as those beautiful places, but Napa Valley is uniquely its own. A predominantly agricultural community, its lifestyle and livelihood are dictated by the seasons.

East Coasters may boast about their fall colors, but here in Napa Valley we can look at a vineyard and practically pinpoint the month by the appearance of the vine. Winter begins with bare canes waving in the wind while the green ground cover creates a lush carpet between rows of vines. By February the canes have been pruned, and the mustard begins to bloom. As spring hits, bud break, an almost magical appearance of new growth, prospers into lengthening canes that become heavier with leaves and small grape clusters as the weather warms up. By midsummer the clusters develop into full-sized clumps of berries, and as harvest nears the grapes morph into a spectrum of green and purple.

The year-round climate is ideal for growing grapes, working and playing outside, and cooking and dining outdoors. It rains November through

March, with plenty of sunshine between wet days. And typically after a few intermittent rainy days in spring, we enjoy a dry summer and autumn. Other than a dozen days of hard frost or extreme heat, the temperatures are moderate and comfortable year-round. The days are warm and mornings and evenings chilly, mostly the result of the cool marine influences from nearby San Francisco Bay.

Navigating Through the Valley

Napa Valley is a slim stretch of land approximately thirty miles long. It's crowned by Mount St. Helena at its northern tip and bordered by the San Francisco Bay on its southern edge, and in between there are six towns that range in population from three hundred to sixty thousand.

Two roads travel the entire length of the Valley, the St. Helena Highway at the base of the western mountain ranges and the Silverado Trail on the eastern side. The roads are separated by less than half a mile at the shortest point and only three miles at the longest, and the Valley itself is only one mile wide at its narrowest point and five miles at its widest.

Most visitors enter the Valley from the south, immediately entering the city of Napa, the gateway to the Valley and its largest township. Its lovely streets are filled with historic Victorian homes and stone buildings. The downtown area, which includes Copia: The American Center for Wine, Food, and the Arts, is compact enough to explore on foot.

Traveling north, the next town is Yountville. Though small, it has so many fabulous restaurants on its main street that it is often called the "gourmet ghetto" of Napa Valley. It too is pleasant to stroll through.

Oakville is so small that you will most likely pass it without realizing it. It has only one business other than wineries, the eponymous Oakville Grocery. The hamlet of Rutherford, barely larger than Oakville, has a market, a hotel, and a couple of restaurants.

The Victorian town of St. Helena is interesting and just large enough that you could spend a few days there without venturing farther and just small enough that it is easy to traverse on foot. It is bursting with superb restaurants, shops, and wineries.

At the very end of the Valley is Calistoga, looking like a set for a Western movie. Park your car and spend the day strolling the pretty, tree-lined side streets as well as the assortment of shops and restaurants on the main drag. Calistoga also is the most active of all the towns at night.

Although the Valley is relatively small, traveling from one spot to the next can be time-consuming due to the relatively small roadways versus the traffic on those roads. When planning your itinerary, consider breaking your days into two or three blocks of time and focusing on one area for each block, including breakfast and lunch. For dinner, consider dining near your lodging, as the roads at night can seem very long.

How to Use This Book

I've written this book as though I were making suggestions for a friend. I chose places and products that time and time again demonstrated quality and reliability. That's not to say that some not featured in these pages don't have appeal.

This book is not an all-inclusive list of every food-related business in the Valley. Instead, it is a subjective collection of eateries, producers, individuals, and other businesses that appeal to food lovers, compiled from my own experiences and suggestions from friends and colleagues.

As you read through this book, you will find a few listings that have an address in a neighboring town or county. I've included them because they sell a product that is worthy of recognition and is available here.

A book of this nature always battles time. By the time this book is published, some businesses may no longer exist and others will have sprung into life. For this reason, and also because many businesses are seasonal, I recommend always calling ahead to check the hours and accessibility of any place you want to visit.

Addresses and hours are listed only for businesses open to the public. Napa Valley is home to a great number of cottage producers, some of whom don't even have a published phone number. When this is the case, I have included a list of retailers or restaurants where their products are available as well as at least one way to reach them for further information.

Please check my Web site, www.foodinista.com, for regular postings of new businesses and other Napa Valley culinary news.

THE NAPA VALLEY

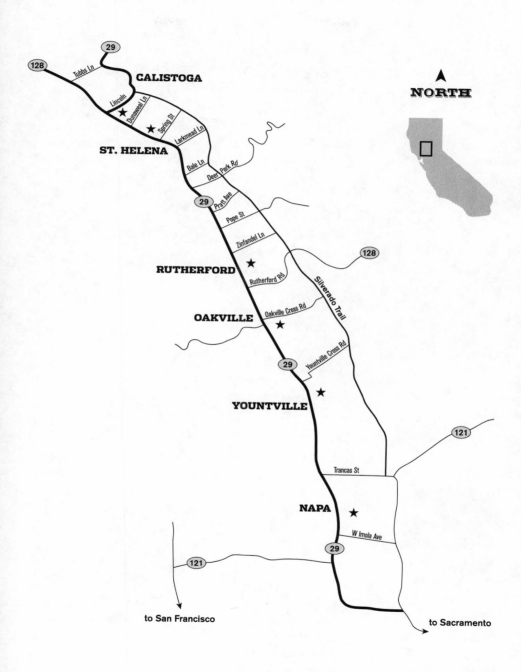

CORNUCOPIA

Where to Eat, Drink, Shop, Learn,
and Generally Make Merry in the Napa Valley

Model Bakery's brick ovens.

BAKERIES

We are bread eaters here in Napa Valley, and we have been since Edward Bale was shipwrecked, found his way to St. Helena (then still under Mexico's government), and built a gristmill to turn the Valley's grain, corn, and wheat into flour. Today, Napa Valley is the home to a wide variety of bakeries, from Model Bakery, which bakes staples like sourdough bread, to Perfect Endings, which is renowned for its elaborate, show-stopping wedding cakes. Whether you are in the market for a luscious blackberry pie (ABC) or the best peanut butter cookie in the world (Sweetie Pies), you will find it here.

Alexis Baking Company and Café

1517 Third Street, Napa
Mon–Fri 6:30am–6pm, Sat 7:30am–3pm, Sun 8am–2pm

(707) 258 1827

ABC, as regulars call it, is a study in understatement. The to-die-for baked sweets are displayed in a glass case almost hidden underneath the counter where orders are taken. The other treats are merely listed on a handwritten menu board and include homemade English muffins, focaccia sandwiches, and Caesar salads. Standing at the counter offers a peek into the kitchen and at the two Airstream-trailer-sized ovens, from which emerge ABC's signature breads, including the coveted potato bread rolls. These soft, yeasty rolls are used for the breakfast sandwiches—the ham, white Cheddar, and egg can't be beat—and the lunch fare, including juicy burgers and grilled chicken sandwiches. For dessert, choose a snickerdoodle, chocolate chip, or shortbread cookie, or a slice of cake. Their chocolate caramel cake is addictive, and the carrot and coconut cakes are the stuff dreams are made of. (Alexis also bakes superb wedding cakes.) If you can't make it to the cheerfully painted bakery itself, Dean & DeLuca, Sunshine Foods, and Cal Mart all carry goods from ABC.

Butter Cream Bakery

2297 Jefferson Street, Napa
Open daily 5:30am–7:30pm

(707) 255 6700

The garish pink-and-white-striped **Butter Cream Bakery** is a Napa institution. There isn't a child in the Valley that didn't cut his or her teeth on Butter Cream's doughnut holes. Their doughnuts have been made with the same family recipe since the doors opened to let in the first crowd of customers. Equally popular are their old-fashioned bakery sheet cakes, including their signature Champagne cake. Layers of light, airy white cake are filled and frosted with a frosting that tastes like spun sugar and chardonnay grapes, and decorated with a buyer's choice of greeting and design, everything from clusters of purple grapes to colorful clowns. Less well known is the superb English muffin bread, the pumpkin pies sold during the holidays, and the dinner rolls that melt in your mouth. The fifties-style diner inside the bakery is a great place to grab a quick breakfast or pair a pastry with a cup of coffee.

Model Bakery

1357 Main Street, St. Helena
Tues–Sat 7am–6pm, Sun 8am–4pm

(707) 963 8192

Do not go to **Model Bakery** hungry, or decision making will be excruciatingly painful. There are just too many loaves of tempting bread lined up against the wall, scrumptious pastries on the counter, and mouthwatering creations in the refrigerator case. Everything looks appetizing. The coup de grace is the rustic Italian-style breads made with organic flour and baked in the two brick ovens installed when the bakery was built in 1920. Enjoy a slice of dense sourdough made with wild yeast from wine grapes, or the light, airy ciabatta, with a bowl of homemade soup. In the morning, try their sour cream cinnamon muffins, pecan sticky buns, cranberry buttermilk scones, or their renowned Good Morning Buns. Don't let the afternoon slip by without one of their toothsome cookies, immodest concoctions including peanut butter cookies studded with semisweet chocolate, almond macaroons, and molasses ginger cookies. Or go for one of their mile-high lemon bars, apricot-oatmeal bars, or brownies. And if you go at the end of the day, all the baked goods are half price.

Passini Sciambra French Bakery

685 South Freeway Drive, Napa

(707) 252 3072

Owner Carl Sciambra's claim to fame is that he introduced the baguette to Napa Valley. In 1982, friend and vintner Darryl Sattui returned from a trip to Europe at the same time Carl and his wife, Barbara, bought **Passini Sciambra** and moved it to Napa. Darryl convinced the Sciambras to create a baguette like those he ate in France. The Sciambras followed his advice and in turn launched a thriving business. Their bread is served at nearly every deli and is available in most grocery stores in Napa Valley.

Perfect Endings

912 Enterprise Way, Napa

(707) 259 0500 Would you eat a red ski boot? What about a baby grand piano? A diner-style jukebox? You would if it was baked by **Perfect Endings**, because underneath its unbelievably realistic appearance would be one of the moistest, lightest, most delicious cakes that you have ever tasted. Perfect Endings is one of the most prestigious cake bakers in Northern California because owner Sam Godfrey always followed his grandmother's credo of using only the best ingredients. At her side he learned to cook watching Julia Child on television—her ploy to keep him out of trouble in the North Richmond neighborhood where they lived. A serendipitous foray into chocolatier Alice Medrich's famed Cocolat in Berkeley in the eighties transformed Sam's life. His love affair with cooking had a new focus: pastries. After baking his way through high school, Godfrey spent a month at Cordon Bleu in Paris, returned to the States, and began baking up a storm at supermarkets around the Bay Area. Soon he was baking cakes on his own, and in the mid-1990s he moved shop to Napa, where he's worked his pastry magic for Sophia Coppola, Oprah Winfrey, and George Lucas, to name a few. Of the up to fifteen hundred cakes that Perfect Endings bakes each year, wedding cakes are a large percentage of the output. Multitiered architectural masterpieces are assembled out of layers of square cakes, round cakes, and custom-shaped cakes, sometimes reaching heights as high as eleven feet. Each magnificent structure is then iced with an ambrosial buttercream or fondant and decorated with opulent displays of organic flowers, handmade sugar flowers, extravagant grape clusters, crystallized fresh cherries, or autumn leaves made with buttercream. The choices include banana cake with layers of cream cheese filling; carrot cake made with freshly ground spices; and yellow cake with lemon mousse filling, cream cheese, and whole berries or apricot purée. Then there are their chocolate cakes, which instantly reveal pastry chef Michael Martin's passion for his work. Choose from a mocha sponge cake with a chocolate Bavarian center, a chocolate cake with a bittersweet filling, and a chocolate cake with chocolate-hazelnut frosting. Brides are encouraged to call up to six months ahead to order wedding cakes. Others wishing to purchase a special-occasion custom cake should call two to three weeks in advance. A retail operation is in the works.

Schat's Bakery

1353 Lincoln Avenue, Calistoga
Sun–Mon, Wed–Thurs 6am–6pm, Fri–Sat 6am–10pm

(707) 942 0777

Before opening **Schat's Bakery,** Jan Schat practiced his craft at Il Fornaio and he won first prize in the "Olympics of baking," La Coupe du Monde de la Boulangerie, an elite international baking competition held every three years in Paris. Try his baguette or one of his other bread creations, such as the black mission fig bread made with organic whole-wheat flour, or his deluxe raisin bread, a medley of raisins, candied orange peel, and olive oil. The bakery also offers cookies, European pastries, and gelato.

Sweetie Pies

520 Main Street, Napa   www.sweetiepies.com
*Mon–Wed 6:30am–5pm, Thurs–Sat 6:30am–6pm,
Sun 7am–2pm*

(707) 257 7280

Walking into **Sweetie Pies** in the renovated historic Hatt Building is like taking a step back in time. The warm wood walls, farm tables, and cake-stand display on an oversized breakfront will make you think you've stepped into the Waltons' dining room. The country-kitchen atmosphere invites you to sit down, sip a cup of coffee, and savor each bite of your choice from the wonderful selection of cookies, cakes, and even savory tarts and quiches. The white chocolate cheesecake is their best-selling cake, but their selection of layer cakes, from the cappuccino, a chocolate layer cake filled with chocolate truffle and mocha mousse, to the almond cake, a white cake filled with caramel and pastry cream certainly won't inspire buyer's remorse. They are all delectable. The menu is seasonal, so in winter you'll be able to nosh on such treats as pear spice muffins with pecans, and sunburst cake, a yellow cake filled with blood-orange curd and finished with orange buttercream frosting. And all of the layer cakes are available in individual sizes, so buy a few the next time you entertain and you'll be able to try them all.

CAKE FAIRIES "Everyone should be remembered on their birthday." This is the founding principle of Napa's most popular bakers. The Cake Fairies, begun by altruist Jenny Valassopoulas, is a private group of do-gooders who bake and deliver cakes for nearly one hundred people a month. Thirty to forty cakes are delivered to teenagers at Juvenile Hall, and twice that many go to Los Niños County Preschool, a program for children living below the poverty level with a single parent, and one is delivered to a retirement home for a group celebration. With only her own wind beneath her fairy wings, Jenny conceived and instituted the idea. The Cake Fairies, self-funded plus a few donations, have grown from an original eight to thirty active fairies, who are predominantly women along with a handful of men. When a birthday arrives, the appointed fairy bakes a cake, dons his or her wings and name badge, delivers the cake and a card to the birthday boy or girl, takes his or her picture, puts it in a frame, and leaves. The delivery lasts only five to ten minutes, but the impact can last a lifetime.

Artisan Bakers

750 West Napa Street, Sonoma   www.artisanbakers.com
Mon–Sat 6:30am–3pm, Sun 6:30am–2pm

(707) 939 1765   Pure alchemy is the only way to describe how four basic ingredients—flour, salt, yeast, and water—can be combined to produce **Artisan Bakers'** range of incredible breads. The brother-and-sister baking team of Craig and Elizabeth Ponsfort opened their Sonoma bakery to rave reviews in 1992 and continue to be a favorite in Northern California. Closed only three days during the year, the bakery's staff of twelve bakers work around the clock—twenty-four hours a day, seven days a week—to bake more than a dozen different types of bread as well as cookies, cakes, and pastries. Every loaf baked by Artisan deserves consideration, especially their two best-selling breads, their dry jack and roasted garlic sourdough, a rustic loaf filled with melted cheese and piquant garlic, and their pugliese, light, airy bread with a perfect pale crust. Artisan Bakers' breads are available at Vallergas, Dean & DeLuca, Sunshine Foods, and Oakville Grocery. And a visit to their Web site is nearly as fulfilling as a trip to the bakery itself.

Basque Boulangerie Café

460 First Street East, Sonoma
Open daily 7am–6pm

(707) 935 7687   The apple doesn't fall far from the tree, at least for Françoise Hodges, whose parents opened the Sonoma French Bakery in the 1950s. When my family moved to the town of Sonoma twenty years later, one of the first places we discovered was the Guerras' bakery. The French breads and pastries baked by Françoise's father were heavenly. The bread became a staple in our lives. My parents converted friends and family into fans as well, and we never went anywhere without a loaf of this bread as a house gift. When I moved to go to college, my father always sent a loaf in his care packages. A few years later, the Guerras sold the bakery. And then a sort of culinary miracle occurred. Their daughter, Françoise, who had been reared in the back of her parents' bakery, opened the **Basque Boulangerie Café** a few doors down from where her parents had baked baguettes, pull-away loaves, and pastries. She and her partner, Jack Montaldo, who worked for her father for twenty-odd years, have resurrected her parents' repertoire of recipes and

have expanded the business to include many of the same delicious foods that you would find in a Paris café, from croques-monsieur to niçoise salads. You won't find a better croissant outside of Paris, but you will find Basque Boulangerie breads in several Napa Valley grocery stores, including Vallergas and Safeway.

Della Fattoria

Petaluma
dellafattoria@home.com

(707) 763 5538

"You're a crust eater," Kathleen Weber quickly surmised when I began to tell her which of her breads are my favorites. I had never thought of myself that way, but bakers view the world differently. **Della Fattoria** has built its reputation by developing its own unique method: Kathleen and her husband, Ed Weber, bake their breads in their own backyard, using a starter made with their own grapes, which is fed several times a day. Every night the ovens are filled with wood, and when the ovens are hot enough, the hand-shaped breads are added. The perfectly crusted, extremely flavorful breads are offered in several styles, from their signature rosemary and Meyer lemon topped with rock salt to their campagna, a rustic Italian loaf, and their roasted garlic and cheese to their épi, a crust person's bread. Della Fattoria's breads are sold at Dean & DeLuca, Oakville Grocery, Browns Valley Market, and Sunshine Foods.

Calistoga's delivery truck.

BEVERAGES

Wine of course is Napa's most famous beverage, but not its only one. Springwater was once a major industry. Water collected from natural springs in the ground was bottled and sold to slake the thirst of the health-minded visitors who came to the Valley's spas. Fruit juices made from grapes have a long history in Napa Valley, especially during Prohibition, when many vintners turned their efforts towards nonalcoholic beverages. Milk, cider, soft drinks, beer, brandy, and even whiskey have played a role in the history of Napa's beverage industry. Today, a handful of exceptional drinks are produced here.

Calistoga Mineral Water Company

Calistoga
www.calistogawater.com

(800) 365 4446

The Wappo Indians, Napa Valley's first residents, discovered the mineral waters that pepper the land in Calistoga. They bathed in the mineral pools and drank the water mixed with the juices of wild berries. In 1920, long after Calistoga had gained recognition as a resort town, soda fountain owner Giuseppe Musante made Calistoga water famous by carbonating it. Customers clamored for the effervescent liquid and wanted to buy it for drinking at home. Giuseppe founded the **Calistoga Bottling Works** on Lincoln Avenue. Today, the water is still harvested from geothermal sources in Calistoga and bottled directly from the source.

Napa Valley Soda Company

P.O. Box 1143, Calistoga
www.nvsoda.com

(707) 963 3474

Markley LaPointe had a dream. He wanted to produce an all-natural soda that would be as high in quality as the wines of Napa Valley and just as tantalizing. Like a chemist, he went to work combining as many as sixty to eighty natural extracts with beet sugar and water to create complex sodas that taste as good as any you'll ever try. Each **Napa Valley Soda** is named after a famous wine region, such as Oakville Orange, Rutherford Root Beer, and Chimney Rock Cherry, a grown-up's soda that will thrill your palate. And the glass bottles are fun to serve at parties and backyard barbecues.

Spa Tea

Napa Valley Spa Products
421 Walnut Street, No. 204, Napa

(707) 257 9808
(800) 963 3432

Jeanette O'Gallagher, the founder of Napa Valley Spa Products, developed her **Spa Teas** to complement the spa experience. As your skin is being nourished and moisturized from the outside with scrubs, masks, and oils, these teas work from the inside out. There are three flavors, Green Tea and Lemon Pick-Me-Up, Passion Fruit with Rose Hips and Hibiscus, and Chamomile Rose. The

THE APPELLATIONS OF TEAS Had Sam Brannan, Calistoga's founding father, succeeded with the tea plantation he developed in the late 1800s, Darjeeling, Ceylon, and Pekoe—teas named for the regions where they were originally grown—might have shared more than just geographical naming devices with wine, they may have shared Napa Valley terroir. Ironically, tea and wine do have traits in common, such as both are high in antioxidants and just as all wine grapes are grown from *Vitus vinifera*, all black, green, and oolong teas are permutations of the same plant, *Camellia sinensis*. The only question is, what do you pair with a cup of Earl Grey, red meat or fish?

❖

first, the only caffeinated one of the bunch, is a vibrant burst of citrus with white grape seeds, spearmint, green and black teas, lemon and orange peel, and lemongrass. The second, an almost-sweet elixir that tastes like a tropical paradise, is made from red wine grape seeds, hibiscus, chicory, and rose hips. And the third literally makes you stop and smell the roses, since that's one of the primary ingredients along with red and white grape seeds, chamomile, and orange peel. They are available at Auberge du Soleil, Meadowood, and Health Spa Napa Valley.

NOTEWORTHY NEIGHBORS
Mighty Leaf Tea

480 Gate 5 Road, No. 118, Sausalito
www.mightyleaf.com

(415) 331 3409 **Mighty Leaf Tea,** founded by husband-and-wife team Jill Portman and Gary Shinner, features three kinds of whole-leaf teas: black, green, and herbal. All are sold in soft fabric tea bags, which feel luxuriant in your hand and are designed to enhance the steeping process. The open weave of the fabric allows the water to surround the tea leaves better. And while the teas steep, they release intoxicating aromas, especially those flavored with herbs, flowers, and other botanicals. Vanilla Bean, for example, pairs Madagascar vanilla beans with Ceylon and China black teas, and the Ginger

Twist lists Guatemalan lemongrass among its herbal ingredients. The mint tea's flavor is so vivid that it's almost like drinking a tea made from freshly crushed mint leaves. These teas deliver what they promise: mightiness in aroma, body, and taste. They are served at Sweetie Pies and the Meadowood and Auberge du Soleil spas and restaurants.

Straus Family Creamery

P.O. Box 768, Marshall   www.strausmilk.com
Mon–Sat 7am–7pm, Sun 7am–6pm

(415) 663 5464   **Straus Family Creamery** makes shakers or spooners out of people—either you shake a bottle of milk to dislodge the dollop of cream resting on the top or you open a new bottle just to reach in with a spoon and scoop it out. In addition to whole, low-fat, and nonfat milk, they produce cream, half-and-half, chocolate milk, European-style butter, yogurt, and cheese. Straus is also the first dairy to introduce a yogurt smoothie that is free from any preservatives or additives. The ambrosial concoctions of nonfat yogurt, nonfat milk, and fruit or vanilla bean powder are sold in single serving sizes—perfect for a healthy snack on the run. The smoothies taste as rich as the cream that floats on top of their milk, and if they have separated, a little shake will make them ready to drink. Buy Straus's milks and yogurts at Vallergas and Dean & DeLuca.

Wolf Coffee

Sonoma County
www.wolfcoffee.com

(800) 808 7089   Strong, full-bodied, and yet smooth with a creamy mouth feel, **Wolf Coffee** is to the breakfast table what a quintessential Napa Valley cabernet is to the dinner table, a powerful taste sensation. After more than a decade and four Sonoma County stores, owners Rick and Jeanne Mariani have moved into Napa territory with sales of their beans at a few stores. Their coffees are dark roasted and robustly flavored, much like Peet's, the popular Bay Area roaster and retailer, and aren't for the fainthearted. Look for Wolf Coffee at Longs Drugs.

The historic façade of the Silverado Brewing Company.

BREWERIES AND BREWPUBS

"It takes a lot of beer to make good wine," the favorite motto of many of the Valley's wine makers, is a sentiment that clearly reflects the quality and taste of the beers made here. Beer has long been a popular beverage in Napa Valley, beginning with the efforts of James Dowell in the mid-1800s. According to Lin Weber, in her book *Old Napa Valley,* not only did Dowell plant hops and grains and brew beer, he also held an annual Hop Pickers Ball. Lin also points out that a man named George Blaufuss is reputed to have brewed Golden Ribbon Beer later, during Prohibition, at his brewery, on Soscol Avenue while the authorities looked the other way. Today, Napa Valley's brewers are legal and all offer a great pint of beer—the perfect palate cleanser after a day of wine tasting.

Calistoga Inn

1250 Lincoln Avenue, Calistoga   www.calistogainn.com
Open daily 11:30am–11pm

(707) 942 4101

When the **Calistoga Inn** began brewing beers in 1987 they were the first to do so commercially in Napa Valley in more than half a century. The beers brewed on-site, including Wheat Ale, Pilsner, Red Ale, and Porter, have been recognized in several brewing competitions. But award-winning beer is only one reason to visit the Calistoga Inn. Its location in one of Calistoga's historic buildings, an inn that was built in the early 1900s, offers a rustic pub setting in which to enjoy a pint. An outdoor garden area is the perfect location to enjoy a cold drink and respite from the grueling heat of summer—Calistoga is the hottest location in the Napa Valley, with temperatures often rising above the 100-degree mark. Another draw for tourists and locals alike is the rollicking live music played in the pub on Friday and Saturday nights.

Downtown Joe's

902 Main Street, Napa   www.downtownjoes.com
*Mon–Thurs 10am–12am, Fri 10am–2am, Sat 8:30am–2am,
Sun 8:30am–12am*

(707) 258 2337

Downtown Joe's is a popular place to meet friends on Friday night, to listen to live music on Saturday night, or to take in a game during brunch on Sunday. Joe Ruffino, the owner of this lively gathering spot, is a third-generation Napa restaurateur. His lively brewpub is located in the century-old Art Deco Oberon Building, on the edge of the Napa River. The brewmaster makes beer on the premises at least four times a week, ensuring that every glass poured by the chatty staff will be fresh. They have a beer for everyone, from their Victory Dark Ale, a beer made with just enough chocolate malt to add a robust, dark-roasted flavor, to their Golden Ribbon American Beer, a light-bodied domestic-style beer named after one of the Valley's first breweries.

Mount St. Helena Brewing Company

21167 Calistoga Street, Middletown   www.mtsthelenabrew.com
Sun–Thurs 11am–8:30pm, Fri–Sat 11am–9pm

(707) 987 3361   Named for the mountain that separates the brewery from the Napa Valley, **Mount St. Helena Brewing Company** makes their beers with water mined from 150 feet of rock and soil. Unlike their Valley counterparts, Mount St. Helena's beers are bottled and sold throughout the Valley. Their Palisades Pale Ale is clean and refreshing, and their India Pale Ale is exactly what it should be: a dry, hoppy beer with the essence of flowers and citrus. They also make an authentic English-style brown ale and honey wheat ale.

Silverado Brewing Company

3020A North St. Helena Highway, St. Helena
Open daily 11:30am–9:30pm

(707) 967 9876   The 1890 building that houses the **Silverado Brewing Company** is an awesome structure made of lava rock mined from nearby Glass Mountain. It was originally built as a winery for Josephine Tychson, the first woman vintner in California. She sold it a few years later, and after changing hands a couple more times, it became the Freemark Abbey Winery, a conflation of the owners' names. Its current incarnation as a brewery is fitting, given that the area was once a thriving wheat- and grain-growing region and just a few miles down the road was the area's most prolific hops fields. All six beers, which are brewed a few times a week, are organic, including their most popular, the whimsically named Certifiably Blond, the lightest of the bunch. Owner Mike Fradilizio is so passionate about his craft that he's captured the attention of the Culinary Institute of America, which he's working with to develop a beer curriculum. This is a great spot to hang out with cellar rats and wine makers at the end of the day, and why not? Their beers are delicious, there's always a game on, and live music fills the air on Friday and Saturday nights. Another reason to patronize Silverado is that they sell kegs in varying sizes.

DO-IT-YOURSELF Napa Fermentation Supplies is the wine maker's department store. They sell virtually everything a wine maker or beer brewer needs, from crushers to bottle tops, from grapes to hops, from books to barrel thieves. Owner Pat Watkins, a wine- and beer-making instructor at Napa Valley College, is usually on hand to offer advice about supplies and techniques. If you want more comprehensive instruction, Pat can be coerced into teaching a private class or two. Napa Fermentation Supplies is located right inside the fairgrounds at 575 Third Street, Napa, (707) 255 6372. Mon–Fri 9am–5pm, Sat 10am–5pm.

The ever-popular Taylor's Refresher.

BURGERS

Burgers are personal, like a preference for a perfume or a particular brand of toothpaste. If you fancy a gourmet version, Taylor's has one for you. If you want a classic—a big beef patty stacked with the standard toppings—Big D's or Red Rock is a good bet.

A&W Restaurant & Ice Cream Parlour

501 Main Street, St. Helena   www.a-wrootbeer.com
Sun–Thurs 10am–9pm, Fri–Sat 10am–10pm

(707) 963 4333   It would be easy to dismiss **A&W** as a relic supported by the high school across the street. But the icy cold root beer that tastes the same as it always has and is still served in the familiar frosty mug makes it a destination for lots of folks. The sandwiches and fries aren't bad for fast food, and when you finish your lunch with a root beer float the whole experience can be a treat. The first A&W, coincidentally, was started in 1919, in Lodi, California, the town where Robert Mondavi spent his adolescence.

Big D Burgers

1005 Silverado Trail, Napa
Mon–Fri 11am–8pm, Sat–Sun 11am–7pm

(707) 255 7188   **Big D** is definitely the place to get a workingman's lunch. The parking lot is always filled with trucks, and men in uniforms and boots are lined up two to three deep at the counter. The fare is pure American: burgers, fries, and milk shakes. Burger sizes start at one-quarter pound and move up the scale to a full pound. There are also chili dogs, corn dogs, fish and chips, tuna salad sandwiches, deep-fried burritos, BLTs, twister fries, crinkle-cut fries, chili fries, onion rings, and soup with garlic bread. You can't miss the building, with its vintage images of a boy and a girl each holding a plate of food high above their head.

Red Rock and Back Door BBQ

1010 Lincoln Avenue, Napa
Summer: 11am–10pm; Winter: Mon–Wed 11am–9pm,
Thurs–Sat 11am–9:30pm

(707) 226 2633   There are those who swear by the restorative properties of a **Red**
(707) 252 9250   **Rock** burger after a night of overindulgence. Their burgers are piled high with shredded lettuce, sliced tomatoes, dill pickles, and your choice of other toppings, including blue cheese, bacon, and grilled onions. The fries are crisp but aren't salted, so you'll have to adjust the seasoning to your liking. They have a variety of other

items on the menu, and most are kid friendly for those with children in their group. The barbecue half of the business offers the usual fare, from ribs to chicken and sides.

Taylor's Automatic Refresher

933 Main Street, St. Helena
Open daily 11am–9pm

(707) 963 3486 Part kitsch, part nouvelle burger cuisine, **Taylor's** is a Napa Valley landmark, founded in 1949. Five decades and at least that many owners later, Joel and Duncan Gott purchased it and gave it a face-lift. They added a wine bar, and an excellent one at that. They transformed the burger menu into an extravaganza of choices, including the Blue Cheeseburger, Bacon Cheeseburger, Western Bacon Blue Ring, Texas Burger, and a classic patty melt. And burgers are just the tip of the iceberg. There is a hot dog, chili dog, mini corn dogs, grilled cheese (the best), veggie burger, ahi burger, pulled pork, tuna melt, and three delectable, albeit messy, chicken sandwich creations. Try the Miss Kentucky (chicken, jack cheese, grilled onions, mushrooms, tomato, slaw, barbecue sauce, and ranch dressing), a dry cleaner's dream. And it goes on. There are tacos, fish creations, chili, salads, milk shakes, fries, garlic fries, and onion rings. The onion rings aren't only good, they're absolutely addictive. Don't pass them up. At lunchtime the place is packed. But there are several picnic tables on the property, and you never know who you'll be sharing them with; it could be Joe Montana and his brood or the acclaimed wine critic Robert Parker Jr., who famously bestowed a very high rating on the burgers.

NOTEWORTHY NEIGHBORS

Happy Dog

18762 Sonoma Highway, Sonoma
Tues–Sun 11am–8pm

(707) 935 6211 **Happy Dog**'s burgers are so good they could bring Wimpy to tears. The secret is the barbecue sauce that is squirted on the burgers while they are still on the grill, just before they are placed on a perfectly toasted bun. A burger at Happy Dog is the only reason anyone who loves burgers needs to make the thirty-minute drive to Sonoma.

Gordon's in Yountville.

CAFÉS AND CASUAL RESTAURANTS

It's hard to get a bad meal in Napa. The challenge is picking just one restaurant per meal.

Here are several restaurants and cafés that cook up an unforgettable plate of food and

serve it in a relaxed atmosphere that won't stress your wallet.

Café Kinyon

Vintage 1870, Yountville
Open daily 11:30am–2pm

(707) 944 2247

Café Kinyon's dining room is much too nice to be hawking a sandwich and salad menu. But it does, during the lunch hour. The rest of the time, the brick-walled room with its metal sculptures by artist Jack Chandler is rented for events. Pop in for lunch and choose between a Cobb salad, a shrimp Louis, or a Thai chicken salad. From the sandwich side of the menu, choose the five-layer club, roast beef au jus, or the Thanksgiving turkey that's served every day. Their menu claims "the world's best" for a few items. This may be a little overstated, but they do show incomparable small-town hospitality. When my bill came and I realized they don't accept Visa, I was told I could send them a check when I got home—that doesn't happen often in the City.

Café Lucy

1408 Clay Street, Napa
Lunch: Tues–Sat 11am–3pm; Dinner: Thurs–Fri 5:30–9:30pm

(707) 255 0110

The word *quaint* describes this small café with its menu of country-French-inspired dishes. The lunchtime crowd is mainly folks who work in the area and want something different than the typical sandwich. At night, **Café Lucy** is a sweet locale that invites lingering over final sips of wine after dinner. The eclectic menu, all of which is prepared in a thimble-sized kitchen, includes such dishes as Fresh Peach, Plum, Fig, Navel Orange, Red Onion, and Basil Salad; Roast Pork Loin with Olive-Dijon Crust and Caramelized Onion Sandwich; and Oven-Roasted Salmon with Herb Pesto and Gratinéed Potatoes. There are lots of small plates, including Provençal Onion Tart, Rustic Chicken Liver Pâté with Balsamic and Capers and Crostini, and a medley of seasonal vegetable dishes. Many of the ingredients are organic and grown locally, including greens from Canyon Acres. The wine list includes mainly French wines with some domestic labels added to the mix. Dine outside in the vine-canopied yard when the weather is nice.

Café Sarafornia

1413 Lincoln Avenue, Calistoga
Open daily 7am–3pm

(707) 942 0555   Named for the famous slip made by town founder Sam Brannan, who when explaining his plans for the area stated he would make it the Calistoga of Sarafornia. **Café Sarafornia** hums with morning chatter of the guests, many of whom look as though they are used to city brunches. The menu includes local eggs and Forni-Brown-Welsh greens. Try the Huevos Benedict, a Mexican take on the breakfast classic, or their signature 2,2,2: two bacon strips, two eggs, and two pieces of French toast or two flapjacks.

Cantinetta Wine Bar

1050 Charter Oak Avenue, St. Helena
Open daily 11:30am–6pm

(707) 963 8888   The **Cantinetta** is the most comprehensive wine bar in Napa Valley. They offer over 110 wines to taste and buy—many of which are rare and difficult to find, much less sample. Wines are available by the glass and by the bottle. Flights of wine are grouped together creatively, including their alumni flight, which comprises wines made by past or present employees. The Cantinetta features *bocconcini per vini*, "little bites for wine," which range from a cured meat plate and a bruschetta sampler to anchovies with a celery and fennel salad. You can easily create a full meal to savor in the most alluring courtyard in all of Napa Valley, which is shared with the attached restaurant, Tra Vigne.

Compadres Mexican Bar & Grill

6539 Washington Street, Yountville
Mon–Fri 11am–9:30pm, Sat–Sun 8am–10pm

(707) 944 2406   **Compadres** is a popular destination for lots of visitors, but it's also a watering hole for locals, who stop in for the Back Bar Margarita, an ambrosial mixture of Cuervo Gold, Grand Marnier, and a splash of OJ mixed with sweet-and-sour. The food is Tex-Mex with a California twist, like the Baja Quesadilla filled with sautéed spinach, shrimp, jack cheese, and a smoky barbecue sauce. The fajitas are popular, but the lesser-known dishes like the chicken

mole, the fresh fish tacos, and the tequila-cured chicken are equally tasty. All of the portions are large, so unless you are ravenous you may want to consider sharing.

Gordon's Café and Wine Bar

6770 Washington Street, Yountville
Breakfast: Tues–Sun 7:30–11am; Lunch: 11am–3pm;
Pastries and coffee: 3–6pm; Dinner: Fri only 6–8:30pm

(707) 944 8246

What can I get you, love?" These six words, spoken by owner Sally Gordon as you step up to the counter to order, are assurance that you are about to start your day right. **Gordon's**, with its country-store façade and its interior filled with farm tables and high-backed chairs, is the ideal setting to enjoy a great breakfast and a peek at Valley dwellers. At breakfast, there is smoked salmon with rye bread and all the fixings, croque-madame on brioche, bread pudding, and a daily house omelet. Keep your eye on the line; it's always filled with vintners, chefs, and other high-profile residents, exchanging the gossip *du jour*. At lunchtime the crowd is much the same, and the menu features gourmet sandwiches, such as house-baked roast beef with Brie, three cheeses and tomato, and Caggiano sausage and fontina. Their salad with mesclun and baked goat cheese is perfectly complemented by crostini topped with tapenade. Friday-night dinners at Gordon's are a real treat. The weekly changing menu, based on seasonal local ingredients, shows Sally's flair for creating sophisticated, satisfying dishes.

Green Valley Café

1310 Main Street, St. Helena
Lunch: Tues–Sat 11:30am–3pm; Dinner: Tues–Sat 5:30–9:30pm

(707) 963 7088

St. Helena's answer to the neighborhood café is not much bigger than a wide hallway, with a few tables lined up against the southern wall and a counter that fills the first half of the room with six or so stools. **Green Valley** is a no-frills kind of place, and the food is great. Midweek, it fills up with locals during lunch and dinner, and the weekends are busy with tourists who have the right instincts for fresh Italian food. The sandwiches on the lunch menu are hearty, reminiscent of a time when big lunches were needed to power you through a day of labor. The Italian sausage sandwich will definitely fill you up, as will the portobello sandwich. Their pasta dishes, including the mushroom ravioli and the penne with potatoes, green beans, and pesto, an authentic Ligurian dish, are great for lunch or dinner, as is the eggplant parmigiano, thin layers of eggplant cooked until the texture is almost creamy, layered with béchamel, mozzarella, and homemade tomato sauce. At dinner the sandwiches are replaced with meat and fish entrees. There is grilled New York steak; calamari sautéed in tomatoes, garlic, and herbs; braised lamb shank with polenta; and more. My friend Sheila Franks sums it up this way: "Green Valley's food is so good it's worth going off a diet."

Mary's Pizza Shack

3085 Jefferson Street, Napa
Sun–Thurs 11am–10pm, Fri–Sat 11am–11pm

(707) 257 3300

Neapolitan-style Italian cuisine is the hallmark of this pizza place. The flagship restaurant, in neighboring Sonoma, was started in 1959 by the late Mary Fazio. Literally a shack on the highway until it outgrew its space in the seventies, the business has grown to include several locations, most of which are managed by Mary's grandchildren and long-time employees. **Mary's** pizzas are superb. The dough is handmade, and shaped into a disk with a flourish by being tossed into the air (among the restaurants' timeless features are counter stools where children can sit and watch the dough being thrown). The pizza is topped with a robust tomato sauce and flavorful cheese. Select your choice of toppings, or order one of the house specials. Toto's Combination piles on sausage, salami, pepperoni, cotto salami, and linguiça—a meat lover's nirvana—while Anna's Mediterranean, a pizza for the health-conscious, includes fresh spinach, sliced eggplant, feta, and fresh thyme. They also offer great pasta: Their spaghetti and meatballs may be better than even what your own Italian grandmother can make.

Moore's Landing

6 Cuttings Wharf Road, Napa
Tues–Thurs 11am–8pm, Fri 9am–9pm, Sat 9am–5pm, Sun 9am–3pm

(707) 253 2439

Moore's Landing is the place to eat lunch or grab a late-afternoon snack when you go wine tasting in Carneros, despite its bait shop

BEFORE THE RESTAURANT REVOLUTION

Napa Valley's first restaurants were most likely established during the Gold Rush as a matter of supply and demand. Later, fancy restaurants were operated at the spas frequented by visiting San Francisco socialites; proof of this are the menus from Napa Soda Springs and White Sulpher Springs on display at the Napa Valley Museum. Over the years, both upscale and casual restaurants have come and gone. Some have left an indelible mark, and a couple of restaurants are still in business. **The Depot Hotel** was started sometime around the turn of the century and later owned by a woman named Theresa Tamburelli, a legend in her own right for acting as a private banker out of her kitchen. More than one hundred years later, it's owned by members of the original family and the place is still packed on weekends. Customers who want to order takeout are encouraged to enter through the back door right into the kitchen. An older, lithe man takes your order, and unless you bring your own pot, puts it in a clean recycled container, takes your money, and sends you on your way. The same policy has been in place for more years than anyone can recall. 806 Fourth Street, Napa; (707) 252 4477.

Having just celebrated its fiftieth anniversary, there is every reason to believe that **Jonesy's Famous Steak House** will be here in another fifty. It has played an important role in many a Napan's life as the place to celebrate a birthday, an anniversary, and a family reunion. Located at the airport, it is a relic of bygone days when cottage cheese was considered a salad. It's still on the menu at Jonesy's and is wheeled out to the table on a plastic cart along with the burgers, steaks, iceberg lettuce salads, and their signature hash brown patty topped with a melted slice of American cheese. Their French fries are no doubt frozen but are cooked just the way a French fry should be, crisp and golden brown on the outside and creamy on the inside. An order of those and I could watch the planes land and take off all day. 2044 Airport Road, Napa; (707) 255 2003.

❖

façade. Set on a slough in the southernmost reaches of the Valley, it offers a unique view of San Francisco Bay to the south rather than the usual backdrop of vineyards. During the week you'll find it filled with vineyard managers, the office staff of nearby wineries, and longtime patrons. And on the weekends it's a diverse group of fishermen, local residents, and a few stray tourists. The no-frills lunch menu is an eclectic mix of Mexican food, burgers, and Caribbean-flavored sandwiches. The jerk talapia sandwich is cooked so well that the fish is moist and flaky, without a trace of oil. The choice between French fries or potato salad is a tough one, given that the fries are crisp on the outside and almost creamy on the inside. The potato salad is silky, the potatoes are cooked perfectly, and it has just the right amount of mayonnaise to bind them, with green onion and pickles that add flavor but don't overwhelm. Everything they serve, from chicken piccata at dinner to their burgers, displays a deftness behind the stove that is hard to find even in restaurants much fancier than this one.

Pacific Blues Café

6525 Washington Street, Yountville
Open daily 8am–9pm

(707) 944 4455   There are three main reasons to patronize **Pacific Blues:** They have a great list of draft beers; their shaded patio is the perfect place to enjoy such a beverage; and during the warm-weather months there's live jazz on Saturday afternoons. Get there early and plan on staying for lunch or dinner; otherwise tables are hard to come by. But if you don't get a table you can still get a beer, an order of gourmet nachos, and a seat on the grass below the patio.

Pearl

1339 Pearl Street, Napa
Lunch: Tues–Sat 11:30am–2pm; Dinner: Tues–Sat 5:30–9pm

(707) 224 9161   **Pearl** is the quintessential neighborhood eatery. The food is always tasty, the dining room is small and lively, and owners Pete and Nicki Zeller are always there and smiling. She does her work behind the stove while he waits tables up front. They have a large wine list, including those offered by the glass, and an eclectic mix of dishes that are substantial and imaginative. Soft tacos with

flank steak, green onion corn cakes with smoked salmon, and Asian noodle and vegetable salad are a few of their beloved starters. Their main-course choices are equally sensational. Try their Chicken Verde with Lime Cream, the Triple Double Pork Chop brined in an apple-Dijon elixir, or the N.Y. Steak au Poivre with Blue Cheese and Roasted Garlic Butter. The daily specials will seduce you with such dynamic creations as Grilled Mahimahi with Rock Shrimp in Green Curry Sauce with Ginger Rice. And do not miss the Caesar salad. Some Caesar aficionados consider it the best in the Valley.

Red Hen Cantinetta

5091 St. Helena Highway, Napa
Sun–Thurs 11am–9pm, Fri–Sat 11am–9:30pm

(707) 255 8125   On hot days, there are few places that could rival **Red Hen** for the respite of its patio: comfortable tables in the shade, refreshing drinks, good food, and a mister! Yes, the patio is covered with tiny hoses that spray the lightest mist over the shorts and tank top–clad crowd. When the thermometer hits 90°F and above, that cool mist can feel like heaven. The food is not haute cuisine, but this is a fun place if you're with a group and want some relatively cheap eats without the hassles of making a reservation.

Saketini

3900 Bel Aire Plaza, Suite B, Napa
Lunch: Mon–Sat 11am–2pm; Dinner daily 5–9pm

(707) 255 7423   Chef and partner Tod Michael Kawachi built his reputation in Napa as the genius behind the stove at Brix, where guests clamored for his Black and Blue Tuna, a perfectly seared fillet served with a creamy wasabi sauce. He now serves the same dish at **Saketini** at a great price, along with other Asian-fusion and American dishes. The Crunchy Beef Spring Rolls are served with a Wang Chung Chili Sauce that is full of verve and vigor, not to mention a little fire. The udon noodles, rice bowl, and hibachi-style salmon taste like Japanese dishes you might order in a Tokyo eatery. Every day there is a sushi and sashimi special as well. The stark dining room is the perfect contrast to Tod's colorful dishes. And the adjoining lounge is a fun place to visit before or after dinner.

ASIAN CUISINE The San Francisco Bay Area is home to a widely diverse Asian population. As a result, there is a panoply of outstanding Asian eateries that beckon when a craving hits. In Napa the choices are fewer. For Chinese food try **Golden Harvest,** 61 Main Street, St. Helena, (707) 967 9888; **Peking Palace,** 1001 Second Street, Napa, (707) 257 7197; **Soo Yuan,** 1354 Lincoln Avenue, Calistoga, (707) 942 9404; **Wah Sing,** 1445 Imola Avenue, Napa, (707) 252 0511. **Bombay Bistro** offers Indian fare: 1011 First Street, Napa, (707) 253 9375. For Thai, visit **Siam House,** 1139 Lincoln Avenue, Napa, (707) 226 7749.

Soscol Café

632 Soscol Avenue, Napa

Mon–Fri 6am–2pm, Sat 7am–2pm, Sun 7am–1pm

(707) 252 0651

You can gain weight just looking at the menu at **Soscol Café.** If you don't, you will once you start eating, because everything is cooked in clarified butter. Butter adds flavor, and that's just one secret to owner Javier Ceja's success. Watching Javier and his small crew maneuver around each other in the shoe box–sized restaurant as they plate breakfast after breakfast is a little like watching a ballet: lots of orchestration and finesse. A crowd of jean- and sweatshirt-clothed customers is always waiting to snag one of the six booths or the dozen seats at the counter so that they can tuck into one of Javier's serious breakfasts. His omelets are the fluffiest I've ever seen. The huevos rancheros—poached eggs nestled on black beans topped with house salsa and guacamole—are flawless. The breakfast burrito—scrambled eggs, bacon, black beans, and cheese wrapped in a fresh tortilla—will make you want to go back to bed until it's digested—about two days. The choice of two different gravies for the biscuits will make you long to be a trucker or anyone else who might eat this kind of breakfast every morning without guilt. Fine dining it's not, but a better breakfast would be hard to find. Don't mind the wait; it's worth it.

Uva Trattoria

1040 Clinton Street, Napa

Tues–Thurs 11:30am–9:30pm, Fri 11:30am–10pm,
Sat 5–10pm, Sun 10:30am–9pm

(707) 255 6646

If you've been to Italy, **Uva** will remind you of trattorias there. It isn't fancy. It is conveniently located, the prices are right, and the food is soul satisfying. The carefully made pasta dishes, like lots of other dishes on the menu, are available in two sizes. If a low-key and simply good meal appeals to you, Uva will more than meet your expectations.

Dean & DeLuca's vast selection of cheeses.

CHEESE

Napa Valley's earliest farmers, the Californios (Spanish and Mexican nationals), introduced cattle to the area two centuries ago. Since then, dairies have come and gone. Today, dairy ranches are practically nonexistent, with a few exceptions, such as the "Oreo" cows at the Stewarts' dairy on Highway 29 and the remnants of the Lewis dairy out in Coombsville. There is, however, Goat's Leap, a goat dairy and the sole Valley cheese maker, and Laura Chenel's farm, on the border of Napa and Sonoma in Carneros, both of which produce outstanding goat cheese.

Goat's Leap

St. Helena
www.goatsleap.com

(707) 963 2337 The twenty or so La Mancha goats that make up the **Goat's Leap** herd take a winter vacation every year, compliments of owners Barbara and Rex Backus. It's during this time that the goats finish gestation. They begin to kid around Valentine's Day, then return to work to produce the five distinctive types of goat cheese that the Backuses sell to grocery stores, cheese shops, and restaurants. The goats are milked every morning and every evening. The milk is stored in five-gallon milk cans—the kind that look like a movie-set prop—and is turned into cheese every third day. One cheese that Rex and Barbara produce is Sumi, a flat-topped pyramid covered with vegetable ash, which hides an almost firm, smooth cheese with a subtle acidic accent. Their Hyku is a plump disk with a creamy center and a bloomy mold outside. Kiku is a small seasonal cheese wrapped in sauvignon blanc–soaked fig leaves. Goat's Leap Carmela is a cheese that improves with aging, which might be as long as a year. The Backuses also produce a wheel of fresh goat cheese made to order—their version of chèvre logs.

Laura Chenel

4310 Fremont Drive, Sonoma

(707) 996 4477 **Laura Chenel** can easily be called the mother of American goat cheese. In the mid-1970s she began to make cheese using the milk from goats she was raising on her farm in Sebastopol. This hobby parlayed into an intense interest in French cheeses, and she traveled to France to apprentice at four goat-cheese farmsteads. After returning to Northern California, she perfected her methods and took a sample of her cheese to Chez Panisse in Berkeley, which was about to define an entirely new style of food, California cuisine. The rest, as they say, is history. In addition to giving birth to the artisanal cheese movement, Laura Chenel's fresh goat cheese inspired the now-famous salad of greens topped with a baked slice of herb- or bread-crumb-coated chèvre. Today, white logs of her creamy, piquant goat cheese are ubiquitous as milk in dairy cases. She also produces fromage blanc, Chabis, taupinière, crottin, and tomme. Her five-hundred-head Nubian-goat farm is just a few feet from the Napa County line in Sonoma. (See the recipe for Laura Chenel's Roasted Asparagus with Goat Cheese on page 260.)

Skyhill Farms

Napa

(707) 255 4800
(800) 567 4628

Amy Wend began her business in the Browns Valley area of Napa, but later moved her goats. Today, the Nubian and Alpine goat's milk she uses to make her fresh goat cheese, feta, and yogurt comes from neighboring Solano County. She praises the Nubians for their mild, creamy, and rich milk, which is used to make **Skyhill Farms** cheese, and the Alpines for the subtly flavored milk that is ideal for her mild, tangy yogurt. With twelve years under her cheese-making belt, Amy has created a niche for flavored goat cheeses, including her Smoked Pepper Crust Chèvre, which is lightly smoked over grapevines and apple-wood chips and then rolled in freshly cracked pepper. **Quick bite:** *Top a baked potato with Skyhill goat cheese or spread it over a bagel in place of cream cheese.*

NOTEWORTHY NEIGHBORS

Bellwether Farms

9999 Valley Ford Road, Petaluma

(707) 763 0993
(888) 527 8606

The Callahan family began raising sheep on their Sonoma County ranch as a retirement plan. That notion soon gave way to producing aged sheep's milk cheeses. Eventually they added Jersey cows to the ranch, and cow's milk cheeses followed. These are no ordinary cheeses; they are exemplary, made using artisanal methods adopted from Europe's great cheese makers. In fact, many of **Bellwether**'s cheeses are modeled after great Italian cheeses, like their pecorino pepato, an aged, nutty sheep's milk cheese dotted with black peppercorns. Their Jersey milk Carmody is a mild, creamy soft cheese, meant to be eaten as a table cheese like its Italian cousins. The Callahans also make both a sheep's milk and a cow's milk ricotta that will discourage you from ever buying a mass-made brand again. Bellwether cheeses are sold in almost every cheese section in Napa Valley, including Oakville Grocery, Sunshine Foods, Palisades Market, and Dean & DeLuca, which built a cheese cave to age them. (See the recipe for Crostini with Pecorino Pepato, Honey, and Orange Zest on page 315.)

LEWIS DAIRY
PL
PAUL LEWIS & SON

California Gold
DAIRY PRODUCTS
California Cooperative Creamery
PAUL LEWIS JR.

Sonoma Cheese Factory

2 Spain Street, Sonoma   www.sonomajack.com
Mon–Fri 8:30am–5:30pm, Sat–Sun 8:30am–6pm

(707) 996 1000

I can't recall a time when my family didn't have a wedge of **Sonoma Cheese Factory** creamy jack cheese in our fridge. We ate it out of hand, on sandwiches, over crackers, and melted on tortillas. When people came to visit us in the town of Sonoma, where I grew up, we would take them on a tour of Sebastiani Vineyards, the Sonoma French Bakery, and the Sonoma Cheese Factory, where you could watch them making the cheese. Under the management of David Viviani, grandson of founder Celso Viviani, they've added several flavors, including garlic jack, pepper jack, and Mediterranean jack, a great mixture of herbs and seasonings that complement the buttery cheese. They also have a Teleme that is superb: soft, milky, and nutty. (See the recipe for Grilled Pita Pizzas on page 275.)

Vella Cheese Company

315 Second Street East, Sonoma   www.vellacheese.com
Mon–Sat 9am–6pm

(707) 938 3232
(800) 848 0505

Growing up, I spent every Saturday doing the week's grocery shopping with my mother. Having embraced the country life, she loved going straight to the producer. We started at an egg ranch on the western side of town and zigzagged across our valley until we ended up at **Vella**'s, a seventy-year-old cheese factory. Originally built for the Sonoma Brewing Company, the landmark building was used as an ice plant and as a creamery, as well as to make steam beer. During Prohibition, the beer and ice production ended, but the building looks much the same as it did then, at least on the outside. Inside, the small sales room is plastered with ribbons, medals, and plaques awarded to Vella Cheese for their fresh and signature dry jack cheeses. They produce three types of dry jack cheeses. Mezzo Secco, which they recently resurrected, was originally made in 1930 as a softer, easier-to-slice cheese. Formed into a large wheel, it is coated with oil and pepper and then aged until partially dried. Vella's Dry Monterey Jack and Special Select Dry Monterey Jack are shaped into ten-pound wheels and brushed with oil. They are then coated with a mixture of ground pepper and cocoa powder. The Dry Jack is aged for seven to ten months until it's hard, pale yellow, and tastes sweet and nutty. The Special Select is aged a little longer, resulting in a slightly sharper taste. (See the recipe for Dry Jack and Red Pepper Biscuits on page 298.)

Napa Valley Coffee Roasting Co.'s St. Helena location.

COFFEEHOUSES

The Napa Valley isn't a place where folks spend a lot of time in cafés nursing a cup of coffee, but quality is essential. There are several coffeehouses that provide an outstanding cup of joe, and two coffeehouses, Calistoga Roastery and Napa Valley Coffee Roasting Company, roast their own beans. Between them they furnish nearly every restaurant in the Valley with a private-label blend, many of which are available for sale.

Browns Valley Yogurt and Espresso Bar

3265 Browns Valley Road, Napa
Sun–Tues 6:30am–8pm, Wed–Sat 6:30am–9pm

(707) 252 4977

Mah-jongg anyone? **Browns Valley Yogurt and Espresso Bar** is the exception to the hang-out rule. On any given morning you will find a cross section of Napa Valley's population filling up on caffeine, including neighborhood women playing cards and enjoying a coffee klatch. The coffee and espresso drinks are made with mellow-tasting beans from a South San Francisco roaster. During summer, this is the place to come for frozen yogurt.

Café Society

1000 Main Street, Napa   www.cafesocietystore.com
Mon–Fri 8:30am–6pm, Sat–Sun 10am–6pm

(707) 256 3232

Café Society is for Francophiles. The coffee bar, well stocked with robustly flavored Caffé Roma coffee beans, seduces customers with robust coffee drinks while they shop for French artifacts. This darling little shop sells everything from antique clocks to water carafes, garden sculptures to bistro menus. Sit and have a coffee, but don't get too comfortable because the attractive woven bistro chairs and marble tables in the café are also for sale.

Calistoga Roastery

1631 Lincoln Avenue, Calistoga
Open daily 6:30am–6pm

(707) 942 5757
(800) TRY JAVA

You probably won't find Frasier at the **Calistoga Roastery,** with its beach-shack décor and laid-back atmosphere, but you wouldn't be surprised to look over and see a bluesman strumming a guitar; it's just that funky. The coffee of the day, their proprietary Indonesian blend of six parts dark beans and four parts light, has been served every day for the past ten years. One sip and you know why they haven't changed it: The taste is superb. Along with the other coffee beans that owners and coffee aficionados Clive Richardson and Terry Rich purchase directly from growers all over the world, it's roasted by Clive. Whole beans and ground coffee are available at the store as well. Try Clive's Wake-Up Call, a coffee described as "the secret to [Clive's] nonstop talking capacity. If you've seen him in the café, you'll understand." Too risky? They have decaf, along with coffee drinks, teas, freshly baked goods (including a daily savory bread pudding) and a short list of breakfast and lunch items. Enjoy them in one of the window seats or out on the patio. With a slogan like, "No wine, no mud, just great coffee," you can't pass up a cup of joe here.

Napa Valley Coffee Roasting Company

[1]948 Main Street, Napa   *Open daily 7am–6pm*
[2]1400 Oak Avenue, St. Helena   *Open daily 7:30am–6pm*

[1](707) 224 2233
[2](707) 963 4491
(800) 852 5805

With two locations, one in downtown Napa and the other in St. Helena, a satisfying cup of coffee from **Napa Valley Roasting Company** is never more than a few miles away in the Valley. Sit down and enjoy a café crème served in a bowl; Denise's Double Short Latte, an espresso served with a dollop of steamed milk and a swirl of chocolate; or one of the specialty coffees created to celebrate the season or the weather. The first to open a Napa Valley coffee shop with proprietor-roasted beans, Denise Fox and Leon Sange set a standard for coffee here. They hand select their beans, often buying and roasting beans from a single farm. Napa Valley Roasting Company has created many of the private blends that are used by restaurants in the Valley and are also available for sale at the two shops. Take home a pound of the French Laundry, Tra Vigne, or Oakville Grocery blend.

Napa Valley Traditions

1202 Main Street, Napa
Mon–Fri 7:30am–5:30pm, Sat 9am–5:30pm, Sun 10am–4pm

(707) 226 2044

Equal parts gift shop, party-favor supplier, wine bar, and coffeehouse, **Napa Valley Traditions** is hard to define. But given that it was Napa's first coffeehouse, opening its doors as Whitter's Tea and Coffee in the seventies, that identity has stuck. Owner Cheryl Richburg and her husband bought the business in 1993 and expanded the merchandise to reflect her family's long retail history in the Valley (her grandfather owned a grocery store in Calistoga in the 1940s). They carry a creative mix of kitchen and entertaining goods, from decorative napkins to dried herbs from Herbs of the Napa Valley and their own line of Cellarmaster's Wife condiments and jellies. The coffee bar serves tasty espresso drinks and an assortment of teas.

FOLLOW THAT VAN! The Bean Machine's van, that is. Samantha Beaudoin has transformed a vintage delivery truck into a charming mobile espresso machine from which emerges some of the richest, most delicious coffees and espresso drinks available in the Napa Valley. Look for the Bean Machine on Salvador Avenue at Highway 29, around the town of Napa, or reserve it for your next event. Napa (707) 226 7119.

The vintage hardware at the Big Dipper.

CONFECTIONS AND FROZEN TREATS

Craving something sweet? Several businesses in Napa Valley can answer that call. Chocoholics will love Alexis Bonbons and Vintage Sweet Shoppe's chocolate-coated wine bottles. And there are plenty of shops offering a scoop of ice cream, a business that has prospered since Prohibition forced saloons to morph into ice cream parlors and coffee shops.

Alexis Napa Valley Estate Bonbons

Swanson Vineyards   1271 Manley Lane, Rutherford
www.swansonvineyards.com

(707) 967 3500

Long before **Alexis Bonbons** were packaged in their attractive, whimsical pink-ribboned hatboxes, chocolate was an integral aspect of the wine-tasting experience at Swanson Vineyards. And even before that, Alexis Swanson Farrer, the winery's marketing director, showcased the exotic and truly divine truffles created by her friend Katrina Markoff—owner of the esteemed Vosges Haut-Chocolat of Chicago—at her own dinner parties. Her fascination with Katrina's ability to infuse dark chocolate with ginger and wasabi, paprika and curry powder, ignited Alexis's desire to concoct the perfect truffle to be served with the winery's proprietary blend of cabernet sauvignon and syrah, called Alexis. It took nine months and several thousand truffles to find the perfect one: a sublime combination of dark chocolate ganache flavored with Alexis wine, coated with a layer of dark chocolate and dusted ever so lightly with curry powder that looks like gold dust—and it might as well be, so magical is the essence of spice and sweet and savory. And as Alexis says, "It makes our guests squeal with elation." If you want to experience chocolate euphoria, Alexis Bonbons are available at Dean & DeLuca, St. Helena Wine Center, Vintage 1870, and JV Beverage Warehouse.

Anette's

1321 First Street, Napa www.anettes.com
Mon–Fri 9:30am–6pm, Sat 10am–6pm, Sun 11:30am–4pm

(707) 252 4228

Veteran chocolate truffle producer Anette Yazidi, along with her brother Brent Madison, has been satisfying the collective sweet tooth of Napa with chocolates and sauces for more than a decade. **Anette's** also makes their own ice cream and sorbet and offers a variety of fountain treats, including the Oakville Grade Blendie, a cross between a soda and a shake, made with your choice of sorbet and their handcrafted syrup.

Ben & Jerry's

1299 First Street, Napa www.benjerry.com
Summer: Mon–Thurs 10am–8pm, Fri–Sat 10am–10pm,
Sun 11am–8pm; Winter: Mon–Thurs 11am–6pm,
Fri 11am–7pm, Sat 11am–7pm, Sun 11am–6pm

(707) 253 0484

No surprises here, just rich, delicious ice cream. Conveniently located in the center of town on First Street, this **Ben & Jerry's** shop offers all of your favorite flavors: Cherry Garcia, Phish Food, Chunky Monkey, and Bovinity Divinity. Ben & Jerry's also has sorbets, frozen yogurts, and smoothies, including an entire lineup of coffee-based smoothies called Capachillo Coolers: nirvana for the caffeine junkie with a sweet tooth. Those who want to indulge in a decadent treat can order an old-fashioned sundae or banana split.

Big Dipper

1336 Oak Avenue, St. Helena www.bigdippersodafountain.com
Mon–Sat 11:30am–6pm

(707) 963 2616

At first glance, it might seem odd that this old-fashioned soda fountain is one block off the main street of St. Helena. At three o'clock the reason is revealed: Two elementary schools in as many blocks are right across the street. Maury Gilbert, former owner and father of current owner Wayne Gilbert, boasts that the **Big Dipper** is the only place in America where Coca-Cola is still mixed by hand, the way it was in 1935. The walls are covered with soda fountain artifacts; the tables and ice cream parlor–style chairs are straight off a movie set; and a giant Wurlitzer jukebox shares floor space with a pinball machine made in 1934. Coca-Cola memorabilia is everywhere, from bottles collected from around the world to trays and bottle openers. There is a huge display of ice cream scoopers, each identified with a date. But behind the counter is where the real gems are: Vintage green milk-shake mixers churn out milk and ice cream blended into a lump-free, smooth elixir. There is also a shaved-ice maker, a carbonation contraption, and "Ask Swami" napkin holders.

Candy Cellar

1367 Lincoln Avenue, Calistoga
Open daily 10am–9pm

(707) 942 6990

Aptly named for its huge wine barrels spilling over with all kinds of candy, from twenty-two varieties of saltwater taffy to chocolate coins, the **Candy Cellar** is an Eden for sugar lovers. Most of the candy is the stuff of nostalgia. Remember Chick-O-Sticks? Necco Wafers? Bit-O-Honey? And they make their own fudge, with a flavor for everyone, including Chocolate Cheesecake, Mint Chocolate Swirl, Vanilla Walnut, Rocky Road, Fudge with Peanut Butter, and Calistoga Mud, which is just pure chocolate. Walking through the store will make you feel like a kid again, so don't pass it by the next time you are in Calistoga.

Kernel Mustards

1080 Coombs Street, Napa
Summer: Open daily 10am–8pm, to 9:30pm on Fri;
Winter: Mon–Sat 10am–6pm, Sun 11am–5pm

(707) 255 6633

Tucked away on the eastern side of Napa's downtown center, **Kernel Mustards** is a surprise to many people who pass it on their way to and from somewhere else. Frozen-yogurt lovers know where it is and make their way there to choose among the six flavors, three of which are staples: chocolate, vanilla, and strawberry. The other three flavors rotate, but there is always a sugar-free and a nonfat option. They also offer half a dozen sandwich choices and hot dogs.

See's Candies

1301 Trancas Street, Napa   www.sees.com
Mon–Sat 10am–6pm

(707) 257 6261

See's Candies, a Northern California institution, was established in 1924 in South San Francisco. Over the last century, new candies have been added, but the originals have never changed. The three most popular candies in Napa are the Bordeaux, a heavenly combination of brown sugar and buttercream covered with chocolate sprinkles; the Scotchmallow, fluffy marshmallow stacked with chewy caramel and coated with chocolate; and the Butterscotch Square, crunchy, firm brown sugar with vanilla buttercream. This is the most popular place in Napa the day before Valentine's Day, Easter, and Mother's Day, so shop early if you want to beat the crowds and bring home something sweet for the ones you love.

Vintage Sweet Shoppe

3261 Browns Valley Road, Napa   www.vintagesweetshoppe.com
Mon–Sat 11am–6pm, Sun 11am–4pm

(707) 226 3933

It's easy to like a candy maker. It's even easier to like one as personable as Deborah Dever. Deborah grew up making candy with her seven siblings under the guidance of her mother. Today her mother and children help make the candy and run **Vintage Sweet Shoppe,** which Deborah and her husband, Hank, own. Her homemade toffee is delectable, with a crunchy center, a chocolate coating, and hand-roasted peanuts sprinkled evenly over the outside. The cabernet truffles, dark chocolate morsels flavored with the essence of a fruity cabernet sauvignon, are one of their most popular candies. They are so popular, in fact, that a batch was flown to Ireland for guests to nibble on at actor Pierce Brosnan's wedding. Deborah's chef d'oeuvre is her chocolate-covered wine bottle design. She devised a way to shrink-wrap a bottle of wine, coat it entirely with chocolate, and wrap it in cellophane to protect it. Wineries love her creation and order them by the dozens. If you have a special bottle that you want covered, Deborah welcomes all wines.

Greystone's formidable structure.

CULINARY CLASSES

The cooking classes offered in Napa are an extension of the hospitality the Valley has become renowned for. Whether you simply want to hone a particular skill (the Culinary Institute of America, Cakebread Cellars, and Copia all offer focused classes), become a professional chef (courses are taught at the Napa Valley Cooking School), or pursue a greater understanding of wine and food (Robert Mondavi Winery, Far Niente, and Beringer all offer intensive opportunities), you'll be treated to an education in an environment like no other. You'll gain access to private wineries, cook with the freshest local ingredients, and learn from some of the best chefs in the country, all set in the splendor of the wine country.

Cakebread Cellars

8300 St. Helena Highway, Rutherford
www.cakebreadcellars.com

(707) 963 5221
(800) 588 0298

Jack and Dolores Cakebread, owners of **Cakebread Cellars,** are staunch advocates of the marriage of wine and food. To that end, they employ two talented chefs, Brian Streeter and Richard Haake, who are the cornerstones of the winery's day-to-day culinary programs. The winery holds half a dozen cooking classes a year, exploring such topics as fowl, grilling, knife use, and farmers' market shopping. Classes are taught by Brian, Richard, and a guest expert on the subject of the day. With limited class size, they stay small, offering an intimate forum for learning. Guests are often asked to roll up their sleeves and participate by following the instructor in cutting up a duck, sharpening a knife, or selecting ingredients from the garden. Each event offers a tour of the winery, a recipe booklet, a wine tasting, and a Cakebread Cellars–logo apron. Each class concludes with a sit-down lunch paired with wines. And the Cakebreads don't believe that adults should have all the fun, so they offer cooking classes for children as well. These instructive classes teach children about cooking techniques, food flavors, and kitchen safety. Cakebread's service expert, George Knopp, also teaches the children proper table setting. And best of all, each child gets to invite one parent to enjoy the fruits of their labor. Classes fill up quickly, so reserve your spot in advance. (See the recipe for Brian's Orange-Braised Chicken on page 323.)

Copia, *see under* Museums.

Culinary Institute of America at Greystone

2555 Main Street, St. Helena
www.ciachef.edu

(707) 967 0600
(800) 333 9242

During a single week, there can be as many as a dozen different activities occurring simultaneously at the **Culinary Institute of America at Greystone,** from weeklong courses on restaurant budgets to one-hour demonstrations of roasting root vegetables; the CIA offers classes that appeal to cooks of all levels. Designed as continuing education for culinary professionals, many of the courses award credits and focus on improving skills, but the passionate nonprofessional cook is always welcome to take a class or simply visit the school. Classes are taught in the historic former Christian Brothers winery building, a formidable hand-cut stone structure built against a hillside north of St. Helena. The teaching kitchens take up half of the third floor. The massive space is filled with a battery of professional equipment for the cook and the baker. Weeklong hands-on courses include such topics as Asian flavors, Mediterranean cooking, and making stocks. For the pastry chef, baking classes include artisan-bread baking and cake-decoration courses. And for the devout, a three-month baking and pastry arts certification program is offered. There is also a bevy of wine courses, including Mastering Wine with Karen MacNeil; Food and Wine Pairing for Chefs; and The Crush, an intensive course during harvest that explores all aspects of growing and making wine. Daily cooking demonstrations are offered at the school's DeBaun Theater. Each demonstration includes a sampling and a take-home recipe. If a cooking class doesn't appeal to you, a visit to the CIA is worth it just to amble through the elaborate terraced herb garden planted in front of the school or the production garden: Both are organic and both are used as a hands-on educational experience for students. More than 145 types of vegetables, 60 culinary herbs, 27 varieties of fruits, and 11 types of berries are grown and harvested for use in the school and the restaurant.

Culinary Convergence

Far Niente   1350 Acacia Drive, Oakville
www.farniente.com

(707) 944 2861   **Culinary Convergence** offers cooking enthusiasts the chance to visit a private winery that is one of Napa Valley's oldest and most beautiful. Led by Far Niente executive chef Michel Cornu, the day-long classes begin with a tour of the winery estate and gardens, which were designed by John MacLaren, who also designed San Francisco's Golden Gate Park. Afterwards there is a cooking instruction and discussion with chef Cornu, a French-born and -trained chef and the former executive chef of Auberge du Soleil. Lunch follows the morning tour outside in a lovely area built for just such an occasion and includes a guided wine tasting with Far Niente wine maker Dirk Hampson. Following lunch, students apply

their morning lesson during an afternoon hands-on session that culminates in a four-course dinner paired with current and rare vintages of Far Niente wines. Students can invite a guest to attend the dinner for an extra fee.

Napa Valley Cooking School

1088 College Avenue, St. Helena
www.napacommunityed.org-cookingschool

(707) 967 2930   For more than a decade, aspiring chefs have earned their whites and toques at the culinary arts department of the Napa Valley Community College, the only training program in Napa for aspiring professional chefs. **Napa Valley Cooking School,** located in the college's Upper Valley campus, consists of two rooms. One is the kitchen—a space that includes two Wolf ranges, two convection ovens, a large demonstration area, an assortment of professional equipment, and plenty of elbow room. For those seeking professional certification, a fourteen-month training program is offered every year, and nine months at the school are followed by a five-month externship at a restaurant of the student's choice. The class size is limited to sixteen students with two chef instructors leading the class through such topics as safety and sanitation, essential skills, the pantry, butchery, stocks, soups, and sauces, nutrition, wine and food, regional cuisines of various countries, and food and beverage cost control. The school also offers Gourmet Food and Wine Experiences, a series of classes offered to those interested in honing their home-cooking skills or learning more about a single topic such as wine, Asian food, or artisan breads. These classes are taught by visiting chefs from local restaurants, the nearby Culinary Institute of America, and wine professionals John Thoreen and Ronn Wiegand.

Master Series on Food and Wine

Beringer   200 Main Street, St. Helena
www.beringer.com

(707) 963 7115   Beringer hosts the **Master Series on Food and Wine,** a ten-class series of cult-focused experiences for wine and food enthusiasts who want entrée into the private homes, wineries, and cellars of

Napa Valley. Groups are limited to twelve students who attend three- to five-day programs that include visits to such exclusive wineries as Grace Family Vineyards, Araujo, Long Meadow Ranch, Pahlmeyer, and Shafer Vineyards. Lunches and dinners are served at the wineries by celebrated chefs of the Napa Valley and the Bay Area, including Donna Scala, Hiro Sone, Sean Knight, Bruce Aidell, and Nancy Oakes. Each class also includes a cooking demonstration followed by lunch at the winery's historic Hudson House.

Pinot Blanc

641 Main Street, St. Helena
www.patinagroup.com

(707) 963 6191
(888) 269 5269

Students join executive chef Sean Knight in his kitchen for a lesson in bistro cookery at **Pinot Blanc.** The classes are held the first Saturday of the month, from February through June. Chef Knight demonstrates a three-course menu, which is served for lunch following the demonstration. Or, you can spend a day in the kitchen cooking shoulder to shoulder with the staff preparing a five-course menu that you along with seven friends enjoy at dinnertime.

Robert Mondavi Great Chefs Program

Robert Mondavi Winery   7801 St. Helena Highway, Oakville
www.robertmondavi.com

(707) 251 4097

Everything the Mondavis do is done well. The personal style and panache that Robert Mondavi and Margrit Biever Mondavi exude is evident in every aspect of their business. Their generosity and graciousness are legendary, and evidenced at any of the myriad of events held throughout the year at their winery, from their summer concerts to their **Great Chefs** program. Held twice a year, this program was begun on the tenth anniversary of the winery in 1976. Famous chefs Simone Beck and Jean Troisgros were the first to hold court, and in the ensuing years, such culinary luminaries as Julia Child, Marcella Hazan, Alice Waters, Lidia Bastianich, Barbara Tropp, Jacques Pépin, Jean-Georges Vongerichten, Thomas Keller, Paul Bocuse, Wolfgang Puck, Alain Senderens, Diana Kennedy, and Martha Stewart have all taken a turn under the demonstration mirror. Great Chefs takes place over a long weekend. Guests arrive Friday night and attend a welcome reception and dinner in the winery's Vineyard Room, an architectural marvel with a retractable glass ceiling that's great for stargazing. After a superb meal prepared by the Great Chefs cooking team, guests are bid goodnight. On Saturday morning, they reassemble in the Vineyard Room kitchen. After an in-depth demonstration during which the chef prepares a selected menu, shares worthwhile information about equipment, and doles out professional tips, there are other educational experiences, everything from focused wine tastings to floral design. Then it's off to lunch at a local restaurant and a free afternoon. Saturday evening is a gala black-tie dinner. Few places are as romantic as the Vineyard Room at night. Flowers, candles, and crystal that shine, sparkle, and glow provide the perfect backdrop for the elegantly dressed guests, who are treated to champagne and hors d'oeuvres before dinner. The Mondavis have assembled a stellar crew that serves dinner flawlessly, presenting each stunning course with an exquisite wine selected by Margrit. On Sunday morning, guests find their way back to the kitchen for another demonstration. That's followed by further explorations of wine topics. The event is then capped with lunch. Following each Great Chefs weekend event is a Monday program. Like a mini version of the weekend, guests are invited to a demo in the kitchen, a wine tasting, and lunch in the vineyard room. Perfect for the gourmand with a busy schedule.

Trefethen Vineyards

1160 Oak Knoll Avenue, Napa
www.trefethen.com

(707) 255 7700 **Trefethen Vineyards** boasts the oldest winery cooking school in Napa Valley, having offered classes for more than thirty years. Three to four times a year, guests descend on the winery on a Sunday to partake of a day's gastronomic activities. The building, one of four designed by Hamden McIntyre—the other three are at Far Niente, Niebaum-Coppola, and Greystone—is a registered landmark that was restored by the Trefethen family in 1968. Returning the building to its former glory included planting a culinary garden that is the first destination for cooking school students. Led by Janet Trefethen, guests are encouraged to taste the garden's abundant offerings as they learn about its origins and maintenance. Guests then sit down for a pairing of Trefethen wines with local

foods, followed by a cooking demonstration by Janet and a guest chef; past participants have included Reed Hearon, Michel Richard, and Julia Child. Guests are then guided through the three-story historic winery before participating in a comprehensive wine tasting. The day culminates in dinner served outside in the sweet Napa air. Students are encouraged to invite a guest to join them for the multiple-course dinners served with rare wines and fine company.

NOTEWORTHY NEIGHBORS

Wine Boot Camp

Affairs of the Vine   696 Elliott Lane, Sebastopol
www.affairsofthevine.com

(707) 874 1975

Shine your boots and press your shorts and tees. A one-day intensive course designed to give you a hands-on experience growing and making wine, **Wine Boot Camp** is for the serious wine lover. Affairs of the Vine gathers "troops" for a full day that begins in the vineyard, where guests participate in seasonal activities, from pruning and shoot positioning to harvesting. After the work is finished, the troop is led through a workshop that can cover such broad topics as aromatic identification, demystifying wine descriptions, and wine and food pairings. Then it's on to lunch in a vineyard before returning to work in the cellar. The cellar portion includes blending your own wine and a tasting. At the end of the day, there's dinner at one of the participating wineries. If you want to learn as much as you can about wine in as short a time period as possible, Wine Boot Camp is for you.

GREYSTONE
THE CULINARY INSTITUTE
OF AMERICA

Calistoga's Palisades Market.

DELICATESSENS

Delicatessens in Napa Valley are hardly your run-of-the-mill sandwich shops. They offer much more than usual cold cuts slapped between a couple of slices of bread. There is Genova's signature muffaletta and zucchini torta, First Squeeze's refreshing smoothies, and Palisades' well-planned wine, cheese, and dessert selections. For a quick lunch, a picnic meal, or a myriad of dishes to serve as finger food at your next cocktail party, any one of these delis will set you up with something scrumptious.

Calistoga Natural

1422 Lincoln Avenue, Calistoga
Mon–Sat 9am–6pm, Sun 10am–5pm

(707) 942 5822

It seems redundant to use the phrase *natural foods* in the Napa Valley, where there is such an emphasis on natural ingredients everywhere you shop or eat. But there are a few stores that fall into that niche, and **Calistoga Natural** is one. In addition to the usual mix of vitamins, organic foods, and odd elixirs, Calistoga Natural also has a tempting deli that is always crowded at lunchtime. Try one of their Calistoga Special sandwiches, a healthy combination of carrot, sunflower seeds, avocado, tomato, and sprouts, or a Zorba the Greek wrap, a medley of vegetables, feta cheese, red onion, and kalamata olives in a spinach or whole-wheat tortilla. They also have a diverse menu of smoothies, coffees, chais, and juices—all organic, and all delectable, and all juices are marked down 50 cents during "happy hour" (3–5PM during winter).

First Squeeze Café & Juice Bar

1126 First Street, Napa
Mon–Fri 7am–3pm, Sat–Sun 8am–3pm

(707) 224 6762

First Squeeze surrounds you in whimsy, from the twelve-foot carrot hanging on the wall to the tomatoes painted on the floor. That same playfulness is behind the names of the smoothies. For example, the Berry Bonds, an alluring tonic of blackberries, strawberries, apple juice, and frozen yogurt, is heralded as much for its namesake as it is its divine taste. The eponymous First Squeeze smoothie is a blend of strawberries, bananas, orange juice, and frozen yogurt. Their menu grows more serious with the sandwiches. Try the Herb Garden, herbed cream cheese spread on twelve-grain bread and topped with black olives, grated carrots, avocado, and sprouts. The Mendocino is a mouthwatering combination of sliced chicken breast, sun-dried tomatoes, and pesto served on a sourdough roll. You can also have a custom sandwich built, choosing from a menu of meats, spreads, and veggies. Or, if breakfast is what you crave, First Squeeze serves one of the latest, until 2PM every day. The tofu scramble is a favorite among the health-minded crowd, their honey-wheat pancake appeals to everyone, and for the meat eater, there is the chorizo scramble, with Mexican sausage, jack cheese, and Cheddar cheese.

Genova Delicatessen

1550 Trancas Street, Napa
Mon–Sat 9am–6:30pm, Sun 9am–5pm

(707) 253 8686

Genova is packed during the lunch hour, especially on the weekends, but the line goes pretty fast and the sandwiches are worth the wait. The people behind the counter are a well-trained army of sandwich makers, and they can build a custom creation or one of their house specials in minutes. Their Italian-inspired combinations include Ham, Fresh Mozzarella and Sun-Dried Tomato Pesto; Mortadella, Provolone, Roasted Peppers, and Artichoke Hearts; and Prosciutto, Mozzarella, and Grilled Eggplant. Everything is cooked on the premises, including their roasted turkey breast, baked ham, and roast beef. A cold case runs the length of the store and is filled with a vast selection of goods, from chicken salad to fruit salad, artichoke hearts to frittatas, and Greek salad to fresh pasta, and they have hot soup, polenta, and eggplant parmigiano as well. Genova also carries an extensive line of Italian products. Shop here for pasta, Italian wine, condiments, homemade ravioli and sauces.

ONE MILLION RAVIOLI AND GOING STRONG

It seems a little odd to walk into **Lawlers,** a nondescript liquor store, and see people standing around the cash register holding pots and pans. They're there to pick up dinner from the deli hidden behind the Lotto machine and milk case, a tradition for the more than seventy years since Ray Lawler first opened the liquor store. Every day, the current owners, the Iberhan family, prepare the same kind of ravioli, malfatti (a northern Italian gnocchi-like pasta), and minestrone that Ray himself served. A rolling pin hanging on the wall in the kitchen is identified by a note on an aged piece of paper stuck above the window of the deli. Ray wrote, "This roller rolled its first ravioli in 1905 by Rosi Martini. Rosi gave it to her daughter Jen Lawler in 1952. Since that time, Jen Lawler and this roller have rolled over one million ravioli. It is now after 75 years of service, today in 1981, being retired." Lawlers Liquor Store, 2232 Jefferson Street, Napa, (707) 226 9311. Deli hours: 11am–8pm.

Oakville Grocery

7856 St. Helena Highway, Oakville   www.oakvillegrocery.com
Summer: Mon–Fri 8:30am–6pm, Sat–Sun 8:30am–6pm
(espresso bar opens Mon–Sat 7am, Sun 8:30am);
Winter: Mon–Fri 10am–5:30pm, Sat–Sun 9:30am–5:30pm
(espresso bar opens Mon–Fri 7am, Sat 8:30am, Sun 9:30am)

(707) 944 8802   **Oakville Grocery** is a foodie haven. As you enter the always-crowded store you are practically pushed into the first display of food set out for sampling. There are a couple of dozen open jars of olive oils, jams, mustards, and other condiments all begging to be tried. By the time you end up at the counter to order, you may be full, but one look into the case where the prepared foods are displayed will revive your hunger. You can put together a meal of their bite-sized ham sandwiches, couscous salads, roasted garlic heads, grilled chicken, cheeses, olives, and loaves of breads, or you can order one of their gourmet sandwiches. The Roast Beef and Blue is not only delicious, they usually have some prepared and wrapped if you're in a hurry. If time isn't an issue, try one of

the hot sandwiches. Be sure to leave room for dessert, because the cookies and pastries are superb. And as much as I love the grocery's lunch fare, the best time to visit is in the morning. Order a cup of coffee and a pastry, and then take a seat on the bench outside and you'll be treated to watching the who's who of Napa Valley grabbing their morning brew.

Palisades Market

1506 Lincoln Avenue, Calistoga
Open daily 7:30am–7pm

(707) 942 9549

I never go to Calistoga without stopping in at **Palisades Market** to pick up one of their homemade Ding-Dongs, a rich chocolate cake filled with freshly whipped cream and topped with a dark chocolate frosting—and they are just one of the charms of this gas-station-turned-market. The store was transformed into the premier picnic place in Calistoga by Victoria Gott and her sons, Joel and Duncan, when they bought it in 1993. Their diverse merchandise, from baked goods to the shelves of olive oils, caters to sophisticated palates. They have a hunger-defying selection of sandwiches, including their Mediterranean Veggie; Rustic Ham and Gruyère; and Peanut Butter and Jelly. And there are plenty of other edible attractions, such as house-made salads, local cheeses, and artisan-baked breads. The wine inventory is small but mighty, and includes Joel Gott wines: big, gutsy zinfandels and cabernet sauvignons that are priced right. And if carrying your lunch fare in a brown bag is too mundane for your taste, they have a fun collection of baskets for purchase. Be sure to also spend a few minutes browsing through the assembly of goods for the home, garden, and body. The rotating inventory of unique items includes ceramic tableware and whimsical toys.

Pometta Deli & Catering Co.

1810 Monticello Road, Napa   www.pometta.com
Mon–Fri 6:30am–7:30pm, Sat–Sun 9am–6pm

(707) 255 3953   For more than fifty years, **Pometta Deli** was a fixture on the Oakville Grade. At lunchtime the overflow from the parking lot nearly reached the highway. And then the lease ran out and it closed. But less than a year later, Pometta found a new spot on the northeastern side of Napa. The familiar wooden cows with the whimsical sign reading "Tastes Like Chicken" are gone, but Pometta's famous barbecued wine-marinated chicken sandwiches are on the menu, as are a few new specialties, including the Wagon Wheel BBQ Beef Sandwich.

Small World

928 Coombs Street, Napa
Mon–Fri 8am–6pm, Sat 9am–4pm

(707) 224 7743   **Small World,** a hole-in-the-wall eatery, is the only place in town that offers falafels, gyros, and baklava. There are half a dozen vegetarian pitas and full plates to choose from. Order one of the pitas bulging with chickpea croquettes, tahini sauce, hummus, and a salad bar assortment of veggies.

Soda Canyon Store

4006 Silverado Trail, Napa
Summer: Mon–Fri 6am–7pm, Sat–Sun to 6pm;
Winter: Open daily 6am–6pm

(707) 252 0285   The Silverado Trail was built in the 1850s to bypass the Valley floor when it flooded. It has remained the less traveled of the two thoroughfares, and it can be a very long road if you are in search of refreshments. A bit of an oasis on the trail, the **Soda Canyon Store** was built in 1946 and is perfect for fueling up at the espresso bar, sandwich counter, or vast beverage coolers. And if you are in the mood for wine tasting, a rotating selection is offered daily.

The stunning courtyard of Niebaum-Coppola.

EVENT VENUES

The wine country is a perfect location for a special event. Several wineries and other venues offer memorable backdrops for corporate events, private parties, and other gatherings. Wedding locales are more difficult to find, but they do exist, such as the Hatt Building and Copia. Most wineries that rent space for events have two requirements. One is that only their wines are served, and two is using a caterer that they approve of. This is usually a benefit to hosts because it means that their preferred caterers not only have a valued relationship with the venue manager, but that they are also familiar with the wines and therefore will be able to create sublime marriages of food and drink.

Christian Brothers Retreat and Conference Center

4401 Redwood Road, Napa
www.christianbrosretreat.com

(707) 252 3706

Mont La Salle is home to the **Christian Brothers,** a Catholic organization, which leads you to expect priests wandering the grounds in robes. A few brothers do, but most likely you'll spot brothers in khakis and sports shirts. This kind of contrast is present throughout the entire location. The historic site, the always-in-bloom courtyard, and the serene chapel combine to make this a peaceful and reverential retreat with state-of-the-art facilities. Built in 1931 and restored in 1989, the Spanish Romanesque and Mission–style center is perched on a knoll above a sweeping expanse of vineyards and verdant hillsides. The chapel tower and the other buildings inspire spirituality, which is a little at odds with the fact that this is an awesome spot for a party. And party is what those who rent the space do. A picnic area nestled under hundred-year-old California redwood and oak trees features a pool and can be rented for outdoor parties—you supply the lifeguard. Despite its religious association, weddings are not allowed, but sixteen contemporary rooms are available for overnight visits—perfect for corporate meetings, family reunions, and parties with out-of-town guests.

The indoor conference center and dining room are available for as few as ten or as many as one hundred. The center provides on-site catering for all indoor functions, which includes nonalcoholic beverages; for outdoor events you may hire the center's food-service operations or bring your own food or caterer. There are grills but no kitchen facility for the outdoor area. All alcoholic beverages must be provided by the event host.

Clos Pegase

1060 Dunaweal Lane, Calistoga
www.clospegase.com

(707) 942 4981

Clos Pegase, the Michael Graves–designed winery, is a feat of daring color and shape and the home of spectacular art. Add to that the European landscaping and the wine caves in the knoll behind the winery, and the result is a magnificent backdrop for special events. From elegant dinners illuminated by candles in the caves to a garden party on the lawn in the courtyard, Clos Pegase lends personality to any function. And it doesn't stop with the location.

In addition to meetings, seminars, lunches, and dinners, Clos Pegase offers an array of interactive events, such as cooking demonstrations, wine seminars, and wine-and-food-pairing workshops.

Up to 120 guests can be accommodated indoors and as many as 300 for an outdoor event. Events include site fee, catering fee, tables, linens, chairs, glasses, plates, utensils, reception and dinner wines, as well as a winery tour.

Copia: The American Center for Wine, Food & the Arts

500 First Street, Napa
www.copia.org

(707) 259 1600 **Copia: The American Center for Wine, Food & the Arts** features a wavy roof, a glass atrium that looks onto the river, and an awesome garden that joins the front of the building to the sidewalk—a striking setting for all kinds of events. From small meetings in the Founder's Room, with its groovy design and adjoining balcony, to huge affairs that flow through the entire ultra-modern center, Copia offers a wide variety of venues to host a soirée. The different locations are based on evening and daytime availability and are priced according to the space. The theater and demonstration areas of the center are more than suitable for presentations and meetings, and the expansive first and second floors can be used for receptions and/or sit-down meals. Julia's Kitchen, the center's acclaimed restaurant, is available for private parties on the days when it is closed to the public.

Depending on the space chosen, a specific room can accommodate as few as twenty people, or up to one thousand people for a standing reception. Caterers must be selected from a preferred list that includes McCall & Associates, which manages the food and beverage operations at the center. Copia allows both weddings and receptions.

Culinary Institute of America at Greystone

2555 Main Street, St. Helena
www.ciachefedu.com

(707) 967 0600
(800) 333 9242

The grand stone building that is Greystone was built in 1888 as a storage and aging facility for local vintners. Later it served as the Christian Brothers winery, then was restored to its original glory to house the **Culinary Institute of America,** which opened its doors in 1995. Its thick hand-cut stone walls are a striking backdrop for events held in the barrel room on the second floor or the big hall on the third floor. I have seen these rooms transformed into an Asian spice market, a French-château tasting room, and an extravagant banquet setting. They are often used for corporate events, social associations, and fundraisers.

Invite as few as six or as many as three hundred of your friends to the CIA for your special event, including weddings. All catering must be arranged with the CIA's food-service operations. You may bring your own wine and champagne; however, a corkage fee is charged.

Domaine Carneros

1240 Duhig Road, Napa

(707) 257 0101

Domaine Carneros, which is owned by the French champagne house Taitinger, is a sensational château set right in the center of the Carneros district (the southernmost wine appellation in the Valley). Its massive foyer and adjoining tasting room can accommodate a standing reception or a sit-down dinner. An outside terrace also can be used, but only when the cool marine climate that makes the area's grapes so happy or the signature winds of the region don't encroach on guests' comfort.

The winery is available for use after business hours. Its capacity indoors is 130 seated and 300 standing. The caterer must be selected from their preferred list. Included in the fee for use are tables and chairs, menu selection with wine pairing, a wine educator to discuss the wines, a tour of the winery, and glassware for a reception. Only Domaine Carneros wines are allowed.

Merryvale

1000 Main Street, St. Helena
www.merryvale.com

(707) 968 3429 **Merryvale's** Historic Cask Room is a dazzling location for a sumptuous feast. Events here are filled with pomp and flair, and begin when guests are led from a reception, glasses in hand, on a tour of the winery, then gathered before iron gates backed with red velvet curtains. The curtains are opened to reveal a stunning scene: a two-story room lined with century-old casks and lit by candelabras arranged down the length of a single table. It is a romantic, enchanting setting for a wedding rehearsal dinner (but no weddings), an anniversary celebration, or an awards dinner.

Merryvale offers a unique selection from three tiers of wine service for all parties. Each tier is designed to be paired with a four-course meal. The Classic consists of Merryvale's varietal Napa Valley wines; the Reserve is selected from current vintages of reserve wines; and the Prestige is Merryvale's lineup of highly sought-after proprietary blends. Caterers must be selected from their preferred list. There is a minimum requirement of 50 people with a capacity of 112. Fees include reception and dinner wine, tables, chairs, white table linens, glasses, wine-service staff, candelabras and candles, sound system for music, and event coordination.

Mumm Napa Valley

8445 Silverado Trail, Rutherford
www.mummcuveenapa.com

(707) 942 3434
(800) MUM NAPA
A decent argument can be made that sparkling wine is the most food friendly of all wines, yet it is rarely poured once dinner is served. Not so at **Mumm Napa Valley,** and for that reason alone, an event here is a gourmet adventure. The winery can arrange lunches and dinners in three primary staging areas: the expansive lawn area, the salon, and the photo gallery.

Up to two hundred people can be seated outdoors and up to one hundred in the salon. Event hosts are welcome to select their own caterer or choose one of the winery's preferred caterers. Hosts can also select from a menu of event styles, including a prix fixe event that the winery creates and the à la carte events, which are custom-tailored gatherings designed with the help of the winery's special events department. All wines served are Mumm Napa Valley wines.

Napa River Inn in the Hatt Building

500 Main Street, Napa
www.napamill.com

(707) 251 8500

The **Napa River Inn** has a colorful history, beginning with its development in the 1880s by Captain Albert Hatt, who paid one dollar for the property the building rests on. Hatt was a man with varied interests, a businessman who owned a steamship company and held social gatherings at his skating rink on the second floor of the inn (the white rock maple planking from Chicago that he had installed is still visible in the guest rooms adjoining Hatt Hall). Finished in 2000, the building renovations took nearly a decade. The results are extraordinary. The inn is beautifully furnished; the restaurants and market are first rate; and the venues for special occasions are one of a kind. Hatt Hall can be used for a business presentation or a wedding reception. Set right on the river, the Hatt Building is not only scenic, it is also conveniently located downtown.

Nighttime use of Hatt Hall requires the rental of the eight surrounding rooms. Hatt Hall can accommodate one hundred for receptions and theater-style seating and sixty for a sit-down banquet. The hotel caterer must be used, but hosts can provide their own beverages via arrangements with the caterer.

Niebaum-Coppola Estate Winery

1991 St. Helena Highway, Rutherford

(707) 968 1100   Francis Coppola restored the Inglenook winery to its original splendor and has made it one of the loveliest spots in the whole Valley. Both the courtyard, with its awesome fountain, and the spectacular barrel room, which has one of the largest capacities among all of the winery venues, are available for an event. **Niebaum-Coppola** is an ideal location for a holiday party, corporate affair, or wedding rehearsal dinner.

The barrel room can accommodate as many as 220 seated guests and the courtyard as many as 500. The winery caterer must be used, and Niebaum-Coppola wines are required for serving.

Rutherford Grove

1673 St. Helena Highway, St. Helena
www.rutherfordgrove.com

(707) 963 0544   The ivy-covered building that houses **Rutherford Grove** is framed in front by blooming flowers, a fountain that sounds like a babbling brook, and a stone path. Its pleasing design makes the rest of the world seem very far away. If you walk past the tasting room, the path leads you to a large grassy area; when I look at it, I can't help but imagine it filled with colorful paper lanterns for a casual outdoor party. With the right props and a little imagination it could be transformed into anything from a costume-theme party to a lavish picnic. Inside, the tasting room also serves as a venue. Its contemporary space would be fabulous for a dinner or reception.

Rutherford Grove wines must be served. A minimum of twenty-five people is required for evening events. The picnic area can accommodate up to five hundred people for a standing reception.

Rutherford Hill Winery

200 Rutherford Hill Road, Rutherford
www.rutherfordhill.com

(707) 963 1871

Rutherford Hill Winery offers several areas, including their caves and three different picnic grounds, as locations for special events. In addition to their site facilities, Rutherford Hill offers two different options sure to make your event a memorable occasion. The Sunset Picnic program takes advantage of their hillside picnic sites, which showcase commanding views of the Valley floor. At dusk, these are among the most romantic places to be in the Valley. The second exciting program is their Wine Maker for a Day. Guests are provided with six different wines and guided in the blending process to create their own merlot.

All catering is coordinated through the winery, which provides a reception, private tasting, menu, wines, tables, chairs, linens, Riedel crystal, candelabras, flowers, sound, event planning and service staff, and personalized menus. The minimum number of guests is twenty, and the maximum varies according to location and program. All wines served are Rutherford Hill wines.

Following pages: The barrel room at Robert Mondavi Winery.

Summer's best for sale at the St. Helena's Farmers' Market.

FARMERS' MARKETS

There is no better place than a farmers' market to watch a season progress, and ours are no exception. The opening of the markets in late spring is marked by the arrival of asparagus, fava beans, cherries, and apricots. Spring crops are soon replaced by summer's first batch of corn and tomatoes, which fade just about the time that fall rolls in with its gourds, chestnuts, persimmons, and apples. I often visit both the Napa and St. Helena markets because they are as much an opportunity to see friends and colleagues as they are to shop. For visitors they are a glimpse into the lifestyle of Valley dwellers, and for chefs they are pure inspiration, which is why you'll find so many of them there.

Calistoga

At the Gliderport, Calistoga
June–Sept, Sat 8:30am–12:30pm

(707) 942 4343   Calistoga's market could potentially suffer from a too-small complex if it weren't for the sheer magnetism of the produce and other foods sold. The selection includes seasonal vegetables from nearby farms, potted plants, and craft items.

Downtown Napa

West Street at Pearl Street, Napa
May–Oct, Tues 7:30–11:30am

(707) 252 7142   This market is the bustling epicenter of Napa on Tuesday mornings. Everyone makes it a destination. Farmers from Napa and surrounding counties sell their wares, from stems of sunflowers to zucchini blossoms, organic salad greens to ceramics, and popcorn to lavender oil. One of the main reasons to patronize this market is the wide variety of heirloom and hybrid tomatoes available through almost the entire season. Farmers from outside Napa Valley that are of interest are Bera Ranch, which grows an astounding number of plums and a lovely mix of microgreens. Keep an eye out for the mushroom stand, and don't pass up their morels or chanterelles. The berry people from Sebastopol bring plump, succulent blackberries, blueberries, and raspberries, and the apple juice from Sebastopol is great. Philips has the best selection of asparagus and cherries in spring, and Les Landeck grows the most flavorful arugula I've tasted outside of Rome, and his romaine, when it's available, will spoil you.

St. Helena

Crane Park, St. Helena
May–Oct, Fri 7:30–11:30am

Locals gather every Friday morning in Crane Park to pick and choose among seasonal fruits and vegetables, from spring garlic to pears and pumpkins. Every week vendors bring handcrafted, homemade, or home-grown items such as ostrich eggs, orchids, stuffed grape leaves, Indian foods, and a variety of garden and home items. Take a break and have a cup of coffee and one of the pastries from the Valley's bakeries. Be sure to sit facing the market; it has terrific peoplewatching because everyone who lives and works "up Valley" (considered a tonier address), from well-known vintners to local food writers, makes his or her way there. And don't miss these vendors: Prather Ranch, with organic beef that is dry-aged and free-range, and grass-fed veal twice a year; Napa Valley Ornamental Nursery for their potted herbs, grasses, and flowers; and Neufeld Farms for the most intensely flavored dried fruit you'll ever eat.

Yountville

Vintage 1870 parking lot, Washington Street, Yountville
May–Oct, Wed 4–8pm

This market is fine if you need basics and can't get to the morning markets. It is very small—only a dozen vendors—but worth the visit for the farm-fresh produce. Make an evening of it, visit the farmers' market, then head across the street and enjoy an early dinner on the patio of Bouchon, or walk down the street to Bistro Jeanty or Piatti.

THE ROWDY BUNCH You will either love or hate the Chef's Market held in downtown Napa every Friday night from Memorial Day to Labor Day. It has the look and feel of a street fair with live music, food stalls, and a gregarious crowd that all share space with the handful of farmers who set up shop in the party atmosphere. Make a night of it by meandering from one end to the other, take a walk through it on your way to dinner for a peek at a cross section of Napa life, or quickly dip in and out to pick up some fresh produce for the weekend.

❖

STRAWBERRY FIELDS FOREVER Napa's strawberry stands are famous among berry lovers. Two of the most popular stands are within a few hundred yards of each other on opposite sides of the street, attracting customers in a nonstop flow from the minute they put out their first basket in late spring until they shut their doors for the last time in fall. The sweet, juicy, red berries are grown in the fields directly behind the stands and are so fresh, they are still warm from the sun when they are packed in their little green baskets. The stands are on the Silverado Trail, about one mile north of Trancas Street in Napa. Both shacks open early in the morning, around 8am, and stay open until the evening.

❖

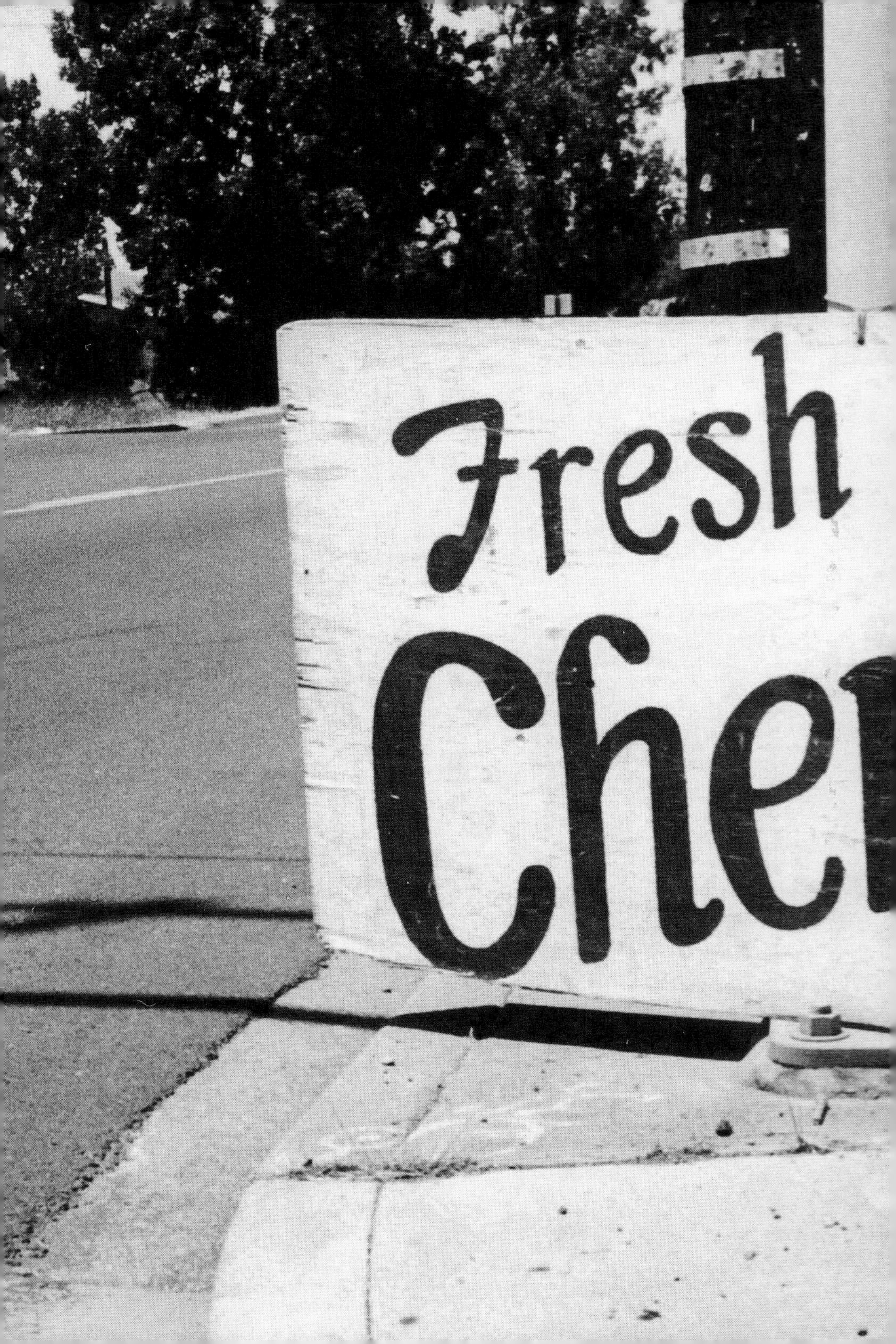
Fresh

Cakebread Cellars' produce shed.

FRUIT, VEGETABLE, AND HERB GROWERS

Napa farmers who don't grow grapes are quickly becoming extinct. Land is too expensive to plant it with low-income-producing crops like the once-abundant prunes, the long-ago prolific walnut groves, and the peach and apple trees that once filled Browns Valley. Vestiges of this pastoral existence can be found on the Silverado Trail, where a peach orchard remains in St. Helena at the Deer Park Road four-way stop. Fortunately, there are still a few farmers left, and most of them sell their wares at the farmers' markets, offering a true taste of Napa Valley *terroir.*

Big Ranch Farms

Napa

Mark Haberger, a fixture at all of the farmers' markets in the Valley, has been farming and selling his fruit and vegetables for nearly a decade. He's been involved with Napa agriculture since the 1960s, when his parents bought and operated a Christmas tree farm—a popular vocation at the time for many Napa folks who owned small parcels of land. **Big Ranch Farms** offers mainly summer crops, which range from red-leaf lettuce to herbs and cucumbers, and Mark is knowledgeable about each one. During the tomato season he grows more than twenty-seven varieties of heirloom tomatoes. Toward the end of summer he also has a small crop of Gem squash—dark green and globe shaped—which are ideal for hollowing out and stuffing. (See the recipe for Feta-Stuffed Gems on page 280.)

Cakebread Cellars

8300 St. Helena Highway, Rutherford
www.cakebreadcellars.com

(707) 963 5221
(800) 588 0298

Dolores **Cakebread**'s garden is spectacular. A backyard-sized rectangle, it's located behind the winery and yields vegetables and herbs year-round. During the warm-weather months when the crops are most abundant, fruits and vegetables are available for sale on the honor system in the produce center, which is a shed in the parking lot. Tomatoes, squash, melons, and cornstalks (perfect for autumn decorations) are some of the items you'll find.

Canyon Acres

5835 Dry Creek Road, Napa

(707) 944 9375

Bradley Kantor, the human earth mover at **Canyon Acres,** is a man with a mission to preserve biodiversity. He's doing a good job of this on the halfacre of land he farms. Aided by a unique microclimate that includes soaring midday temperatures in the summer that drop down rapidly in the afternoon shade of Mount Veeder to the west, and cold, mainly dark winters, Bradley is able to grow cold-climate-loving greens year-round. Ninety percent of his crops are open-pollinated heirlooms, including exotic Asian greens and a variety of radicchios—favorites of Bradley's. A niche grower, Canyon Acres is widely regarded for its pot greens: mustard greens, chard, kale, and other braising greens. Canyon Acres' goods are available for sale at the Napa and St. Helena Farmers' Markets and are served at Café Lucy in Napa.

Farm Fresh Produce

Silverado Trail at Deer Park Road, St. Helena
Open daily 9am–5pm

(707) 963 8551   The Ramirez family operates **Farm Fresh Produce,** a roadside stand, year-round. In winter, they import produce from neighboring Green Valley, but during the rest of the year they grow their own just behind the stand. They offer spring garlic, tomatoes, onions, green beans, corn, peppers, strawberries, peaches, watermelons, cantaloupes, apples, and Asian pears at a fair price. If you don't go for the produce, go for the handmade grapevine baskets woven by Mr. Ramirez, the patriarch of the family. There is always a satisfying selection of shapes and sizes, but if you don't see what you want, he can custom-make one.

Forni-Brown-Welsh

900 Foothill Boulevard, Calistoga

(707) 942 6123   Minnesota Midget. Mammoth Russian. Hollybrook Luscious. Bloody Butcher. With product names like these, it would be easy to surmise that **Forni-Brown** is a training camp for billiard players or wrestlers, instead of the mecca it is for chefs and gardeners. The former worship the farming trio for their impeccable greens, lettuces, and herbs, grown organically using the most stringent of practices. The latter revel in the annual plant sale held in April, when the gate is thrown open and customers can pick among the hundreds of fruit, vegetable, herb, and flower plants put up for sale. Founders Peter Forni and Lynn Brown began the farm on a patch of land out on the Silverado Trail. When Barney Welsh joined their

team, they moved to their current six-acre location. Their crops, which include hybrids and heirlooms, are grown using French intensive-farming methods, a style that includes broadcasting seeds in the fields to start plants as well as nurturing others in the many hothouses that dot the land. Once mature, the plants are harvested and crops are rotated to replenish the soil. The result of their efforts is a pantheon of edibles, including eggplant, peas, melons, peppers, sunflowers, cucumbers, baby lettuces, tomatoes, tomatillos, corn, pumpkins, and squash. Whether you like to dig in the earth or just dig into delicious food, Forni-Brown-Welsh grows something that will tickle your fancy. (See the recipe for Herb Gougère on page 259.)

Harms Vineyards & Lavender Fields

Napa

(707) 257 2606 **Harms Vineyards & Lavender Fields** grows Provence and Grosso lavenders, two varieties praised for their culinary versatility. Patricia Damery and her husband, Donald Harms, originally planted their two acres of lavender plants as part of their vineyard ecosystem. They grow the lavender on their ranch without herbicides, pesticides, or chemical fertilizers, in a habitat made friendly for the birds, butterflies, and bees that the ranch relies on for pollinating. The result is thousands of flowering lavender stalks that are harvested, dried, and sold in a variety of forms. The dried florets that Harms sells in bulk can be kept in an airtight container in the pantry for several years and used as an ingredient in all kinds of dishes. They can also be used for a variety of both practical and indulgent uses, such as making sachets to scent clothing, as pest control, and as a bath additive. Their lavender "fire sticks" can be used on the grill for imparting an herbal essence to whatever you are cooking. And their lavender wands are an aromatic and decorative accent that will brighten any kitchen. Patricia also produces essential oils and a lavender water (Hydrosol), which is essentially a by-product of the oil distillation process and which many believe has antibacterial properties. It can be used as an atomizer for your face and skin (great for flying) or for spraying sheets, towels, and rooms. Harms lavender is available at Olivier Napa Valley and St. Helena Olive Oil Company.

Herbs of the Napa Valley

St. Helena

(707) 963 7096

History does repeat itself sometimes. It did for Alston Hayne Sr., who worked for Spice Islands in 1949, and forty years later, after an illustrious career in the State Department, retired and returned to the seasoning business when he planted a halfacre of culinary herbs. Soon, the crop was so prolific that he began peddling his wares at the St. Helena Farmers' Market. So many peopled oohed and aahed that he enlisted the help of his son, Alston Jr., to help him dry and bottle the herbs. Today **Herbs of the Napa Valley** are sold primarily as proprietary blends, including Herb Dip Blend, Erbe alla Toscana, and Salad Herb Blend. They are sold at the Oakville Grocery, Napa Valley Traditions, and Vallergas.

Hoffman Farm

Napa

(707) 226 8938

The Hoffmans, Margaret and John, bought their property in 1949 and began farming twenty-three acres of walnuts, prunes, and pears. In 1964, they moved away and didn't return until 1981, when they picked up right where they left off. Over the years, **Hoffman Farm** has built a small but loyal following of customers who visit every year to pick their own Bartlett pears in August and walnuts in October and November. Please call first to make sure the produce is available. (See the recipe for Banana-Walnut-Chocolate Tart on page 328.)

Living Water Farms

P.O. Box 3538, Yountville
www.livingwaterfarms.com

Living Water Farms grows a phenomenal mix of microgreens. Their Lilliputian size belies the powerful flavor they pack, especially the wild rocket. Yowza. For everyone who turns up their nose at the use of such frivolous-looking leaves, I implore them to sprinkle a handful over a bowl of drab-tasting winter lettuce and

then decide whether or not they like them. Living Water Farms practices sustainable, natural farming methods and is one of the largest producer of heirloom tomatoes in the area, with thirty different types. Owner Guy Cameron also grows mixed greens, head lettuces, baby spinach, arugula, chard, mâche, and upland crest. His microgreens are sold at Vallergas. The tomatoes and other produce are sold at the St. Helena Farmers' Market and are served at a handful of restaurants, including Bistro Jeanty, Celadon, and Copia. (See the recipe for Crab Cakes with Roasted Red Pepper Pureé on page 320.)

Long Meadow Ranch Rutherford Gardens

1796 South St. Helena Highway, Rutherford
www.longmeadowranch.com
Thur–Sun 11am–5pm when produce is available

(877) 627 2645

Ten-year veterans of the St. Helena Farmers' Market, Ted, Laddie, and Christopher Hall opened **Long Meadow Ranch's Rutherford Gardens** just down the hill from their current organic garden in the summer of 2002. With the help of gardener extraordinaire Jeff Dawson, the Halls' have improved on the site's existing vegetable garden by adding more than sixty types of heirloom tomatoes from Jeff's extensive seed collection as well as sunflowers and a variety of melons. They also harvest basil, sweet corn, and a handsome crop of figs, which is divided between restaurants and the stand's customers. True land stewards, the Halls are to be commended for restoring and revitalizing the diversity of such a highly valued piece of property that could easily be turned into world-class grapes. Stop by in the fall and let your children or your inner child pick their own pumpkin from the two-and-a-half-acre pumpkin patch.

Napa Valley Lavender Company

P.O. Box 2509, Yountville
www.napavalleylavendercompany.com

(707) 257 8920

Lavender is widely reputed to have unrivaled restorative features. For Jennifer Ash, it not only provided much-needed therapy for her chronic fatigue syndrome, it also gave her a new career as a

EDIBLE LAVENDER The aromatic qualities that lavender lends to skin-care and bath products become more green-herbal—think rosemary and peppermint—when added to food. That's not surprising, given that they all belong to the same plant family. There are more than fifty types of lavender, and all of them are edible, but some taste better than others. The two types commonly touted as culinary lavender are Provence and Grosso. English lavender is also recommended by some growers. These three are less camphorous, sweeter and more herblike. The entire lavender plant is edible. The leaves, the flowers, and even the stems can be used for cooking, although the leaves are very pungent and the stems can be woody and tough (they are best used in the grill for smoking). Lavender's culinary uses are endless. It can be ground up with salt or sugar to be used as a flavoring, like any other savory herb, for seasoning chicken, marinades, and butter, and it can infuse the liquid used to make sweet dishes like ice cream, shortbread, and crème brûlée. When cooking with lavender, add it in small amounts to gauge its effect. Lavender is loaded with oil, so it can become overpowering if added in large quantities.

lavender farmer. In search of products made with lavender essential oil, Jennifer decided to plant her own on a small hillside behind her in-laws' home. Four years and uncountable hours of research in France and England later, she grows several types of lavender. **Napa Valley Lavender Company**'s plants begin to bloom in May, and for six to eight weeks the hillside is covered in every color of purple imaginable. All of the harvesting is achieved by hand, as each stalk is cut and bundled into bunches, then hung from chicken wire to dry in a hot barn on the property. Some of the florets are used to fill the company's signature pillows—delicate white linen adorned with hand-painted lavender flowers—as well as a variety of pillows made with French Provençal prints. The multi-shaped and -sized pillows, including sachets, eye pillows, and neck rolls, are as functional as they are decorative, because when they are held and pressed, the florets release their oils and consequently their aroma, a natural mood enhancer. Jennifer's beautifully made hand-printed linen designs have been transformed into stunning pajamas and robes that are so gorgeous you could easily get away with wearing them out to dinner. Napa Valley Lavender Company's products are available at St. Helena Olive Oil Company, Meadowood Spa, and Auberge du Soleil. (See the recipe for Risotto with Lavender, Meyer Lemon, and Chicken Sausage on page 263.)

KID STUFF Wine tasting holds little appeal for folks under the age of twenty-one, but a trip to Napa Valley doesn't have to preclude children, especially during harvest. Two places that are very inviting for young ones are Rutherford Gardens' You Pick 'Em Pumpkin Patch (see page 107) during October, and the Harvest Festival at Connolly Ranch held in late September. Dress the kids in farm clothes (there will be contests for the best attire) and bring them to the ranch for a day of activities that includes apple cider making, scarecrows, and visits to the animals. Connolly Ranch; Browns Valley Road at Thompson Lane, Napa; (707) 224 1894.

❖

Wine Forest Mushrooms

Yountville

(707) 944 8604 Connie Green is known simply as "the mushroom lady." A wild-mushroom expert, she began foraging for mushrooms after marrying a man of Eastern European descent, whom she describes as being more passionate about mushrooms than any Italian. Now, **Wine Forest Mushrooms** supplies essentially everyone in the Napa Valley with wild mushrooms, some of which she personally picks, including chanterelles that grow in hidden locations here in Napa. She also works with a network of reliable foragers who, like Connie, are hostage to Mother Nature for their crops, and often begin work in cold, damp, dark forests as early as 4AM Connie's wild mushrooms are sold at retail at Dean & DeLuca. (See the recipe for Pan-Roasted Salmon on Pasta with Chanterelles on page 264.)

NOTEWORTHY NEIGHBORS
Bates & Schmitt

The Apple Farm   18501 Greenwood Road, Philo

(707) 895 2461 Don and Sally Schmitt are Napa Valley icons who migrated north to a sixteen-acre apple farm in 1994. Long before a relatively unknown chef by the name of Thomas Keller came to the Valley, the Schmitts started a restaurant called the French Laundry and propelled it into culinary stardom with Sally's exceptional cooking. When they sold the restaurant they moved to property in Philo, which their daughter and son-in-law, Karen and Tim Bates, had been steadily developing into a self-sustaining farm for the previous ten years. Today, the **Apple Farm** is a full-family affair that reaps eighty types of apples, including many heirloom varieties as coveted by Northern Californians as a space in one of the farm's cooking classes. The family has also ventured into sharing their harvest in the form of chutneys, jams, juice, hard cider, and vinegar, including a balsamic vinegar hybrid. The juice, jams, and chutneys are relatively easy to find at Vallergas, Sunshine Foods, and Keller's, but the vinegar must be ordered over the telephone. *Quick bite: Cut a sturdy, tart apple into thin wedges. Toss with a liberal amount of extra-virgin olive oil and grill over medium-high heat until grill marks appear, 1 to 2 minutes per side. Arrange on fresh baby spinach leaves. Sprinkle with crumbled blue cheese and chopped pecans. Add a splash of* **Bates & Schmitt** *Apple Cider Balsamic Vinegar. Toss and serve.*

Riverdog Farm

P.O. Box 42, Guinda

(530) 796 3802 Tim Mueller and Trini Campbell began a small farm in Napa Valley more than ten years ago. When the farm grew and available land diminished, they moved their operations to the Capay Valley. Fortunately for **Riverdog Farm**'s faithful customers, Tim and Trini have continued to sell their fully organic produce at the St. Helena Farmers' Market and through a weekly box-delivery service. They grow over two dozen different types of fruits and vegetables each season, including fava beans and green garlic in spring, eighty varieties of tomatoes in summer, bok choy and sweet potatoes in fall, and Russian banana potatoes and baby Brussels sprouts during winter. A typical summer box might include a yellow watermelon, heirloom tomatoes, summer squash, Finn potatoes, cucumbers, basil, torpedo onions, and garlic. A winter box might contain baby cauliflower heads, spinach, broccoli rabe, Valencia oranges, beets, and sun-dried tomatoes. Each box contains a flyer that describes the goings-on at the farm, a description of the contents, and several delicious recipes.

ROADSIDE TREASURES Some of Napa's freshest produce can be found right alongside the roads. Keep your eyes peeled for stands selling the copious yields from backyard gardens or orchards. Persimmons, figs, and pomegranates are a few of the crops folks will set out for sale on the honor system. Or late in the summer, fill a pail with ripe blackberries from the prolific brambles that saturate the Valley's landscape. As long as the fruit isn't on private property, it's finders keepers, and there isn't anything that tastes sweeter than a just-picked, juicy blackberry. Just be careful of the thorns—they're sharp.

EGGPLANT
$2.00 LB.
LONG

Historic Main Street in St. Helena.

GROCERY STORES

There is a fine distinction between a supermarket and a grocery store. Size immediately comes to mind. Other differences are more subtle, like the way longtime customers still run a tab on account, and the foods are selected by the owner, not someone in a corporate office. Truth be told, though, even the large supermarkets here in the Valley are outstanding, with an impressive inventory of high-quality products—but it is the smaller grocery stores that are a true pleasure to shop in.

Browns Valley Market

3263 Browns Valley Road, Napa
Open daily 8am–8:30pm

(707) 253 2178   **Browns Valley Market** is a market for folks who want a home-cooked meal but don't want to do the prep work. Among the high-quality choices in the butcher shop is premixed meatloaf, stuffed lamb roasts, and lots of marinated meats, poultry, and seafood ready to be thrown on the grill. The deli, Giovanni's, the original name of the store, is stuffed with a large selection of prepared foods, including individual servings of salads, wraps, savory entrées, and desserts. A complete section of dips and other snack foods will bring a sigh of relief to a host in a hurry. Their cheese department is comprehensive, and each cheese has a note that offers a wine suggestion. All produce is identified on a tag that declares not only whether or not it is organic, but also where it is from. The market is fairly small, and thus the aisles filled with staples are limited; fresh food is clearly the draw at this store.

Cal Mart

1491 Lincoln Avenue, Calistoga
Open daily 7am–9pm

(707) 942 6271   **Cal Mart,** the only grocery store in Calistoga, stocks a wide variety of staple items, with lots of local products appearing in every aisle. It's a reliable market for residents or for anyone looking for everyday provisions.

Dean & DeLuca

607 St. Helena Highway, St. Helena   www.deananddeluca.com
Mon–Sat 7:30am–7pm, Sun 9am–7pm

(707) 967 9980   I have always loved the **Dean & DeLuca** stores in New York. Our Napa Valley store offers the same aesthetics and bounty as the flagship SoHo location. The staff wears the same official-looking uniforms, the shelves are the same industrial steel towers stuffed with the exotic and the everyday, the immense cheese selection includes domestic and imported types, and the desserts section is a towering display of seductive sweets located near the coffee bar.

Though Dean & DeLuca has New York roots, the St. Helena store may be our best resource for local products. Nearly every grower, manufacturer, and baker lists Dean & DeLuca as a retail location for his or her products. This store also has an alluring display of prepared foods, including a bevy of gourmet sandwiches (the chicken sandwich ranks as a favorite among locals). The Napa Valley location also has what the New York stores can only dream about: a large cheese-aging cave and a wineshop. The wineshop, nearly half the size of the entire store, offers a phenomenal collection of wines. For those who like to grocery shop, Dean & DeLuca is to marketing what a Rolls-Royce is to driving: incomparable.

Keller's Market and Ernie's Meats

1320 Main Street, St. Helena
Mon–Sat 8am–8pm, Sun 8am–7pm

(707) 963 2114

Keller's epitomizes the American success story. Owner John Sorensen began working at the market as a bag boy when he was fourteen; today he owns it. Keller's carries the basics with a few local products mixed in, such as Forni-Brown-Welsh greens, Sparrow Lane vinegar, and Skyhill goat cheese. John also owns **Ernie's Meats,** a longtime meat shop and deli in the corner of the store that is a St. Helena lunchtime fixture. Ernie Navone was the butcher behind the counter for more than forty years, before retiring to become a grape grower. His reputation as a dear, sweet man is often corroborated by his well-known gesture of handing out chocolates to girls of all ages whenever he is out and about. Ernie is missed at the meat counter, but his well-loved roasted-chicken and grilled-steak sandwiches are still available. There is also an enticing display of interesting salads, homemade chicken potpies, and a shrimp cocktail with chunks of avocado crowding the bowl. But order fast; John, who is often behind the counter now, is a member of the St. Helena volunteer fire department, so you'll never know when he might be called away.

Sunshine Foods

1115 Main Street, St. Helena
Summer: Open daily 7:30am–9pm; Winter to 8pm

(707) 963 7070

Anytime **Sunshine Foods** is brought up in conversation, the first thing mentioned is the seafood department. Its extensive selection is more than impressive—it is truly awesome. They have golden trout, fresh sand dabs, Hawaiian swordfish, day-boat scallops, wild and farmed salmon, lobster tails the size of a baseball bat, thresher shark, and what seems like forty-seven different types of shrimp, including hopper prawns from the Florida Gulf. But you may never make it to the seafood department, because as you enter the store, the extensive cheese display on the left and the dessert case on the right vie for your attention. Sunshine takes the term "specialty foods store" to new heights with their stock of salted anchovies, duck confit, USDA prime beef, and tubs of candied walnuts, all only a few feet from the front door. Farther inside is the produce department. Stacks of fresh, crisp vegetables are arranged as though a photographer were expected at any moment. There is micro arugula, white asparagus, purple asparagus, beets of every color, and rows of peppers. Other aisles contain shelves of vinegar and olive oil, Peet's coffee, and Straus Family Creamery products. And if you don't feel like cooking, Sunshine throws something on the grill every day, from hot dogs or lobster tails. Whatever it is, it will be delicious.

Vallergas

[1]Solano at Redwood, North Napa   www.vallergas.com
[2]First Street at Silverado Trail, East Napa
[3]Imola at Jefferson, South Napa
All stores open daily 6am–10pm

[1](707) 253 2621
[2](707) 253 2780
[3](707) 253 7846

Vallergas is like the yellow pages; if something isn't there, it probably doesn't exist. They offer a full deli with sandwiches, a huge selection of salads and prepared foods, and sushi made fresh right there. The cheese inventory reads like the United Nations roll call, and there are more than fifty different types of breads and half a dozen coffee brands, all artisanal roasters. You'll find an unbeatable selection of organic products in every department, and the produce department is cared for like a baby nursery. What differentiates Vallergas from other markets is the brands they carry. The shelves are filled with local labels, from Herbs of the Napa Valley, Straus Family Creamery, and Salute Santé Grapeseed Oil to Living Water Farms microgreens, Tsar Nicoulai caviar, and Gerhard's sausages. They also have an extensive selection of high-quality pasta, hard-to-find Asian ingredients, cured olives, gourmet vinegar, and the best chocolate: Scharffen Berger. The meat and seafood counter carries free-range chickens from Petaluma, fresh seafood from local resources, beautiful cuts of meat, and an array of marinated meats and poultry. The butchers are incredibly helpful and extremely knowledgeable, so if you don't see it, ask. They can usually get anything you need, from fowl to game. There are a lot of reasons why Vallergas is outstanding, but the most important is that service seems to be their highest priority, from helping you find an item to carrying out your purchases. The entire store focuses on catering to the needs and desires of its clientele. The staff, many of whom have been with the store for two decades or more, are friendly and attentive. There are three locations on the parameters of Napa, making it easy to get to one.

Sonoma Market

500 West Napa Street, Sonoma
Open daily 6am–9pm

(707) 996 3411   **Sonoma Market** should be the role model for all grocery stores. A relatively small store, every department is bursting with a selection of the best foods available in the area, most of which are from local producers, including Artisan Bakers, Bellwether Cheese, Della Fattoria, and Wolf Coffee. This store takes the doldrums out of going to the market and is one of the best places in Sonoma to put together a picnic, with a huge selection of cheese, mountain of breads, and endless shelves of wine.

Shackford's distinctive storefront.

KITCHENWARE

Where there are great cooks there must be great equipment. The kitchenware stores in Napa Valley prove this. In fact, some of the stores here offer such a broad variety of items for cooking and baking that they draw customers from all over the Bay Area. Whether you have an unusual kitchen item on your shopping list, want to buy a gift for a foodie, or just like to meander through sizeable kitchenware displays, be sure to visit one of these stores.

C&C Distributing

253 Walnut Street, Napa
Mon–Fri 8am–4pm, Sat 9am–1pm

(707) 257 2274   **C&C** is Napa's restaurant supply store. They carry just about everything you would expect to find in a professional kitchen, and many items you'll want in your home kitchen. Shop here for heavy aluminum sauté pans, hotel pans, industrial cleaners and cleaning equipment, bulk paper and plastic goods, giant storage containers, mixing bowls, tongs, spoons, spatulas, and so much more.

Cravings

Vintage 1870, Yountville
Open daily 10am–5:30pm

(707) 944 8100   This tiny shop is hard to define. **Cravings** is not so much a kitchenware store as it is a combination souvenir and gourmet food shop, but they carry a short list of kitchen gadgets among their inventory of ceramics and locally produced foods. What makes this shop the most attractive is the extremely nice owner, who is the kind of person I hope every visitor to Napa encounters.

Shackford's

1350 Main Street, Napa
Mon–Sat 9:30am–5:30pm

(707) 226 2132   **Shackford's** doesn't have a color catalog, an 800 number, or a Web address, but the thirty-year-old establishment has everything else a cook, baker, or epicure could ever need. Don't let the hand-painted sign or the sidewalk sales tables deter you from shopping in this store. Donna and Jim Shackford, who share the purchasing and clerking duties with their employees—all of whom can lead you down the aisles of wooden shelves to any item you need—have maintained the integrity of a community shop despite the pressures of retail technology. Even the wedding registers and sales receipts are handwritten, a charming reminder of yesteryear. Yet innovation and evolution are evident in the inventory. On the shelves is every kitchenware artifact of today, from appliance replacement parts to "VCRs" (vertical chicken roasters), permanent parchment paper to cardboard cake trays, and electric knife

sharpeners to milk frothers. Shackford's also carries an extensive supply for the home canner, the candy maker, and the barbecuer. For the brand-conscious, they have an ample selection of All-Clad, Global, Cuisinart, and KitchenAid. Whether you need a cutting board, a pepper grinder, or a stand mixer, Shackford's is sure to have it.

Spice Islands Campus Store and Marketplace

The Culinary Institute of America at Greystone
2555 Main Street, St. Helena   www.ciachef.edu
Open daily 10am–6pm

(707) 967 2309   It's not surprising that the country's most venerable cooking school would also be home to one of the area's best kitchenware stores. They carry a wide range of products for the everyday cook as well as the full-on chef—whether you really are or just want to be. From toques to whisks, **Spice Islands Campus Store** has it all. They offer hard-to-find items like the miniature porcelain molds found at the renowned A. Simon in Paris and used at the French Laundry. One entire wall is devoted to gourmet foods. Another area is dedicated to wine accessories, and sprinkled throughout the store are fun finds such as soaps made from herbs grown at the school, and fancy little plates. They carry a huge inventory of Emile Henri, All-Clad, knives, chef's pants, jackets, hats, and clogs, as well as a phenomenal selection of cookbooks—the Valley's largest at more than two thousand titles. They have an entire wall of baking books and every piece of equipment you would ever need to make any recipe in any book. This is the store for anyone who likes to cook, eat, or read about food.

WINE STORAGE   Once you get home with all the wine you bought while visiting the Napa Valley, what are you going to do with it? Well, you can purchase everything you need to open it, serve it, or store it at **Wine Hardware** in St. Helena at 659 Main Street, (800) 967 5503 or (866) 611 9463. Visit the showroom or call for a catalog.

Steves Hardware and Houseware

1370 Main Street, St. Helena
Mon–Fri 7:30am–6pm, Sat 7:30am–5:30pm, Sun 9:30am–4pm

(707) 963 3423   It's rumored that the hardware section of **Steves** carries dynamite. Perhaps that's for people who want to blow up their kitchens and restock them using the vast collection of kitchen goods that this old-fashioned country store stocks. They have a generous inventory of staples like glasses and microwave ovens, as well as a wide variety of not-so-run-of-the-mill items, including fondue pots, trays, platters, pie stands, wooden salad bowls, cake stands, baby sets, kitchen clocks, and plastic flasks. The store's success is not surprising, as they've had a long time to perfect their business— more than 120 years to be exact. Current owners Gary and Ron Megehon took over the reins of the store from their father, who purchased it from the founder, Warren Steves, in 1955. Take a walk around and you'll be treated to much more than their quirky and practical inventory, you'll also discover a bit of St. Helena history in the memorabilia that grace the walls and shelves, including items Mr. Steves himself purchased.

The herb and spice selection at La Morenita.

LATINO MARKETS

Napa Valley's Latino residents are the backbone of the wine industry as well as the workforce in many of the other labor-driven fields. Their presence is echoed in the handful of Latino markets that sell authentic Mexican food products. They are not only reputable shops for ingredients, but are an opportunity to experience the culture that is so integral to Napa Valley's success and beauty.

Aztec Fruteria

2997 Jefferson Street, Napa
Open daily 9am–9pm

(707) 252 8497 On the rare occasions when I need a ripe avocado and can't find one at the grocery store, I slip into **Aztec Fruteria,** a tiny, rustic produce market. It has a sufficient stock of staple items, as well as the tiny Mexican lime called *limon kila* that will make the best margarita you've ever tasted, countless bins of fresh chiles, and fresh juices made to order. On weekends during the summer, they often sell *helotes cosidos,* an ear of corn on a stick. It's garnished with Mexican *crema* (a mild sour cream), cotija cheese, a drizzle of fresh lime juice, and a sprinkle of chile powder. It alone is worth a visit to the store.

La Luna Market

1153 Rutherford Road, Rutherford
Open daily 8am–7pm

(707) 963 3211 **La Luna** is the only market in the small hamlet of Rutherford, and in 1968, when it was established by the de Luna family, it was the only market in the Valley devoted entirely to Mexican food. In 1994, they added the taqueria, and most days it seems that the traffic in and out of the store is directed there, but plenty of customers visit La Luna for its grocery foods. They also have items you'd expect to find in Mexico, like sombreros, woven shopping bags, and a full array of Mexican candies and pastries. The collection of dried chiles, spices, and herbs is vast. And although the produce selection is small, it offers the staples of Mexican cuisine, such as cilantro, avocados, and limes. La Luna also carries basics, so that locals, like Eleanor Coppola, who's been spotted shopping for milk, can pick up the bare necessities.

La Morenita

2434 Jefferson Street, Napa
Open daily 8:30am–9pm

(707) 255 9068 **La Morenita** is the Costco of Mexican food. They have more than two dozen different types of tortillas, nine varieties of dried chiles,

countless bins of beans and dried corn, four types of tortilla presses, three sizes of *piloncillo* (a cone of brown sugar with a molasses flavor, used for caramelizing rice and other dishes), and three ten-foot-long shelves lined with religious candles six deep. The meat shop in the back has the biggest selection of offal in Napa Valley, from tripe to beef cheeks. In the seafood case there's whole catfish and tilapia and overflowing buckets of fresh shrimp.

Latino Market

2993 Jefferson Street, Napa
Open daily 9am–9pm

(707) 257 7188

Latino Market is crowded with all kinds of Mexican food staples, but its real draw is the *carnecería,* its meat market. The assemblage of meat cuts is immodestly huge, and not a single piece is packaged. You could conceivably assemble an entire animal here if you shopped just right. On Mondays and Fridays, whole cows and pigs are delivered and cut into parts. There is everything you can imagine, from pig's and cow's knuckles to pig's and cow's feet, from pig snouts to cow brains (which are very small, by the way), tongue to skirt steak, smoked pork chops to ground sirloin, tenderloins to thin, thin sheets of beef. They also sell *carnitas,* pork cooked, like duck confit, in its own fat; sheets of fried pork rind; pork marinating in a spicy adobo sauce; and menudo, a special soup made from tripe on Sundays. I shop there for their linguiça sausage, made in the traditional Portuguese style with chopped pork, garlic, cumin, and cinnamon. It's sold both fresh and dry-cured. Although many of the staff are reluctant to speak English, Gabriel behind the meat counter and María at the cash register every day but Thursdays speak English fluently and can answer almost any question you might have about Mexican food. Actually, there always seems to be someone, whether staff or customer, who can describe some delectable dish that can be made with the store's wares. With each recipe they share, a richer understanding of the culture and cooking of Mexico is divulged. If you want a superior cut of meat at a great value, Latino Market has it. And if you want something special, just show up when the meat does and let Gabriel and his staff go to work. (See the recipe for Tri-Tip with Fennel and Peppercorn Crust on page 288.)

Vallarta Market

1009 Foothill Boulevard, Calistoga
Open daily 8am–9pm

(707) 942 8664   **Vallarta Market** boasts a fun collection of piñatas, including characters from the popular cartoon Powerpuff Girls. They also carry cooking implements, including iron griddles for cooking tortillas, stone mortars and pestles for making guacamole or grinding herbs, and steel platters. On the back wall of this market, across from the taqueria, is a large and diverse assortment of dried plants, from eucalyptus leaves, rosebuds, and chiles to herbs and spices. And of course there is also the standard selection of tortillas, various sauces, and other grocery basics.

A pastoral setting in Soda Canyon on the eastern side of Napa.

MEAT, POULTRY, AND SEAFOOD

In Napa Valley it's possible to eat fish for dinner that took its last swim that morning, a juicy, organic steak that was farmed thirty miles away, and duck confit made from birds that roamed free just over the hill. Farmers and shopkeepers work together to provide restaurateurs, chefs, and home cooks with the best the area has to offer.

Browns Valley Market, *see under* Grocery Stores.

Ernie's Meats, *see under* Grocery Stores.

Gerhard's Sausage

901 Enterprise Way, Napa

(707) 252 4117 Gerhard Twele learned his craft as an apprentice of a well-known butcher and sausage maker in Germany's Rhine Valley as a young man, but he has perfected it in Napa Valley. It seems odd to call a sausage healthful, but with **Gerhard's** it's true. They are made without any preservatives or additives, using fresh meat, organic fruits, vegetables, and herbs, and Napa Valley wines. He makes lean chicken sausages that are as comfortable on the breakfast plate as they are on the dinner grill, including Chicken Apple, East Indian Chicken Apple, Chicken with Wild Mushrooms and Sun-Dried Tomatoes, Thai Chicken with Ginger, Chicken with Habanero Chiles and Tequila, and Chicken Apricot. Gerhard also makes a bevy of smoked sausages. He has created a line of sausages that demonstrate a profound sensibility for global flavors and are the most delicious combinations ever found in a casing.

Latino Market, *see under* Latino Markets.

Napa Valley Lamb Company

4320B Old Toll Road, Calistoga

(707) 842 6957 Thanks to Don and Carolyn Watson's sustainable farming methods, the **Napa Valley Lamb Company**'s lambs have dined in all of the best vineyards, including those that belong to Beringer, Domaine Chandon, and Robert Mondavi. They raise one thousand lambs annually for restaurants throughout Napa Valley and the Bay Area, and grow clover and vetch sold as ground cover to the

wineries where the sheep graze. This is a far cry from their original careers of counting beans, not sheep. As a child spending summers in Lake Tahoe, Don watched the annual migration of sheep from Reno to Truckee. It wasn't until a life-altering experience—the death of a close friend—prompted Don and Carolyn to quit their corporate jobs and travel that they discovered a whole new life. After a brief stint in Australia they headed to New Zealand, where they landed in sheep country, and their fate was sealed. A year later they moved to a four-hundred-acre spread in Calistoga that Carolyn's parents had purchased in the early 1960s. They acquired three ewes and three rams, and life as modern-day sheepherders began. Today, they raise delectable lamb. (See the recipe for Baby Lamb Chops with Honey-Mustard Glaze on page 261.)

WHERE'S THE BEEF? In the tradition of Napa Valley's early cattle ranchers, two producers are quickly growing their folds into prosperous businesses that offer grass-fed beef to savvy carnivores.

Long Meadow Ranch owners Laddie and Ted Hall wanted to avoid a monocultural environment when they added Scottish Highland Beef to their roster of farming endeavors. Their cattle is herded back and forth between the valley floor and their mountain property to ensure a rich diet of grasses that helps lead to tastier and healthier beef. They sell their beef at Sunshine Foods, Celadon, and Taylor's Automatic Refresher. Or purchase it online at www.longmeadowranch.com, or call the ranch at (707) 963 4555.

Brothers Jim and Tom Gamble started raising free-range Black Angus on their northern Napa County property as a means of perpetuating the family ranch that was established more than six decades ago. Their cattle is moved from pasture to pasture to take advantage of the best grazing the Valley has to offer, resulting in healthy, humane, tender beef. The Gamble's beef is available at Keller's Market and is served at Miramonte. You can also find it online at www.napafreerangebeef.com, or call (707) 963 6134.

❖

Omega 3 Seafoods

1740 Yajome Street, Napa
Tues–Sat 10am–6pm

(707) 257 3474

The steady stream of customers pouring in and out of **Omega 3** is the first thing you might notice about this small, off-the-beaten-track seafood market. Your second impression will be that everything is so fresh it glistens. Seasonal seafood is brought in every day, from local king salmon to live Maine lobsters. Owner Mathew Hudson started Omega 3 as an import business, bringing fresh seafood up from Baja California. Today, it is the best resource for any type of seafood you might want, from skate, day-boat scallops, and East Coast monkfish to local petrale and rock cod to scallops from the Sea of Cortez. They carry live crayfish from Sacramento, Hog Island Oysters from Marin County, and swordfish from Hawaii. During Dungeness crab season, Omega 3 offers whole live crabs, whole cooked crabs, and fresh crabmeat. They smoke all of their own seafood, from salmon to oysters. Matthew has assembled a staff of fishmongers who know their business, know how to cook, and will be glad to give you ideas. One is Michael Carpenter, a former chef at Wolfgang Puck's Spago and Chinois. He can tell you how to prepare any piece of fish in the shop. Omega 3 also sells sauces and grapeseed oil, and every seafood purchase includes a free lemon. (See the recipe for California Ceviche on page 282.)

Osprey Seafood

1014 Wine Country Avenue, Napa
Wed–Mon 10am–7pm

(707) 252 9120

A longtime supplier for Napa restaurants, **Osprey Seafood** now offers a retail location in the Valley. With its good selection of fish and shellfish, and owner Michael Weinberg-Lynn's promotion of environmentally friendly fishing methods, Osprey is a welcome addition to Napa's food community.

LAMB MADE TO ORDER On the day I went to meet the Watsons and learn how they grow their lamb, Don greeted me at their home in the mountains above Calistoga and asked, "Are you ready for a hike?" We started along the dusty road that circles a small pasture below their house. Don stepped down and released a gate and then stood back as Shelby—the dog called to duty—herded a couple dozen sheep up to the road. We followed the herd of mainly white sheep—black or brown sheep are added for a quick head count—along a dirt trail that led to a larger, unfenced pasture. We stopped as the sheep grazed and the dogs played in the natural springs that dot the property; Don pointed to another flock that looked like specks on the rocky terrain. The sheep that were situated twenty-five hundred feet above us, unlike the herd we were leading out just for the day, stayed out for a week at a time. Between them and us was a steep hillside that climbed up to the dramatic Palisades range.

The pasture we were in consisted of rough, dry ground that looked ordinary until Don pointed out the clover ground cover that is used as the primary feed for his sheep. This is part of the holy trinity that guides their farming practices: breed, feed, and age. As a niche farmer, they breed ewes that can produce twins each year, as well as a breed that gives milk in larger quantities. This serves two purposes: The more milk a lamb drinks the larger it will grow, and excess milk can be sold to cheese makers. And mother's milk is one of the most important components of raising lambs for high-end restaurants. In fact, milk combined with clover and other legume-type plants is the best diet for lambs. It is protein and mineral rich, which results in succulent, tender meat. The clover is especially prominent because the burrs become attached to the sheep's wool and act as seeds when dropped. This perpetuates the right feed wherever the sheep are kept.

When the lambs are born—predominantly in November—they are kept in the Dunnigan Hills in the Sacramento Valley. In spring, many of the lambs are moved with their mothers to the rolling hills of the Sonoma Coast. The remaining lambs, as well as the ewes that give birth in the spring, are transferred to Calistoga. All of the lambs are doted on to ensure that they meet the specifications of the Watsons' chef-clients. Chefs that want a milky taste and finesse that favors gentle seasonings, delicate sauces, and elegant wines are sold milk-fed lambs slaughtered at ninety days. They have a subtle, delicate-flavored meat with an extremely tender texture. By contrast, some chefs prefer meat from more mature lambs—six to ten months old—that have a highly developed flavor and are dry-aged to ensure a tender texture. The robust taste of these lambs can hold up to hearty sauces, bold spices, and lush, full-bodied red wines.

Hog Island Oyster Company

P.O. Box 829, Marshall   www.hogislandoyster.com
Wed–Sun 9am–5pm

(415) 663 9218

I like to tell people that when my sister got engaged, she called **Hog Island** to reserve them for the reception before she asked me to be the maid of honor. They're that good. Hog Island came into being in 1982, when two marine biologists active in the field of acquaculture, John Finger and Michael Watchorn, teamed up to farm two hundred acres of Tomales Bay. Hog Island's meticulous farming practices reap rewards for the ecosystem. For this reason, Hog Island was the first oyster bed ever to be certified organic. And for us consumers, it means that each oyster is as succulent, flavorful, and as fresh as it can possibly be. Hog Island Oyster Company is always one of the most popular food stations whenever they appear at an event. Guests line up to try sweet, smoky, smooth, and complex Hog Island Sweetwater oysters; plump, buttery Kumamotos; French Hogs, a strong, briny-flavored oyster; bluepoints; and salty Hog Island Atlantics—all cultivated at their farms and shucked to order. Their oysters and Manila clams are served at Silverado Country Club, Brannan's, Bistro Don Giovanni, and Pinot Blanc. They can be purchased at Omega 3 if you want to shuck some at home.

Niman Ranch

1025 Twelfth Street, Oakland
www.nimanranch.com

(510) 808 0340

Owner and founder Bill Niman is a cowboy with a cause: to raise animals under the best conditions to produce the best-tasting meat. For more than twenty-five years, he's adhered to this principle and has forged relationships with the best restaurants in Northern California, which serve his beef, pork, and lamb. **Niman Ranch** products grace the menu at many Napa Valley restaurants, including Auberge du Soleil, Bouchon, Brannan's Grill, the French Laundry, Meadowood, Mustards, Piatti, Silverado Country Club, and Silverado Brewing Company.

Sonoma County Poultry

P.O. Box 140, Penngrove
www.libertyducks.com

(707) 795 3797   **Sonoma County Poultry** owner Jim Reichardt is part of a duck-raising dynasty, as his family's duck farm in Petaluma is the oldest in the country. In 1870, a clipper ship from China pulled into San Francisco Bay and unloaded three dozen Pekin ducks (a name probably derived from their point of origin). Two dozen traveled on to Long Island, while the remaining twelve ducks stayed in San Francisco. In 1901, Jim Reichardt's grandfather inherited the progeny of those original ducks when he bought a local duck farm. After playing real-estate hopscotch, migrating to South San Francisco then back to the City, he finally moved the operations to Petaluma. He and his family built their business into a prolific ranch that produces twenty-five thousand ducks per week, primarily for the Chinese community in the Bay Area. Jim, who began working for his family's business in 1981, left after a decade to raise ducks for a smaller market: California's flourishing gourmet restaurants. Larger ducks were in demand by chefs who also wanted the most natural ingredients available for their kitchens. All of Sonoma County Poultry's ducks are raised outdoors, on the ground, without any antibiotics. The result is plump, tasty birds. Sonoma County Poultry ducks are sold in only five retail locations, three of which are here in the Napa Valley: Sunshine Foods, Ernie's Meats, and Vallergas. (See the recipe for Duck Roulade with Cauliflower Purée on page 267.)

Tsar Nicoulai

144 King Street, San Francisco
www.tsarnicoulai.com

(800) 952 2842   Swimming pools in Sacramento Valley, about an hour east of Napa, are almost a necessity due to its intense summer heat. But people aren't the only creatures swimming in Sacramento, now that Mats and Dafne Engstrom raise sturgeon there for producing organic California-farmed osetra caviar, with its buttery flavored, medium-sized grains. Mats and Dafne, founders of **Tsar Nicoulai,** import Chinese and Russian caviar, including beluga (the most prestigious type), sevruga, American sturgeon, gold pearl salmon or trout, imported osetra, American golden, and tobiko. The

Engstroms, who are leading authorities on caviar, are often called on to answer questions about this revered delicacy, and they address some common myths about caviar in their press kit. The last is my favorite: Q: "Caviar is an aphrodisiac?" A: "Well, while there's no scientific proof, caviar certainly adds a touch of elegance to a romantic evening for two. . . . Plus, it's packed with protein—a great source of energy!" Can you imagine a better reason for partaking of caviar?

Copia's modern design.

MUSEUMS

Just as man cannot live on bread and water alone, neither can he just eat and drink. Okay, maybe it's possible, but a little exercise between meals is kind to both body and mind, and the best places to walk off some calories are the museums, which house some of Napa's most extraordinary art and historical wares.

Copia: The American Center for Wine, Food & the Arts

500 First Street, Napa www.copia.org
Call for hours.

(707) 259 1600 **Copia** is to food and wine what the Smithsonian is to Americana: It captures our culture through what appears on our plate and in our glass. A museum, an organic garden, a gift shop, a cooking school, a film house, a concert stage, a wine bar, a restaurant, and so much more, it is a must-see for anyone with epicurean interests. The second floor is devoted to *Forks in the Road,* a permanent exhibition. It features unique, and some interactive exhibits that capture the essence of the American dining scene. The second gallery contains a rotating show of food-related art. Downstairs, Copia offers an all-encompassing menu of educational programs. On a typical day there are as many as eight different programs taking place, such as a chardonnay tasting, a lecture on chocolate, a pastry class, a screening of *Tortilla Soup,* a class on garden-bed preparation, and a poetry reading. There are also two superb places to take a break and eat. Julia's Kitchen is a marvelous sit-down restaurant, and the American Market Café has just the right balance of salads and sandwiches for those wanting a casual bite to eat. Outside is a 3½-acre organic garden filled with fruit, vegetables, and art. Its design alone is worth a visit. Tours of the garden, exhibitions, and entire center are offered throughout the day. This gateway to Napa Valley offers an expansive behind-the-scenes view of the area, from wine-barrel making to lavender growing, all under one roof.

di Rosa Preserve

5200 Carneros Highway, Napa www.dirosapreserve.org
Call for hours.

(707) 226 5991 When people talk about the **di Rosa Preserve**, they smile, and once you've been there you'll smile too. The di Rosa Preserve is an unexpected collection of the blasphemous, the humorous, the far out, and the unthinkable. And it is the brainchild of Rene di Rosa, who took his collection of art, primarily from local and emerging artists, and spread it out over fifty-three acres of land. This museum has no direct relation to food unless you draw a vague connection to Rene selling his acclaimed vineyards (he was the first to grow grapes in the Carneros region) to fund the preserve.

But it is included in this book because it is a must-see for anyone who appreciates modern art. Rene has amassed a collection that reflects his irreverent spirit and playful nature. *The San Francisco Chronicle* described it as "the crossroads of beauty and terror, where whimsy and madness meet." The art fills three buildings, including Rene's former home—he lives above the garage now—and peppers the landscape and, in some cases, like the red Fiat hanging from an oak tree, the sky of the preserve. Many of the pieces Rene collected with his late wife, Veronica, were purchased from artists before they had achieved much recognition, such as sculptor Mark di Suvero, painter Sandow Birk, and photographer Judy Dater. My favorite artwork is one of the first you see: it's Rene's mother's 1967 Pontiac, which has been transformed into art with a V-8, via the attachment of thousands of objects by the artist David Best. Nothing is sacred or too outlandish at the di Rosa Preserve.

Napa Valley Museum

55 Presidents Circle, Yountville   www.napavalleymuseum.org
Wed–Mon 10am–5pm

(707) 944 0500   The very modern building that houses the **Napa Valley Museum** looks out of place on the grounds of the Veterans Administration Hospital where it is located. But inside, its thought-provoking exhibits share space with dioramas of historic Napa—including photos and documents of the veterans' home when it had its own hog farm—that bridge the two entities. In addition to the displays that explain the life of the Wappo Indians and exhibit bottles of six different soda companies, there is also an entire floor devoted to wine. The multimedia display offers an in-depth education about every facet of wine growing, making, and consuming. It is impossible to walk away from this museum without learning some interesting fact about the Napa Valley—past and present.

MUSEUM-WORTHY ART The **Hess Collection Winery** is known for both its art collection and its wines. The winery, which was once part of the Christian Brothers' holdings, was purchased by current owner Donald Hess and transformed into a home for his two passions: wine and art. Two floors are devoted to mixed-media exhibitions, along with views of the vineyards, the tank room, and the bottling room. Artwork by such luminaries as Francis Bacon, Lynn Hershman, and Frank Stella are part of the permanent collection, which is as stimulating and sensational as the Hess Collection of wines. 4411 Redwood Road, Napa, (707) 244 1144. Open daily 10am–4pm.

Copper tanks filled with olive oil at Olivier Napa Valley.

OIL AND VINEGAR

It should come as no big surprise to anyone that olive oil and vinegar production thrive in the Napa Valley. Not only does the climate provide the perfect environment for olive trees, these two ingredients are integral elements in the preparation of the California-Mediterranean cuisine that flourishes here. Additionally, olive oil, vinegar, and wine production work in synergy. As the grape harvest winds down, olives hit their peak of ripeness and acidity and are ready to be picked and pressed into oil. And vinegar is made from wine. The better the wine the better the vinegar, so it of course makes sense to apply a little alchemy to Napa's finest to produce a vinegar worthy of the maker's efforts.

The California Press

P.O. Box 408, Rutherford

(707) 944 0343

When John Baritelle, founder of the **California Press,** talks about his inspiration for making the best domestic nut oils available in the United States, he imitates his grandmother. The image of a large, imposing man walking around flapping his imaginary apron is a sight that is not soon forgotten. His handcrafted, first-pressed nut oils make the same impact on your palate. They are as silky and lush as melted butter, with seductive aromas and even more alluring flavors. Not content with just luscious oils, the California Press also produces a line of nut flours. Both products are made from whole and halved nuts that are toasted, ground, and pressed. After the oil is extracted, the cake is ground again and sifted to form the heady flours. Choose among walnut, filbert, pecan, almond, and pistachio oils and flours to enrich your pantry. California Press products are sold at Vallergas, the Culinary Institute of America, and the Oakville Grocery.

Lila Jaeger

5100 Big Ranch Road, Napa

(707) 255 4456

Lila Jaeger was a pioneer in California's premium olive oil business in the early 1990s, when she decided to harvest the olives growing on the hundred-year-old trees at her winery property. The **Lila Jaeger** olive oil she created is primarily made with Fargas, Spanish olives from the Catalonion region, blended with French and Italian olives. The oil has a complex, round olive taste. Lila Jaeger Extra Virgin Olive Oil is available at Oakville Grocery and Dean & DeLuca.

M. Turrigiano & Company

Napa
mturrigiano@earthlink.net

Michael Turrigiano understands the need to protect olive oil from the elements. An artist who specializes in ceramic sculptures,

Michael had been crafting his earthy ceramic bottles for an oil producer for several years. When the producer changed to glass, Michael decided to make his own olive oil and fared well when a friend planted an *oliveto* (olive grove) at the same time. Made entirely from organically grown Manzanillo and Mission olives, his oil is buttery and voluptuous, with just a hint of pepper. The bottles are much too precious to discard when empty; I use mine as bud vases. **M. Turrigiano** extra-virgin olive oil is available at Oakville Grocery, Merryvale, Niebaum-Coppola, Gordon's, and Vanderbilt and Company, which also carries other ceramic works by Michael. You can also see his work on the tables at Terra Restaurant.

Napa Valley Olive Oil Manufacturing Company

835 Charter Oak Avenue, St. Helena
Open daily 8am–5:30pm

(707) 963 4173

A St. Helena landmark, the **Napa Valley Olive Oil Manufacturing Company** is a family-run operation that looks exactly as it must have when they opened the doors in the 1950s. Housed in an old barn at the end of a dead-end street, it is bordered by prolific citrus trees and has a little yard for picnics. Inside, barrels of dried mushrooms perfume the air. Italian salami, cheese, pasta, vinegar, five-gallon buckets of dried beans, cans of imported tomatoes, anchovies, tuna, and cured olives all share space with dark green bottles of olive oil, which are bottled on the premises from the large tank in the back room. Buttery, fruity, and reasonably priced, it is a good everyday olive oil, available in pint, quart, three-liter, and half-gallon bottles.

Napa Valley Grapeseed Oil Company

1673 St. Helena Highway, Rutherford
www.rutherfordgrove.com

(707) 963 0544

Napa Valley Grapeseed Oil Company is the only producer that uses Napa Valley grapes to produce their oil. Founded by the Pestoni family, the oil company was developed as a by-product of the family's other business, producing organic grape compost. The Pestonis decided to separate out the grape seeds and cold press them to extract the subtle, nutty oil. Grapeseed oil is revered for its health benefits—a boastful amount of antioxidants, vitamin E, and omega-6—and its versatility. It has a high smoking point, so it can be used to sear meat, seafood, and poultry over high heat. Unlike olive oil, grapeseed oil has a very subtle flavor, so it can also be used as an ingredient in salad dressings, mayonnaise, and for sautéing delicately flavored foods like scallops. Also it doesn't turn cloudy or clump in the refrigerator like olive oil. (See the recipe for Napa Valley Grapeseed Oil's Warm Winter Pear Salad on page 318.)

ODE TO GRAPE SEEDS Grape seeds release a fetching oil ideal for the body—inside and out. Extracting the oil, though, is backbreaking work. After the wine is pressed, the pomace, a mixture of grape skins, seeds, and sometimes stems, is gathered and sorted to collect the seeds. (The seeds are smaller than a lemon seed in most cases, and the pomace can measure in the tons.) The seeds are then dried and pressed to release 3 percent of their weight in oil. It's a lot of work for just a little reward, but so worth it.

Olivier Napa Valley

1375 Main Street, St. Helena   www.oliviernapavalley.com
Mon–Sat 10am–5:30pm, Sun 11am–5pm

(707) 967 8777   **Olivier**'s long, graceful bottles filled with herbs, spices, and oil are so beautiful you may be tempted to display them as art rather than open them. I know. I've had a bottle of their Herbes de Provence oil on my kitchen windowsill for more than five years. There is something about the way the sun shines through the golden oil that is transfixing. I have opened other bottles and have been equally wowed by their taste. The shop where they sell their wares is stylish and chic—very Provençalesque—and the perfect stage for their posh merchandise, which includes fourteen infused olive oils. One entire wall is lined with custom-made copper vats filled with six single-varietal oils, a house blend, and a grapeseed oil that you bottle yourself. The store—a veritable showroom for goods from the olive oil–producing regions of the world—is filled with large oak tables and lavish displays of olive oil accoutrements. The floor is painted with olive branches and in colors that evoke an antique Tuscan villa. Paper cups are lined up next to every bottle and tank for tasting, and when you are finished, tossed into earthenware pots that are much too pretty to be trash cans—not surprising, given how beautiful everything in the store is.

Prato Lungo

Long Meadow Ranch   1775 Whitehall Lane, St. Helena
www.longmeadowranch.com

(707) 963 4555   Long Meadow Ranch is an ecological marvel. The winery and *frantoio* (olive oil mill) are housed in an architecturally daring structure constructed almost entirely of recycled materials. The walls are made with the dirt that was extracted to form the caves. The redwood beams were rescued from a warehouse in Oakland, and the industrial-looking lamps are made from steel enjoying a second incarnation. Ted and Laddie Hall, owners of Long Meadow Ranch, employ stringent organic farming practices, have developed an integrated system that involves every aspect of the ranch, and have restored a 120-year-old olive orchard that was planted by some of the Valley's earliest settlers and then forgotten. **Prato Lungo,** their estate-grown, ultra-premium extra-virgin olive oil, also has the fine distinction of being made in California's only winery

and *frantoio* combination. The on-site eight-ton Italian granite olive crusher and world-class Pieralisi equipment ensure that the hand-picked olives are pressed within hours under the supervision of olive-oil maker Mick McDaniel. The oil, made when olives are at the stage of ripeness that yields the desired low acid, is clean and fresh, with the essence of tropical fruit and a lingering peppery essence. It is oil worthy of the orchard's history.

St. Helena Olive Oil Company

8576 St. Helena Highway, St. Helena   www.shooc.com
Open daily 10am–5pm

(707) 967 1003

The **St. Helena Olive Oil Company**'s home feels like a rustic country barn. In the back you can watch the oil being bottled, and out front you can wander the shop and sample the different oils and vinegars they produce, including their estate oil, made entirely from Napa Valley olives. The store also carries goods that look as though they were stolen right off a farm in Provence. Traditional oil cans, thick woven linens, and enamelware evoke a languid lunch set in the French countryside. And if that appeals to you, you can re-create that feeling at home, complete with the olive trees and topiaries that are for sale. If you are leaning more towards the practical, check out the chef-sized half-gallon containers of oil and vinegar. There are several different berry-flavored balsamic vinegars, Napa Valley cabernet and chardonnay vinegars, a California extra-virgin olive oil, and an extra-virgin lemon olive oil. This store demonstrates the generous nature of owner Peggy O'Kelly, who carries a good variety of other local products, from Napa Valley Lavender Company pillows to Made in Napa Valley mustards.

Quick bite: *Pour ¼ cup olive oil into a small decorative bowl. Add a splash of balsamic vinegar, a pinch of dried lavender florets, and a pinch of crushed red pepper. Let sit for at least 1 hour. Serve as a dipping oil for bread.*

Salute Santé Grapeseed Oil

Food & Vine   68 Coombs Street, Suite 1-2, Napa
www.grapeseedoil.com

(707) 251 3900

When grapeseed oil first began to hit the shelves in the United States, it was considered a novelty, but it has been used in Mediterranean kitchens for centuries. Today it is a staple in the kitchen of almost every Napa Valley chef. **Salute Santé Grapeseed Oil** produces several different types of grapeseed oil in Europe, including an unfiltered cold-pressed oil with 100 percent chardonnay grape seeds (the remainder is extracted using a precise oxygen- and light-deprived process that results in a more neutral flavor). Salute Santé is available in almost all Napa Valley grocery stores, as well as at Omega 3 Seafoods.

Silverado Vineyards

6121 Silverado Trail, Napa

(707) 257 1770

Silverado Vineyards makes its estate olive oil from their own *oliveto,* or olive grove. A patch of land filled with the lush, shimmery trees, it has its own romantic albeit tragic tale. The original trees, planted nearly a century ago, attracted a young man to the ranch in the early 1920s. He bought it as a home for himself and his wife-to-be. On their wedding day, she failed to appear. He remained on the property for the rest of his life waiting for her to return, tending the silvery, seductive trees. Today, their fruit is used for Silverado's extra-virgin olive oils, which are sold at the winery, Oakville Grocery, and Genova.

Sparrow Lane

St. Helena
www.sparrowlane.com

(707) 815 1813

Sparrow Lane vinegar is following the same path wine did in the seventies, from generics to varietals. The result is distinctive vinegars that reflect the regions where they are made. All of Sparrow Lane's vinegars are made entirely of Napa Valley grapes and produced in small lots. Their chardonnay vinegar is aged in oak for eighteen months to develop a smooth mouth feel, with hints of oak and citrus in the aroma. The cabernet vinegar has a caramel essence with a balanced acidity. Tart and bold are the dominating characteristics of their champagne vinegar. They also make a zinfandel vinegar, an apple cider vinegar, a balsamic, and the crown jewel, a golden balsamic made from muscat grapes that exhibits a mesmerizing honeysuckle quality. It adds vim and vigor to all kinds of foods, from salad dressings to reduced sauces. Sparrow Lane vinegar is available at Vallergas, Sunshine Foods, Keller's, and Cal Mart. (See the recipe for Heirloom Tomato Salad with Capers and Golden Balsamic Vinegar on page 278.)

ESTATE OILS Gnarled old olive trees have grown synonymous with winery landscaping, so it should come as no surprise that many wineries also produce an estate olive oil. When visiting wineries, look for their proprietary oils in their tasting room. Many produce only a few hundred cases annually. The oils make thoughtful gifts, and small bottles weigh less than a bottle of wine—handy for those who are traveling. A few wineries that produce an oil are Robert Mondavi Winery, Cakebread Cellars, Roy Estate, Harlan Estate, Beaulieu Vineyards, and Duckhorn Vineyards.

Storm Ranch

Katz & Company   101 South Coombs Street Y-3, Napa

(707) 254 1866
(800) 676 7176

Another tiny producer, **Storm Ranch,** makes only about one hundred cases of olive oil a year. The olives are grown on a 120-year-old cattle and dairy ranch in Pope Valley, an appellation known for hot, dry summers and cold winters. Owner Bonnie Storm planted one thousand trees that she imported from Tuscany in 1994 and produced her first vintage seven years later—150 years after her great-grandfather settled in Auburn, California, planted olive trees, and fed his family with the fruits of his labor. True to its Tuscan roots, Storm's olive oil is mildly bitter, with the aroma of freshly mown grass.

Vine Village

4059 Old Sonoma Road, Napa

(707) 255 4006

Vine Village olive oil and vinegar have the fine distinction of benefiting a worthy cause. Vine Village is a home for disabled adults situated in the Carneros countryside. The proceeds from the oil and vinegar are used to sustain the organization, which employs many of the residents in the farm, vineyard, and product operations. Their seasoned wine vinegar and extra-virgin olive oil not only taste good, they'll make you feel good too, knowing you've enhanced the lives of Vine Village's residents. Vine Village products, including some of their estate-grown vegetables, are sold at the Napa Farmers' Market, and at many grocery stores throughout the Valley.

NOTEWORTHY NEIGHBORS

McEvoy Ranch

5935 Red Hill Road, Petaluma
www.mcevoyranch.com

(707) 778 2307

When Nan McEvoy decided that she wanted to plant her 550-acre ranch to olive trees, she didn't fool around. She revived a then-dilapidated ranch in northern Marin county, hired an expert, Maurizio Castelli, to help select the right trees, imported the trees from Tuscany, assembled an enviable *frantoio,* and went to work producing one of the most respected California olive oils available. Every year the olives hit their peak of ripeness—when the acid is just below 1 percent—around the beginning of November. The olives are hand harvested and carried to the two-thousand-pound granite press on the property and processed within hours. The large stone crusher releases aromas that are so robust you can almost taste the oil. The first harvest of **McEvoy Ranch**'s Tuscan-style olive oil was 1994, and in 2000 they produced their first vintage of *olio nuovo,* "new oil," a peppery, cloudy, intense oil bottled immediately after being pressed. (See the recipe for Roasted Brussels Sprouts with Olio Nuovo on page 319.)

The Olive Press

14301 Arnold Drive, Glen Ellen   www.theolivepress.com
Open daily 10am–5pm

(707) 939 8900   Like the co-ops of Europe, **The Olive Press** in Sonoma presses olives for local olive growers, including many of Napa Valley's wineries. Their petite facility offers a view of the olive-pressing process during harvest, November through January. They offer a selection of oils made from olives grown all over Napa and Sonoma Counties. Every Mediterranean country that produces olive oil, from Morocco to Spain, is represented in their merchandise of linens, ceramics, and oil vessels. They also carry a serious collection of books for the cooking enthusiast and the beginning olive farmer.

O Olive Oil

1854 Fourth Street, San Rafael
www.ooliveoil.com

(415) 460 6598   **O Olive Oil** was the first California producer to use the age-old Italian method of crushing olives with fruit to produce an intensely flavored oil. O Olive Oils are quintessentially Californian: They are made of hand-picked organic fruit and late-harvest Mission olives, which are most likely the state's oldest. The first oil they produced made use of founder Greg Hinson's favorite citrus, Meyer lemons. Since then, they have added three more oils made with exotic,

OLIO NUOVO A couple of years ago, I made a pilgrimage to Sicily and tasted *olio nuovo,* freshly pressed olive oil, for the first time. I was in the tasting room—a room in the basement of a neoclassical villa—of the Ravidas, who make estate olive oils from olives grown on their family farm just outside Menfi. Our hostess, Natalia Ravida, offered my friend, Andrew, and me each a small plastic cup of thick green liquid that resonated with the fragrance of freshly cut grass and a peppery finish that gently scratched the back of my throat. Its complex flavors, which were more intense than the oil from the previous year's harvest, captured my culinary imagination. In Italy, *olio nuovo* is taken from the press when the first crop of olives is crushed and is consumed immediately as a celebration of the harvest. Italians have as many uses for new olive oil as Americans do for ketchup. This is especially true in Italy's most prominent olive-growing regions, Tuscany and Sicily. Tuscans pour it over fresh fava beans, raw fennel and artichokes, and grilled meats and fish. Sicilians add *olio nuovo* to pasta with grated pecorino, drizzle it over braised greens, and pour it onto eggs. In fact, there are very few foods in these regions that escape to the table without a drizzle of *olio nuovo.* This oil should never be subjected to heat because hot temperatures can destroy its aroma and flavors; instead it is added to a dish once it has finished cooking but is still hot, so that the residual heat warms the oil and releases its distinctive fragrance. McEvoy Ranch in Northern California has begun to bottle and sell their *olio nuovo.* It is usually available at the end of November and is available for a short time—only two to three months. After that, the oil does the same thing that aging oil does: the solids settle in the bottom of the bottle and the taste begins to mellow. *Olio nuovo* is bottled unfiltered, and as a result it is dark green, a little cloudy, and very pungent. Like all olive oil, it should be stored in a cool, dark place.

❖

tantalizing types of citrus, including Blood Orange, Tahitian Lime, and Ruby Grapefruit. The year after his first olive oil harvest, Greg made his first batch of vinegar, O Zinfandel Vinegar, which is, hands down, the best red wine vinegar on the market. He begins its production by aging zinfandel wine in oak barrels for two years, using a traditional vinegar-making method that involves slow evaporation while the alcohol in the wine is converted into acid. Then he adds his signature splash of Bing cherry juice and lets the vinegar sit for six more months before bottling and releasing it. Also produced are a champagne vinegar and a rich, smoky sherry vinegar (using methods introduced to California by Spanish settlers in the early 1800s) that features his own California apricot wine.

The Bale Grist Mill's waterwheel.

PANTRY GOODS

A great meal is only as good as the ingredients used to prepare it. Finding tasty, high-quality goods to fill your pantry is a matter of tasting as many different products as you can and evaluating them. Are they fresh? Are their flavors balanced? Are they grown and produced by people who strive for the best? Napa Valley is just small enough that it offers the advantage of knowing the people behind the product. They are folks who live around the corner, down the street, and the next block over. They are chefs, gardeners, gourmands, and common folk who want to enhance everyone's dining experience. And the products they create are as diverse as hot sauces and preserves, mustards and honey, puréed fruits, and verjus. These are the building blocks for a stellar pantry and a delightful meal.

Bale Grist Mill State Historic Park

3369 North St. Helena Highway, St. Helena
Fri–Tues 9am–5pm

(707) 963 2236
(707) 942 4575

Dr. Edward Bale built the **Bale Grist Mill** in 1846 from stone quarried from the Napa River. A bit of a rogue, Bale found his way to Napa after being shipwrecked on the coast. He quickly married one of General Mariano Vallejo's nieces in order to qualify for a land grant, then built the mill just north of St. Helena. In the 1850s and '60s, wheat and grain were two of the Valley's major crops, and the Bale Grist Mill, along with Joe Chiles's gristmill, George Yount's "Star of the Pacific Premium Mill" in Yountville, and Albert Hatt's mill in Napa, was a major supplier for the entire country. In its early years, the Bale mill was also an important gathering place for residents, who met there to share gossip and news. In 1905 the mill was closed, and for nearly a century its huge waterwheel sat still, until the 1990s, when it was restored and once again the mill began to grind grain. The mill runs five days a week, and visitors can catch a glimpse of it in operation as well as buy any of the five stone-ground flours produced there: white wheat, red wheat, rye flour, fine cornmeal, and coarse cornmeal.

Branches Preserves

Katz & Company   101 South Coombs Street Y-3, Napa

(707) 254 1866
(800) 676 7176

Branches Preserves are not peanut-butter-and-jelly preserves. They are wake-up-in-the-French-countryside-and-spread-a-tablespoon-of-summer's-ripest-fruit-on-your-baguette preserves. They are made with just fruit, sugar, and lemon juice. The strawberry preserves are made from Napa Valley fruit whenever possible. The fruit for the other preserves is purchased from farmers in neighboring counties.

Mammarella, Francis Coppola Brands

1991 St. Helena Highway, Rutherford

(707) 967 0442

Outside of the Napa Valley, Francis Coppola is more widely recognized for his talents behind a camera than for his skills at the stove, but that is gradually changing with the introduction of his own line of Italian food products. His **Mammarella**-brand pasta, sauce, and olive oil showcase his Italian heritage. There are three all-organic sauces: Pomodoro-Basilico, Puttanesca, and Arrabbiata. The four pasta shapes, gemelli, farfallone, quadrefiore, and rosette, are all produced at a Brooklyn facility—the Morisi Pasta Company—that is as historical as the Inglenook Estate that Francis has restored here in the Napa Valley. Mammarella products are available at Niebaum-Coppola, Vallergas, and Oakville Grocery.

Hurley Farms

Napa

(707) 257 3683

When Sheri Hurley moved to Napa in 1997, she didn't know what to do with the abundant fruit that grew on her farm. At first she tried to sell it at the farmers' market, but she was still overloaded. With the assistance of her mother-in-law she began to make **Hurley Farms** preserves from the pears, apples, raspberries, and apricots growing in her orchards and those of her neighbors. The preserves are delicious, resonating with the taste of freshly picked fruit. A welcome addition to any breakfast table, they are available at Vallergas, Dean & DeLuca, and Trefethen Winery.

Made in Napa Valley

Tulocay   101 South Coombs Street, Napa
www.madeinnapavalley.com

(707) 253 7655

Catherine Bergen, the proprietress and genius behind the **Made in Napa Valley** brand, is a stickler for detail. She oversees every aspect of her business, from developing the innovative products that carry her name to ensuring that every single package is identical to the next. With over eleven different products, including vinegars, tapenades, sauces, dressings, rubs, mustards, baking mixes, dipping oils, and dessert sauces, Made in Napa Valley's only limitations are Catherine's imagination, which seems unstoppable. Her Fig and Roasted Shallot tapenade packs a wallop of flavor; her Tangerine Zinfandel Fruit condiment is sort of sweet, sort of savory; and her Citrus Jalapeño Caesar is a beautiful mix of subtle grape-seed oil, tangy citrus, and piquant chiles. Balsamic vinegar lovers will appreciate her Blackberry Balsamic with Pear; Raspberry Balsamic with Lemon; and Fig Balsamic with Dates. (See the recipe for Individual Chocolate Soufflés on page 269.)

NAPA VALLEY MUSTARD ISN'T WHAT YOU THINK IT IS. The bright yellow flowers that carpet the Valley in late winter are mustard, but they are wild mustard and their seed is not used for commercial condiments. Domestic mustards are made with yellow and sometimes brown mustard seeds that are predominantly grown in the northern prairie states and Canada. According to local lore, our wild mustard was imported to Napa by way of José Altimira, a Franciscan missionary, who was carrying a sack of mustard seeds on the back of his burro and either dropped the seeds on purpose as a trail marker or inadvertently due to a hole in the sack. The entire plant above ground is safe for eating. (The roots are sometimes used for dye.) The leaves may be used in braises, soups, and to mix with other greens for salads. The flowers, which can be very spicy hot, can be used like other edible blossoms. And once the flowers have gone to seed, the seeds can be harvested and used whole in vinaigrettes and sauces, or crushed and used to make mustard powder.

❖

Marshall's Farm Honey

Flying Bee Ranch   159 Lombard Road, American Canyon

(707) 224 6373
(800) 624 4637

Marshall's Farm has 650 beehives in one hundred locations throughout the Bay Area, many of which are here in Napa. All of Marshall Farm's specialty honey varieties are distinguished by region as part of their effort to maintain the integrity of each area's distinct environment, in the same way that wine is distinguished by appellation. The hives are harvested many times throughout the year to capture the flavors of each season's bloom. After harvest, the honeycombs are taken to the honey house, where the honey is extracted and bottled. Most of the honey is certified organic, and all of it has its own subtle nuances and flavors unlike any other. Visit their honey-tasting room, or purchase their honey at most grocery and gourmet stores.

Napa Brand Foods

Napa

(707) 258 8772

Gardner Jeff Dawson, the green thumb behind Copia's stunning gardens, the Culinary Institute of America's herb and kitchen garden, and a couple of winery organic demonstration gardens, is also the creator of **Napa Brand Foods'** delicious pepper sauce. After growing Hungarian peppers for a half dozen years, Jeff decided to throw a bunch in a barrel with some vinegar. They sat for six months and then were puréed in a blender. Pleased with the results, Jeff set about refining his method until he reached the right balance of vinegar and peppers. The sauce is a spicy, tantalizing addition to eggs, soups, and marinades and is available at Copia, Oakville Grocery, and St. Helena Olive Oil Company.

Napa Nuts

1755 Industrial Way, Napa   www.napanuts.com
Call for an appointment.

(707) 226 6083

If you've eaten a nut in Napa, chances are it came from **Napa Nuts.** Established in 1947 by the Rosenthal family, Rosenthal, as it was then called, sold eggs and kosher chickens until the 1980s, when it expanded its business to include fruits and nuts. Fifty years after they started, the Rosenthals sold their business to Allan and Maxine Milnso, who continued selling eggs for three more years, primarily to wineries for clarifying red wine. Now, the Milnsos concentrate on dried fruits and nuts, which are collected from all over the world and then sold to Napa restaurants and retail outlets, including Dean & DeLuca and Julia's Kitchen. Walking through Allan's closet-sized work space, which is packed floor to ceiling, is like taking a crash course in nuts. He is a walking encyclopedia of nut trivia. Did you know that toasting nuts releases their fat and reduces 3 percent of their volume? It's true, which is why Allan buys all of his nuts raw and roasts them himself. Did you know that dried fruit may sometimes be coated with oil? That's why it's best to give fruit, especially small berries, a quick dip in hot water followed by a cold bath before adding them to a marinade so that they'll absorb the liquid better. Have you ever wondered why cashews are so expensive? According to Allan, cashews are grown in Vietnam, and each softball-sized pod holds a single nut that grows in a leathery pouch on the bottom of the pod. The pod is poisonous, so the pickers have to climb the tree, drop the pod, burn it, then peel it away to get to the nut. And the very fastest workers pick only six a minute. Napa Nuts is a treasure, not only for the fun facts that Allan shares, but because the products are all gorgeous and high quality. The assortment of nuts, including more than twenty-seven different kinds of almonds, is unbroken and fresh; the two hundred kinds of dried fruit are all plump and flavorful; and the seven different kinds of coconut all taste as though they were just removed from the shell. All of the dried fruits and nuts can be purchased directly from Napa Nuts, by phone or directly at their office by appointment. (See the recipe for Spiced Fruit Biscotti on page 310.)

NapaStyle

801 Main Street, St. Helena   www.napastyle.com
Mon–Sat 10am–5pm, Sun 11am–5pm

(707) 967 0405
(866) 776 6272

Michael Chiarello, the former chef and owner of Tra Vigne, knows food and how to create dynamic flavor combinations. **NapaStyle,** his newish venture, is a line of products that provide home cooks with the same culinary tools he uses in his cooking. Among them are spice blends, including Herbes de Napa, a mixture of dried rosemary, fennel, thyme, savory, bay, and lavender. There are too many products to list them all, but a few warrant mention, and if you are in Napa, a trip to the store to taste them is recommended. Their lavender honey is sweet but not cloying. The Balsamic Reduction is a concentration of flavors in a sauce without the work. The Mission Fig Preserves have a surprising little twist with the addition of rosemary. And the Fritto Misto Flour, which is hard to find elsewhere, is ideal for dusting any type of vegetable, meat, or seafood that you want to fry. NapaStyle goes beyond food products to offer other wine-country items, such as pottery by local potters, olive tree topiaries, and barrel staves that have been transformed into furniture and candle holders. Visit their store or call for a catalog to see all of their wares. (See the recipe for NapaStyle's Crazy Strawberries on page 272.)

Napa Valley Pantry

P.O. Box 50, Oakville

(707) 224 2440
(888) 234 5536

Breakfast is the most important meal of the day for farmers. This statement was true for Kelly Wheeler, who grew up on a farm, and it was also the inspiration behind her delicious line of breakfast foods. **Napa Valley Pantry** consists of three yummy pancake and waffle mixes—Meyer Lemon Pecan, San Francisco Sourdough, and Light Buttermilk—and two luscious toppings, Boysenberry Cabernet Sauce and Brandy Maple Syrup. The pancake and waffle mixes are flavorful and easy to make, though the recipe on the container may need to be adjusted by reducing the milk if you prefer a thicker batter. Start your day with a taste of Napa Valley, or indulge yourself and have pancakes and waffles for dinner. The mixes and toppings can be purchased at Oakville Grocery, Sunshine Foods, and Cravings.

Napa Valley Vintage

Napa

(707) 451 3856

Most cooks have at least one specialty that their friends try to convince them to sell. For Ron Armosino, it was the barbecue sauce that he started making in college. After perfecting his recipe for more than twenty years, he decided to bottle it. He designed and painted the **Napa Valley Vintage** label himself and began selling two sauces, Original and Spicy. Both are smoky, tomatoey, robust blends made with Napa Valley cabernet sauvignon. Look for Napa Valley Vintage at Oakville Grocery and Cravings.

The Perfect Purée of Napa Valley

975 Vintage Avenue, St. Helena
www.perfectpuree.com

(707) 967 8700

Tracy Hayward started **The Perfect Purée** with the intention of developing a product that would prove to be useful to professional and home chefs. Pure puréed fruits and vegetables were the result of her creativity and hours and hours of research. The Perfect Purée makes over forty single flavors, ranging from red raspberry to morello cherry, coconut to lychee, apricot to peach, and roasted garlic to roasted sweet peppers. Use them in any dish that requires a puréed fruit or vegetable, including soufflés, blended drinks, creamy soups, sauces, marinades, and dressings. Although the purées have always been available primarily to chefs, home cooks can purchase them at the Perfect Purée office with prior arrangement. Distribution for retail sales is expected soon.

Sea Star Sea Salt

P.O. Box 55, Oakville
www.seastarseasalt.com

(707) 967 0222

Homer called salt a divine substance, Mark Kurlansky wrote an entire book on the subject, and Holly Peterson Mondavi imported her favorite salt to the Napa Valley and called it **Sea Star Sea Salt.** After cooking in Europe for many years, Holly was convinced that grey sea salt from Brittany, France, has a cleaner taste and healthier attributes than other salts available in the United States, so she set out to provide a reliable source for professional chefs and food enthusiasts. She began working with a Brittany salt farmer, Sylvain Le Duc, who uses traditional methods for harvesting the crystals. His pristine practices have earned him an organic certification, and the taste of his salt has earned him the accolades of those who have become converts. The salt is available in a coarse form, which can be used whole in cooking or ground in a mortar and or a spice grinder. Sea Star Sea Salt is available at Vallergas and Dean & DeLuca. (See the recipe for Holly Peterson Mondavi's Spice-Rubbed Grilled Salmon with Cucumber Salad on page 287.)

Fusion Foods

P.O. Box 542, Rutherford
www.verjus.com

(707) 963 0206
(800) 297 0686

Jim Neal, the mastermind behind **Fusion Foods,** was the original sous-chef at Terra when it opened. After leaving Terra, he spent some time at the now-defunct Oakville Stars, and then took a break from cooking and went to work in the vineyard with David Abreau. It was in the vineyard, while thinning fruit (cutting away clusters of grapes to create a greater concentration of flavor in the remaining berries) that he was struck with the idea of converting the half-ripened fruit into verjus, an ingredient used all over the world wherever grapes are grown, from France to Iran. Verjus, literally translated as "green juice," is made from unripe grapes and tastes like a very tart grape juice. It is used in much the same way as vinegar—in making salad dressings, deglazing pans, poaching fish, and marinating meat and poultry. Bouchon uses it in their steamed mussels, the French Laundry has incorporated it into a sorbet to cleanse the palate, and Jim uses it in almost everything he cooks. Verjus is available in both white and red versions (a small percentage of red grapes are added) and can be purchased at Vallergas, Sunshine Foods, and Oakville Grocery. (See the recipe for Jim Neal's Dried Fruit Compote with Corn Bread Financiers on page 330.)

Jimtown Store

6706 State Highway 128, Healdsburg   www.jimtownstore.com
Mon–Fri 7am–5pm, Sat–Sun 7:30am–5pm

(707) 433 1212   For an old-fashioned country store, **Jimtown** offers some very contemporary edibles. One of their signature foods is their olive salad, a savory mix of chopped olives, oregano, and garlic that can be used in place of tapenade, spread on crackers, or added to a recipe. In addition to their olive salads, there is a spicy chipotle spread, a sweet pepper and tomato spread, and an Asian peanut spread. Jimtown condiments are also available at Vallergas. (See the recipe for Chicken Ragout with Potatoes, Peppers, and Olives on page 309.)

FABULOUS FAKES California bay trees are the imposters of the culinary world. *Umbellularia californica,* a native of the Pacific Northwest and Northern California, has the same aroma and taste as *Laurus nobilis,* or sweet bay, but a greater intensity. Sweet bay is reported to have Asian roots and has a prolific presence in the Mediterranean, where it has been used in Greek and Roman cuisine since antiquity. It is the kind of bay leaf used most commonly for cookery, though California bay leaves can be used in the same ways, adding flavor to stews, soups, and braised dishes. Typically, one California bay leaf has the same potency as three European (often referred to as Turkish) leaves and recipes should be adjusted accordingly.

Morton & Basset Spices

32 Pamaron Way, Novato
www.mortonbasset.com

(415) 883 8530
(800) 646 8530

The quality of **Morton & Basset** herbs and spices is clearly visible: Their glass bottles allow you to see the plump, colorful, whole herbs and spices. Morton Gothelf, a cooking enthusiast, began to make up herb and spice blends for his own use in the mid-eighties. At the urging of his friends, he began selling them, and his company eventually grew to produce a high-quality line of herbs and spices that are all-natural, certified kosher, and nonirradiated. A line of thirty organic products for home use and food service is his latest venture. Look for Morton & Basset (named after himself and his faithful friend, a basset hound) at Vallergas and Sunshine Foods.

Scharffen Berger Chocolate Maker

914 Heinz Avenue, Berkeley   www.scharffenberger.com
Mon–Sat 10am–5pm (call for tour times)

(510) 981 4050

"Food of the gods" is the English translation of *Theobroma cacao,* the tree from which cocoa beans are harvested to make chocolate. Those who have tasted **Scharffen Berger** chocolate would agree that the same phrase could be used to describe the ultra-premium, handcrafted chocolate that Robert Steinberg and John Scharffenberger make. The two, a physician and a wine maker, respectively, select the cocoa beans used for their intensely flavored chocolate products from the finest plantations around the equator. The beans are transported to their Berkeley factory—a square brick building replete with vintage European equipment restored to full working order—where they are processed in small batches. The results are not like any other chocolate produced in the United States. Their chocolate bars, including semisweet, bittersweet, and unsweetened, are available in home chef and professional kitchen sizes. For easy eating they make three-ounce and one-ounce bars. The latter includes their Nibby, a blend of chocolate nibs (roasted cocoa beans, separated from their husks and broken into small pieces) and semisweet chocolate, and Mocha, the same semisweet chocolate infused with the flavor of dark-roasted coffee beans. Scharffen Berger also makes a rich chocolate sauce and a cocoa powder, and sells cans of nibs for home chefs to add to their own creations in place of nuts or chocolate chips. (See the recipe for Jan Janek's Blackberry Ice Cream on page 295.)

RED WINE AND DARK CHOCOLATE—MYTH OR

MAGIC? The ensemble of red wine and dark chocolate is probably the most polarizing food combination there is. There are those who love it and those who disdain the mere idea. Why is this? According to John Scharffenberger, who is both a renowned wine maker and an acclaimed chocolate maker, it's because dark chocolate and red wine have parallel flavor profiles, as well as similar acid content and tannin structure, so although sometimes they work well together, sometimes they fight. Most people agree that chocolate and red wine can exist harmoniously in the same meal if the chocolate is used as an ingredient in a recipe that also has wine as an ingredient or another high-acid component such as tart fruit.

Five Star Productions' inventory in place.

PARTY RENTALS AND SERVICES

Napa Valley's reputation for hospitality dates back to its earliest days. The Californios hosted large fiestas that went on for several days. Later, when the wine industry was in its infancy, guests often came to visit and stayed overnight for grand parties. During Prohibition, Napa Valley, and especially Yountville, was a destination for those seeking illegal alcoholic beverages. Once wineries were flourishing again and the Valley had grown in prestige, parties and special events became not just a way of life but also big business for caterers that could supply the props.

CATERERS

Café Kinyon

Vintage 1870, Yountville

(707) 944 2788   Kinyon Gordon has catered in a tent outside of Copia without a drop of water. He has transformed ho-hum lunches into a fun build-your-own box lunch. And he's developed cooking school dinners, in which he divides party guests into groups and then assigns each a different dish to prepare. And for those who want to entertain but don't want to cook, he offers plattered presentations: an entire meal arranged on decorative platters. All the host has to do is set the table and unwrap the food, and presto! Perhaps the most unique aspect of Kinyon's business is that he also has a space to offer. His restaurant, **Café Kinyon,** and its attached banquet room can fit 175 people for a dinner, wedding, or rehearsal dinner. (See the recipe for Café Kinyon's Beef Tenderloin with a Farci Crust on page 322.)

Knickerbocker's

1314 Oak Avenue, St. Helena
www.knickerbockerscatering.com

(707) 963 9278   For Tony Knickerbocker, owner and chef of **Knickerbocker's** and one of Napa Valley's most respected full-service caterers, food is a common career in his family: His sister Peggy is a well-known San Francisco cookbook author. Tony specializes in creating custom wine-pairing menus for wineries, including Beaulieu Vineyards, Rutherford Hill, Frog's Leap, and Merryvale. His clients rave that he is equally adept at preparing a casual Italian grill feast as he is at executing an extravagant formal French meal.

Melissa Teaff Catering

101 South Coombs Street, Napa
www.mtcatering.com

(707) 254 8160   **Melissa Teaff** has built her reputation by using local products, from Skyhill's goat cheese to Gerhard's sausages, to create seasonal

menus. After more than twenty years of catering, Melissa has produced almost every occasion imaginable, from wine-country weddings to real estate lunches. She can create a couscous that would make Moroccans envious, and her marinated grilled tri tip with spicy barbecue sauce would make a Texan weep.

Mi Fiesta

P.O. Box 2417, Yountville

(707) 963 2449 An authentic Mexican meal is a fun way to liven up an event. And entirely appropriate, given that Napa Valley was by and large settled by Mexican and Spanish nationals. **Mi Fiesta** owner Yolanda Tierrafria is the person to hire for a true Mexican feast. Her salsas are mélanges of vegetables, herbs, and aromatics, with just enough heat to please but not overwhelm. She offers a bevy of different rice, beans, chicken, and pork dishes, including sopes, flautas, and chiles rellenos, and her tamales are so full of flavor it feels like there's a mariachi band playing in your mouth. If you aren't planning a party but still want to taste Mi Fiesta's foods, look for Yolanda at the Napa and St. Helena Farmers' Markets, where you can sample all of her salsas and buy her tamales, which, by the way, freeze beautifully.

Wild and Free Catering

(707) 287 0199 **Wild and Free** may sound like a contrived name, but it is actually the surnames of partners Andy Wild and Carolyn Free. The two met while working at Dean & DeLuca and decided to combine his cooking skills with her pastry chef talents to create a catering firm dedicated to small custom events. Andy's nearly twenty-year cooking career includes stints at the French Laundry, the Culinary Institute of America, and Showley's, a Napa Valley classic that's now closed. Wild and Free offers boundless choices of menus, styles, and flavors.

Wine Valley Catering

875 Sousa Lane, Napa
www.winevalleycatering.com

(707) 256 2900

If there is a caterer to the stars—star wineries that is—Peter McCaffrey is it. His **Wine Valley Catering** has served breakfast, lunch, dinner, and just about every other type of meal or snack imaginable at nearly every winery in the Valley, from Opus One to Cuvaison. His business is less than ten years old, yet it is one of the most sought after in the Valley—no surprise, given Peter's culinary experience. After graduating from San Francisco's California Culinary Academy, he helped open the Portman Hotel, then spent a year working at Louis XV, Alain Ducasse's renowned Monte Carlo restaurant. He moved on to Paris, where he worked for Alain Senderens, before eventually finding his way back to California. Fresh high-quality ingredients are the foundation for his perfectly cooked, flavorful dishes. He can whip up a Mexican feast for Cinco de Mayo, create hors d'oeuvres worthy of Martha Stewart's praise, and serve a sit-down dinner for two hundred with ease.

NOTEWORTHY NEIGHBORS

Isa Caterer & Event Maker

2775 Cavedale Road, Glen Ellen

(707) 935 0723

Finding just the right caterer for a wedding can sometimes be as challenging as finding the right person to marry. When my sister became engaged, my friend Andi Werlin, a veteran of the restaurant business, told me that she had just had the most delicious catered food she had ever eaten. And thus **Isa** entered our lives. Isa is an extraordinarily talented chef with the touch of an artist and the conscience of an ecologist. Her globally flavored cuisine relies on the use of local ingredients that she buys as much as possible directly from Napa and Sonoma County farmers, fishermen, and cheese makers. A year after my sister's wedding, the guests were still raving about the stunning, innovative food. Of course, they were probably also swayed by the gorgeous presentations. An art major in college, Isa's skills range beyond the kitchen to the table, where she creates striking displays of food and eye-catching centerpieces.

Five Star Productions

1952 Iroquois Street, Napa   www.fivestarevents.com
By appointment only

(707) 257 2200
(800) 31 EVENTS

Five Star Productions carries props for every type of theme imaginable: tropical, Asian, Western, fifties diner, wine, Mardi Gras, and game night, to name a few. They have yards and yards of fabric, live trees and plants, gondolas, wrought-iron chandeliers, paper lanterns, coconut trees, corrugated tin, corral fencing, tiki huts—even the giant Wheel-of-Fortune made famous when Robert Mondavi dressed up as Vanna White and gave the wheel a spin at the Wine Auction. Five Star works with its clients from concept to execution and can create events as elegant or as casual as desired. Like magicians, they can transform a plain room into a fantasy setting with the use of light, draping, and a little elbow grease.

Napa Valley Party Services

365 La Fata Street, St. Helena   www.napavalleyparty.com
Mon–Sat 8am–5pm

(707) 963 8001
(707) 944 9403

Napa Valley Party Services offers everything from tables to punch bowls. Chance of rain? No problem; they can put up a tent, hang some walls, and set up an entire kitchen under the big top. They also offer a large selection of plates, glasses, and eating utensils and have a tasteful collection of linens, from sheer organza to sturdy brocade, prints to solids, and large to small in all shapes. Their tabletop rental items include Riedel stemware, candelabras, and a whole range of chargers, from patina to textured glass.

Wine Country Party

1924 Yajome Street, Napa   www.winecountryparty.com
Mon–Sat 9am–5pm

(707) 252 0711
(888) 545 0711

Wine Country Party has a diverse selection of items, from silver-service pieces that'll make your party look like you robbed your grandmother's credenza to an assortment of glass plates the color of precious stones. Their collection of plates includes several colors and sizes of square plates that are a nice change from the standard round ones. Light up your event with any of their candlesticks, candelabras, and beaded shades. Growing to meet the demands of more theme parties, Wine Country Party also rents more elaborate props, such as columns, arches, pillows, lamps, and even birdcages. And of course, they offer the basics in crystal, china, and utensils.

The picnic area at Clos Pegase.

PICNIC SITES

Fortunately, there are only a few winter months that discourage picnicking in Napa. The rest of the year, it is practically impossible to not be seduced by the temperate weather, lush foliage, and awesome vistas that greet picnickers. Bright yellow fields of mustard lined with vivid pink-blooming trees beckon picnickers in early spring. Blue skies and warm sunshine complemented by a slight breeze beg you to eat out of doors in summer. And autumn—harvest time—is the sweetest time to savor a midday meal on a hillside, at a picnic table in the shade, or on a blanket spread out on the lawn. Wherever you are in the Valley, there is sure to be a place to do so.

PUBLIC PARKS

Every town has a public park or two that makes for a practical pic-nic destination. Within each town, laws regarding open containers of alcohol vary. Chances are, if there aren't any signs posted, the discreet consumption of wine is allowed.

Alston Park

End of Trower (heading west) and Dry Creek Road, Napa

(707) 257 9529   There are only a few picnic tables in **Alston Park,** but they are set on the top of small hills. Your effort to make the slight trek to get to the tables is rewarded with a view: an almost panoramic tableau of the Valley from a western perspective. The tables are not shaded, so cooler days are best for dining here. If you have time, walk around the park on its main trail. The view and the varying landscape provide a mini-tour of California: oak trees, wild flowers, grapevines, grass, and depending on the season, plum trees in bloom.

Crane Park

Crane Avenue and Grayson Avenue, St. Helena

(707) 963 5706   **Crane Park** is rumored to have been built as a campground for vis-itors who drove to Napa during Prohibition to purchase booze. It is a large city park that contains the usual attractions: tennis courts, a jungle gym, and an expansive lawn area. The real draw of this park is its bocce ball courts. A favored pastime of Valley residents, bocce ball is as fun to watch as it is to play, so spend a few min-utes before or after lunch taking in a game.

Fuller Park

Between Oak and Laurel on Jefferson Street, Napa

(707) 257 9529   Situated in the center of Napa, **Fuller Park** offers something for visitors of all ages. There are swing sets and playgrounds to play

on and in, lawn and picnic tables to dine on, and beautiful homes on every border to look at. This is a swell spot to take a nap in the middle of the afternoon, host a children's birthday party, or cruise around to check out some of Napa's diverse architectural styles. Alcohol is prohibited in this park.

Lyman Park

Main Street near Adams Street, St. Helena

(707) 963 5706   Located within walking distance of the center of St. Helena, **Lyman Park** is a smallish square with a large inviting lawn ideal for picnicking or just taking a short break on a park bench.

Pioneer Park

Cedar Street near Lincoln Street, Calistoga

(707) 942 2838   The beauty of Calistoga is that you can park your car on one of the town's shady side streets and leave it there for the day. This town is a walking town and **Pioneer Park** is ideal for meandering to with a picnic lunch. Only a couple of blocks off Lincoln, the main street, Pioneer Park is green and shaded, with a large lawn area, picnic tables with grills, and restrooms.

Yountville Park

Washington Street near Madison, Yountville

(707) 944 8712   **Yountville Park** is a pie-slice-shaped public park located at the northern end of Yountville. Those that appreciate the macabre will be pleased to know that the top edge of the park is bordered by the George C. Yount Pioneer Cemetery and Ancient Indian Burial Grounds, established in 1848. Those who don't gravitate toward the park's jungle gym, large lawn area, and picnic tables with barbecue grills might be inclined to visit the cemetery. A stroll among the headstones is a mini-history lesson featuring former residents of Yountville, including its founder, George C. Yount.

WINERIES

Many wineries request that picnickers purchase wine while using their picnic areas and will reserve tables for customers. Buy a glass or bottle in the tasting room and enjoy it with your lunch.

Clos du Val

5330 Silverado Trail, Napa
Open daily 10am–5pm

(707) 259 2225   **Clos du Val**'s picnic area is small: two tables set on a tiny patch of lawn under a large oak tree. But the scenery couldn't be prettier—one side affords a view of the winery with a backdrop of the dramatic hillside; in another direction there is a giant magnolia tree, and in the other the vineyards.

Clos Pegase

1060 Dunaweal Lane, Calistoga
Open daily 10:30am–5pm

(707) 942 4981   **Clos Pegase,** a dramatic building designed by Michael Graves, has a very European feeling, especially the small picnic area surrounded on two sides by vines and on a third by Italian cypress trees. Walnut trees shade the café tables in the summer, offering a respite from the hot temperatures of Calistoga.

Cuvaison

4550 Silverado Trail, Calistoga
Open daily 10am–5pm

(707) 942 6266   On a lush patch of lawn, **Cuvaison** has arranged redwood tables with benches for picnickers. The only drawback is that it is set right on the road; however, the Silverado Trail is the less traveled of the two main arteries in the Valley, and the view of the fields and hills across the road more than makes up for the nuisance of passing cars.

Edgewood Estates

401 St. Helena Highway, St. Helena
Open daily 11am–5:30pm

(707) 962 7293

It is easy to become immediately enchanted by **Edgewood Estates'** tasting room and its adjoining picnic area. The building exudes a European country appeal, and the picnic tables are set under a small grove of trees bordered by roses and vineyards. Pick up lunch at Dean & DeLuca next door, buy a glass of wine in the tasting room, and you'll be set.

Folie à Deux

3070 North St. Helena Highway, St. Helena
Open daily 10am–5:30pm

(707) 963 1160

Four tables are arranged next to **Folie à Deux**'s farmhouse, home to the tasting room. The picnic area is a bit crowded, but the rustic setting is pure California: oak trees, vineyards, and green mountains in the background.

Louis Martini

254 St. Helena Highway, St. Helena
Open daily 10am–4:30pm

(707) 963 2736

The formidable stone walls that border **Louis Martini**'s enclosed picnic spot will make you feel that you are the guest at a French château. The picnic area is off the tasting room and has trees, a lawn, and picnic tables. Because it is set back from the road, it is a little quieter than other locations along the St. Helena Highway.

Monticello Vineyards

4242 Big Ranch Road, Napa
Open daily 10am–4:30pm

(707) 253 2802

At **Monticello Vineyards** a rose garden, olive trees, and vineyards surround eight tables. The colonial-style winery evokes the image of Thomas Jefferson riding up on his horse. Besides style, this picnic area has a conveniently located sink, grill, and restrooms.

Nichelini Winery

2950 Sage Canyon Road, St. Helena
Open daily 10am–5pm, spring and summer only

(707) 963 0717 **Nichelini Winery** was established in 1890 and is the oldest continuously family-operated winery in Napa Valley. The original building, built by its Swiss-Italian founder, is a rustic retreat for those willing to drive the twenty miles east of the Silverado Trail. The route takes you along Lake Hennessy and offers a view of Napa Valley terrain quite different from that on the Valley floor. The picnic tables are surrounded by ancient walnut trees down by a stream that runs along the property. Bring your bocce balls—there's a court.

Robert Keenan Winery

3660 Spring Mountain Road, St. Helena www.keenanwinery.com
Open daily 11am–4pm

(707) 963 9177 There are no two ways about it, **Robert Keenan Winery** is way off the beaten track. The hillside winery is located high above the Valley on Spring Mountain. The picnic tables are set on a tiny stone platform and have a panoramic view of vineyards and mountains. It's reached by a one-lane dirt road that would not be friendly to sports cars, but the unobstructed views are worth the drive. The winery suggests making a reservation if you plan a midweek visit.

Rutherford Grove Winery

1673 St. Helena Highway, Rutherford
Open daily 10am–4:30pm

(707) 963 0544 Don't be misled by the single table in front of **Rutherford Grove Winery.** There is a large, grassy picnic area nestled in a grove of eucalyptus trees behind the building. This is a great spot on a hot day or for a large group.

Rutherford Hill Winery

200 Rutherford Hill Road, Rutherford   www.rutherfordhill.com
Open daily 10am–5pm

(707) 963 7194

Rutherford Hill Winery shares the same view as their neighbor, the exclusive Auberge du Soleil. They have three picnic areas, one set on the crest of an oak-covered hillside that looks directly out onto the Valley floor. This would be an ideal place for a large party. The second is a secluded olive grove, and the third is a private oak grove with views of the winery and the Valley. Reservations are required for a group of ten or more. The winery carries a few picnic items. Those wishing to reserve the picnic grounds for a private party can arrange a fully catered event with Rutherford Hill's special-events department. They offer a choice among three menus—a gourmet picnic lunch, a buffet, and a barbecue—all of which can be prepared for as many as two hundred people or as few as twenty.

St. Clement Vineyards

2867 St. Helena Highway, St. Helena   www.stclement.com
Open daily 10am–4pm

(707) 967 3033

The steep climb up the hill from the parking lot to the Victorian house that hosts **St. Clement**'s tasting room and picnic area is well worth it. An area just off the porch is set up with picnic tables and café tables that are shaded and offer a view of the surrounding vineyards. It is a charming location to spread out a gourmet lunch and pour a glass of wine. The tables can be reserved in summer, although it's not required for groups smaller than ten.

A table set for two at Bouchon.

RESTAURANTS

Napa Valley has become a destination in large part due to the restaurants here. The abundance of seasonal local products, the creativity and dedication of world-class chefs, and the awesome surroundings create dynamic conditions for unforgettable dining experiences. Whether you are simply seeking substance or celebrating a special occasion, you're sure to enjoy the fine restaurants that fill the Valley.

All Seasons

1400 Lincoln Avenue, Calistoga
*Lunch: Thurs–Sun 11:30am–2:30pm; Summer: Dinner daily
6–10pm; Winter: Dinner daily 5:30–9pm*

(707) 942 9111   **All Seasons** is like the town of Calistoga itself: comfortable, with a dose of sophistication. The small dining room is unfussy; the white-cloth-covered tables are surrounded on two sides by large plate-glass windows offering a view of the goings-on outside. The waitstaff treats you like an old friend they're glad to see and are happy to share their enthusiasm for the dishes that emerge from the kitchen. The lunch menu is a mix of gourmet salads and sandwiches, with a few other dishes added for variety, such as Steamed Mussels in a Green Thai Curry Coconut Lobster Broth, House-Smoked Salmon Pasta, and Crispy Half Chicken with Roasted Sunchokes. The dinner menu changes with the seasons. The wine list is chosen from the tiny wineshop in the back corner and has a good mix of domestic and French wines at reasonable prices.

Auberge du Soleil

180 Rutherford Hill Road, Rutherford   www.aubergedusoleil.com
*Breakfast: daily 7–11am; Lunch: daily 11:30am–2:30pm;
Dinner: Mon–Fri 6–9:30pm, Sat–Sun 5:30–9:30pm*

(707) 963 1211   It didn't take being selected as one of America's fifty best hotel restaurants by *Food & Wine* magazine to confirm what those who've dined there know: **Auberge du Soleil** is a wine-country classic. It built its reputation as a fine-dining destination early when its original chef, the late Masa Kobayashi, cooked his first meal there. His extraordinary talent for combining taste, presentation, and fresh seasonal ingredients set the standard for the chefs who've followed him, including current executive chef Richard Reddington. The dining room is a fusion of rustic country lodge with luxury resort. A patio deck runs the length of the dining room and bar and is one of the most romantic places in all of Napa Valley on a warm summer night. Richard's culinary skills are displayed in the prix-fixe menu at both lunch and dinner, which features three and four courses, respectively. (A la carte choices are honored.) A spring menu may include Caramelized Diver Scallops with Cauliflower, Almonds, and Capers, or Wolfe Ranch Quail with a Lentil Velouté. Second and main courses could include Roasted Striped Bass with

a Sunchoke Purée, Crispy Bacon, and Sherry Vinegar Jus; Liberty Farms Duck Breast with Pea Tendrils, Sweet Onion Purée, and Spiced Jus; and Sautéed Salmon with Spring Vegetables, Brandade, and Green Garlic Nage. Dinner options include a six-course chef's menu, a nine-course epicurean tasting menu, and a four-course spa menu. A full breakfast menu is served in the dining room in the morning. For those who wish to indulge in the luxury of sitting on the hillside deck and taking in the view without dining at the restaurant, there is a bar menu. When the weather isn't agreeable, the bar with its fireplace is just as inviting.

Bistro Don Giovanni

4110 Saint Helena Highway, Napa
Sun–Thurs 11:30am–10pm, Fri–Sat 11:30am–10:30pm

(707) 224 3300

Bistro Don Giovanni kindles romance. Despite its large, spacious dining room, the restaurant feels cozy. And its boisterous environment, which some deem noisy, inspires intimacy. The testament to this is the dozens of couples who get engaged here. I think it's because of the tremendous food, flowing wines, and excellent service. It could also be the warmly painted walls inside lined with colorful pottery, or the patio dining room surrounded by grapevines, olive trees, and flowering vines. Whatever it is, at the core of a visit to Don Giovanni is the Italian cuisine that owners Giovanni and Donna Scala showcase on their seasonal menu. Start with their signature fritto misto, a combination of fennel, onions, and calamari, lightly floured, fried to a crisp perfection, and served with a slightly spicy aioli. There are always several pastas on the menu, and they are all good. Try the pasta with duck ragù for a bite of local flavor. The Salmon with Buttermilk Mashed Potatoes is a perennial favorite, and one bite into the succulent fish with its crisp exterior explains its popularity. The pizzas, all baked in a wood-burning oven, are a perfect start to a meal, and the tiramisù is the ideal way to finish it. Lunch guarantees a peek at the Valley's who's who, from chefs to wine makers. (See the recipe for Bistro Don Giovanni's Roasted Beet, Fennel, and Haricots Vert Salad with Roquefort Vinaigrette on page 316.)

DINING SOLO IN A DEUCE TOWN Napa Valley inspires romance. This can be either a little intimidating or a huge source of annoyance for the solo diner. To combat the presence of couples at every other table, I suggest sitting at the bar. There is always someone friendly behind the bar at places like Zuzu, Bistro Don Giovanni, Bistro Jeanty, and Bouchon. It's the best of all worlds: outstanding food, supreme wines, and someone to chat with only if you feel so inclined.

Bistro Jeanty

6510 Washington Street, Yountville
Open daily 11:30am–10:30pm

(707) 944 0103

Philip Jeanty has the Midas touch. With a few coats of mustard-yellow paint, a scattering of Gallic memorabilia, and a seasonal menu that elevates traditional French cookery to greater heights, he's created a gold mine. Modeled after the bistros of Philip's youth in the Champagne region of France, **Bistro Jeanty**'s two rooms evoke images of the French countryside, from the vintage bicycle, complete with a baguette-filled market basket, that separates the front room tables from the waiting area, to the mustard jars on every table. The same is true for every dish that leaves the kitchen. The flawless preparation of *cuisine bourgeoise,* a repertoire of casseroles, meats, and fowl prepared simply but exquisitely using California's freshest, finest ingredients, is a glimpse into Jeanty's twenty-year career preparing fine cuisine at Domaine Chandon before opening his bistro. The Coq au Vin is timeless in its appeal, his Tomato Soup in Puff Pastry is a must-have, and the Kidneys in a Creamy Peppercorn Sauce are comfort food for the Francophile. Don't miss the cheese plates or the crêpes. Reservations are absolutely necessary for individual tables, but there is a community table that is first come first served. (See the recipe for Bistro Jeanty's Tomato Soup on page 303.)

Bouchon

6534 Washington Street, Yountville
Open daily 11:30am–12:30am (abbreviated menus offered between lunch and dinner and late at night)

(707) 944 8037   **Bouchon** is so French it's almost startling when the host speaks English. Named after a Lyon-style café, Bouchon is a city-chic bistro. From the room's design (by famed restaurant designer Adam Tihany) to the menu, which is cleverly folded around a napkin, owner Thomas Keller applied the same meticulous attention to detail that has won him the highest accolades at the French Laundry down the street. The square room is highlighted by a zinc bar, above which are smoky mirrors and a vintage French clock. The back wall hosts a large mural, and the burgundy velvet banquettes crowned with mirrors along three walls are coveted for people watching—you are as likely to see a supermodel and her celebrity boyfriend as you are a Food Network chef visiting from out of town. The menu offers bistro fare that is skillfully prepared. The quiche of the day is so silky it practically melts in your mouth. The blood sausages are as authentic as any you would eat in France. The cauliflower gratin is a glorious dish of tender vegetables in a creamy sauce. A full seafood bar includes lobster, oysters, shrimp, clams, and mussels. The choice of local, domestic, and imported cheeses is carefully selected, and the desserts are designed for those with a sweet tooth and a discerning palate. The wine list features an outstanding selection of Napa Valley vintners, from Blockhedia Zinfandel to Mason Sauvignon Blanc, and the house wine, served in a bistro-style carafe, is always yummy.

Brannan's Grill

1374 Lincoln Avenue, Calistoga
Lunch: daily 11:30am–3pm; Dinner: daily 4:30–9pm

(707) 942 2233   **Brannan's** façade is reminiscent of the Wild West—all timber and adobe. You almost expect to walk in and see saloon girls and a poker game, but instead, the handsome room is filled with large, comfortable deep red booths, Craftsman-style lamps, a gorgeous dark wood bar, and a huge stone fireplace. This Pottery Barn setting is a pleasant place to eat lunch or dinner, but locals swear that Brannan's true value is their talent for making an impressive margarita. The big bar is certainly inviting and should be visited

for a drink or a glass of wine from their profuse collection of California wines—everything from Schramsberg sparkling wine by the glass to bottles of Diamond Creek Gravelly Meadow. But the real appeal of Brannan's, in my opinion, is their ribs. The meat, so tender it slips off the bones when barely nudged with a fork, is painted with a hoisin-based sauce that is everything a barbecue sauce should be: a balance of smoky, piquant, and sweet flavors. It will have you licking your fingers and ignoring the warm washcloth they bring you, guaranteed.

Brix

7377 St. Helena Highway, Yountville
Lunch: Mon–Sat 11:30am–3pm, Sun 10am–3pm;
Dinner: Mon–Thurs 5–9:30pm, Fri–Sun 4–10pm

(707) 944 2749

Brix is a solid restaurant that has steadily served good food and has an attractive dining room and a professional service staff. Unfortunately, it's never carved out a niche in the restaurant scene, despite its inviting interior, the olive groves and vineyards that frame the building, the lovely patio that merges into a marvelous garden, and its lavish brunch. Maybe folks can't get past what can easily be called the best wineshop in the Valley. They carry a huge list of wines that are hard to find, including Amici Pickett Vineyard Old Vine Zinfandel, White Cottage Sangiovese, Downing Family Fly by Night Zinfandel, Tom Eddy and Turnbull Cabs, and Miura Pinot Noir. And those are just the reds. They have just as varied a selection of whites, plus a cold case filled with the stuff. The shop also carries a cornucopia of bright, cheery items like colorfully painted dinnerware, shiny pewter serving pieces, and whimsical bags. There are even mosaic-tiled birdbaths—a little heavy for carry-on, but if you live nearby you could bring one home in your trunk, and fill it with ice and a few bottles of the exquisite wines Brix sells.

Catahoula Restaurant & Saloon

1457 Lincoln Avenue, Calistoga www.catahoularest.com
Brunch: Sat–Sun 10am–3pm; Dinner: daily 5:30–10pm

(707) 942 2275   The fire literally never goes out at **Catahoula,** as there are always a few glowing embers in the wood-burning oven placed center stage in the dining room. The domain of Jan Birnbaum, owner and chef, who is a master of creating bold flavor combinations that comprise his heavily skewed toward Cajun-Southern menu, Catahoula was named for the Louisiana state dog. Ironically, Catahoula sounds similar to catacula, the name of a flour milled at the Chiles mill in the 1800s, perhaps a prescience of the future, given that flour takes a prominent role in many of the dishes cooked at the restaurant. Jan's tongue-in-cheek humor pops up on the menu, which features Soft, Sexy Grits; Oysters with Mignonette and Snortin'-Hot Cocktail Sauce; and Spunky Chicken Stew with Red Bliss Potatoes and Chive Biscuit. The food, however, is serious. The gumbo is outstanding, and I have friends who drive the thirty miles from Napa to Calistoga just to have a bowl. It is smoky, spicy, and especially satisfying on a cold night. When in season, the fried smelt should not be passed up; neither should the Brick Oven Roasted Dungeness Crab. The Crispy Cornmeal Fried Catfish is always a treat, as are the sides billed as More of the Stuff You Really Like! And those in the know go to Catahoula for its very Southern breakfast.

Celadon

500 Main Street, Napa
*Lunch: Mon–Fri 11:30am–2pm; Dinner: Mon–Thurs 5–9pm,
Fri–Sat 5–9:30pm*

(707) 254 9690   When owner Greg Cole opened **Celadon** in downtown Napa it was like an instant oasis: a citylike restaurant in a country town, very cosmopolitan, very hip, and very good. The menu is seasonal, and both lunch and dinner are divided into small plates and big plates that fuse Mediterranean and Asian ingredients. The polenta small plate is two pieces of cheesy polenta stacked on sautéed chard and drizzled with a reduced balsamic syrup. The Cowboy Steak is a huge chunk of meat with a bone like a handle that tempts you to pick it up and start gnawing. And the wine list has as many rare, special wines as it does well-known ones. After several years in its tiny, creekside location, it has expanded in a larger venue in the Hatt Building.

Cole's Chop House

1122 Main Street, Napa
Dinner: Sun–Thurs 5–9pm, Fri–Sat 5–10pm

(707) 224 6328

Cole's shamelessly promotes carnivorous activity with their twenty-one-day Chicago dry-aged steaks and a menu rife with giant cuts of meat. The deal, though, is to look past the fancy cuts and choose the Beef Chop, a flavorful bone-in rib eye that is always cooked to perfection. It may not have the pedigree of its page mates, but it is delicious. Like a true steakhouse, the meat comes unadorned. The menu has a full list of classic sides to round out your meal. Don't pass up the hash browns, a giant skillet of grated potatoes with or without onions. The grilled asparagus with hollandaise is another sure bet, as are the sautéed mushrooms. Save room for dessert. The Bananas Foster is not only scrumptious, it is a showstopper that is served flambéed. The retro-style plates with Cole's logo and the stately surroundings—stone walls, cathedral ceilings, booths, dark wood floors and chairs—will remind you at every glance that you are in a place built for manly meals. The full bar is one of only a few in the Valley, so consider a martini before dinner or dive right into the wines. The wine list has a good half-bottle selection, and a bevy of vintages and vineyard designates from some of the region's best producers, like Phelps, Diamond Creek, Jarvis, and Crocker & Starr.

Domaine Chandon

California Drive, Yountville
Lunch: Wed–Sun 11:30am–2pm; Dinner: Wed–Sun 6–9pm

(707) 944 2892

The restaurant at **Domaine Chandon** defines elegance. One of the first upscale dining rooms in the Valley when it opened in the mid-seventies, it has held its place at the top with a menu that is decidedly French with a California backbone. The seasonal menu is available à la carte or as a tasting menu that includes wine suggestions, many of which are the sparkling wines made at the winery. Domaine Chandon is a delightful stage for special events, such as significant birthdays, an anniversary, or romantic rendezvous. The dining room is built into the slope of the hill where the winery blends into its surroundings so beautifully. Tables are arranged in terraced areas, creating the impression of many small dining rooms. The chairs are large and sumptuous, and the tables are set with glass and silver that twinkle in the soft light. With its long history, Domaine Chandon has amassed a cellar that could bring collectors to tears. It contains old vintages of French wines that most of us have only read about and local wines that are so rare they have attained mythical status.

Flat Iron Grill

1440 Lincoln Avenue, Calistoga   www.flatirongrill.com
Dinner: Sun–Thurs 4:30–9pm, Fri–Sat 4:30–9:30pm

(707) 942 1220   If you can eat steak guilt-free while being stared at by cows depicted in humorous paintings, **Flat Iron** is the place for you. Named for an inexpensive cut of meat that is their signature dish, this smallish restaurant is well appointed and comfortable. Rust-colored walls surround the beige-leather booths and scattered tables. Drapes and metal accents add to the soft glow of the interior. The menu is easy to navigate, with a short list of starters ranging from mussels served with French fries and a tangy lemon aioli to a Caesar salad. For the main course, choose from such hearty dishes as their griddled flatiron steak, a perfectly cooked tender strip of beef served with a cheesy potato gratin; beef brisket; and baby back pork ribs. Nonmeat eaters will be satisfied with the fish and pasta offerings. Desserts are all-American and irresistible, including New York cheesecake, apple crisp à la mode, and peanut caramel sundae.

Foothill Café

2766 Old Sonoma Road, Napa
Dinner: Wed–Sun 4:30–9:30pm

(707) 252 6178   **Foothill Café** has built a loyal following of locals that keep it filled until closing time every night. One of the first casual-upscale restaurants in the Napa Valley, it was an instant hit and its popularity has never wavered. The small, cozy dining room is painted a warm golden yellow that makes you feel as though you are wrapped in a giant sunflower. Their signature dish is their baby back ribs, but just about everything on the menu, from their seasonal heirloom tomato salad to their pasta creations, is equally as scrumptious. Foothill is small and always jammed, so reservations are recommended, even for weeknights.

The French Laundry

6640 Washington Street, Yountville
Lunch: Fri–Sun 11am–1pm; Dinner: daily 5:30–9:30pm

(707) 944 2380

A visit to the **French Laundry** is the dining adventure of a lifetime. Thomas Keller has created a cuisine that is uniquely his own and in doing so has carved out a place for himself in gastronomic history. However, his food is just part of the entire experience. When you arrive at this historic stone building and pass through the small but lush garden and the entrance, you'll realize why it is so difficult to get a reservation: The place is miniscule. It is divided into two small dining rooms, and a third, even smaller, private room. Thomas has the gift of wiping away pretense by offering his version of "diner food": Macaroni and Cheese, for example, is butter-poached Maine lobster with creamy lobster broth and mascarpone-enriched orzo. There is also Tongue in Cheek, Bacon and Eggs, Coffee and Doughnuts, and Chips and Dips. Much has been written about these dishes and all of Thomas's food and with good reason, but I won't do that here, because part of the appeal is the element of surprise as each course is delivered to the table. Instead of food descriptions, let me offer some advice on dining here: Go when you are certain that you will be able to relax and if possible, plan to stay overnight in the area so that you can revel in the memory of your meal rather than watch the road. Although you will have a choice between three prix-fixe menus, including a tasting of vegetables, for the most complete French Laundry experience you should order the chef's tasting menu and let Bobby Stuckey or Keith Fergel, the sommeliers, select the wines. Laura Cunningham, the restaurant's manager, has been part of the French Laundry from its beginning, and has built an impressive wine program that Bobby and Keith execute with exquisite food and wine pairings. Take your time to appreciate every nuance of each course. Look at the size and shape of the plate, examine the architecture of the food itself, and then take a bite. Savor it. Then take another bite, but don't feel compelled to clean your plate. It will be a long meal, so pace yourself; you don't want to fill up early. A tip on getting a reservation (the restaurant is usually booked two months ahead): Time your call for 10AM when the phones open. Be patient and don't let the busy signal dissuade you. Be willing to dine there for lunch or to eat dinner early or late, or you can always call in the afternoon for that night on the chances that there are cancelled reservations. Persevere and you shall be rewarded.

RESERVATIONS PLEASE Napa Valley is one of the best places in the world to eat. It's nearly impossible to get a bad meal here. But dining here does have a few flaws. Many Valley restaurants are quite small, hence they often have tiny or nonexistent bars, and thus very often there isn't any place for diners to wait. This is one reason why reservations are a necessity, especially Friday through Monday. The middle of the week is more forgiving, and diners can often be seated at most restaurants without a reservation. If you have your heart set on a particular place, call them the minute you know you are headed here. If you can't get the reservation you covet for dinner, consider eating like a European and enjoy a long lunch, as many restaurants offer the same menu during the daytime.

❖

Julia's Kitchen at Copia

500 First Street, Napa
Lunch: Thurs–Mon 11:30am–3pm (hours subject to change; call in advance)

(707) 265 5700   Located in Copia, **Julia's Kitchen** pays homage to the doyen of American cuisine, Julia Child. The food, the exposed kitchen, and the ambiance all do her justice. The dining room is light and airy: lots of white, glass, and subdued accents in the décor. Unpretentious and simple, at Julia's Kitchen the focus is on the food. Fresh seasonal ingredients are melded into creations like Roasted Onion and Saffron Soup with Rock Shrimp, Pearl Onions, and Chives; Steamed Black Sea Bass with Enoki and Shiitake Mushrooms, Scallions, and Mushroom Consommé; and Sautéed Calamari Salad with Blood Oranges, Mâche, and Mint. The service is impeccable, the wine list is superb, and the attention to detail is unsurpassed. The experience is worthy of the grande dame whose name it carries.

La Boucane

1778 Second Street, Napa
Dinner: Mon–Sat 5:45–9pm

(707) 253 1177   **La Boucane** is reminiscent of an era when maître d's wore tuxedos and chefs didn't deviate from their classical training. Nostalgia may motivate a visit to La Boucane, but the food will be the reason to return. This is largely due to the sensibility of owner Jacques Mokrani, who has been cooking since 1942. An Algerian by birth, he learned to cook in Marseilles, France, where he grew up. After some time in the Bay Area, he moved to Napa and opened La Boucane in a charming Victorian downtown. It was Napa's first French restaurant, and it remains in the same location with the same good food and the same homey atmosphere. It is a sweet place to indulge in a romantic dinner of Crisp Roast Duckling and Raspberry Soufflé for two. The Salmon Poached in Champagne Sauce is superb, a perfectly cooked fillet with spinach on the side and a silky sauce floating over the fish. When strawberries are in season, Jacques marinates them in red wine and garnishes them with a pinch of red pepper: heaven in a bowl. Jacques's cooking is impeccable and his personality is magnetic. At seventy-three, he is happy to take a minute to boast that he didn't begin his family until he was fifty-nine and that he contributes his virility to good

genes and the good life he leads, including eating and drinking moderately. After a taste of his skills behind the stove, you'll wonder how he's remained so disciplined.

La Toque

1140 Rutherford Road, Rutherford
Dinner: Wed–Sun 5:30–9pm

(707) 963 9770

It is rare that every single item on a restaurant menu looks irresistible. But **La Toque**'s menu is just that: a repertoire that will inspire gluttonous desires because you'll want to try every dish. It's ironic, given the rivalry between Northern and Southern California, that Ken Frank built his career in Los Angeles with his restaurant, also named La Toque, then moved to Napa Valley to create an exemplary menu that is considered one of the most wine-friendly in the Valley. The prix-fixe menu consists of five courses—six if you order cheese—and each course includes two choices, and sometimes three. The wine-pairing menu offers a specific wine for every dish, including cheese and dessert. And the à la carte menu has something for everyone, with its diverse array of perfectly prepared and delicious ingredients from water, land, and sky: dark green spinach soup loaded with buttery lobster, white asparagus with creamed morels, Niman Ranch rib roast with Blue Lake beans, and fresh pappardelle so tender it melts in your mouth. Though the food is fancy, the waiters are unpretentious, friendly, and knowledgeable. La Toque's understated dining décor, with its tan walls, whitewashed pine ceiling, sconces, and matching chandelier suspended above an enormous arrangement of perfectly coifed flowers, complements Ken's delectable food. This is a restaurant for a special occasion or for an occasion that will become special with every bite. (See the recipe for La Toque's Foie Gras with Fuji Apple and Mango on page 304.)

Martini House

1140 Oak Avenue, St. Helena
Open daily: Lunch 11:30am–3pm; Snacks 3–5pm;
Dinner: 5:30–10pm

(707) 963 2233 **Martini House** has a lot to like about it. First, there is the space. Restaurant impresario Pat Kuleto has turned the historic spot—the former home of bootlegger Walter Martini—into a Cowboys and Indians kind of place. It is the only restaurant in the Valley that honors Napa's first residents, the Wappos, with décor that includes chairs covered in fabric made to look like prairie blankets, a giant piece of driftwood hanging from the ceiling used as a candleholder, and lamps that appear to be woven baskets. The dark rooms, further accented by fireplaces, are a little like the set of *Bonanza,* but instead of Hop Sing, executive chef Todd Humphries (don't be misled by his ever-present dishwasher shirt, he really is the chef) is in the kitchen. Todd has created a seasonal menu that shows off his talent for emphasizing flavor, texture, and presentation. The wine list is as bold as the interior decoration and as well composed as the food. It has a foreword that explains the restaurant's philosophy and divides the wines by straightforward categories, including wines made by women and wines made by restaurateurs (Pat Kuleto's wine can be found there). Of course, all of the wines are what you would expect from a high-end wine-country restaurant: some cult, some familiar, and some exotic. The restaurant is wonderful, and the whole experience would be superb if it weren't marred by the attitude that you might encounter from the management and the reservationist. But it is still worth a visit, especially for the prix-fixe lunch. For the price of an entrée, you get a genuine taste of Napa Valley at a bargain price.

Meadowood, The Restaurant and the Grill

900 Meadowood Lane, St. Helena   www.meadowood.com
Grill: daily 7am–10pm; Restaurant: Mon–Sat 6–10pm,
Sun 10am–2pm

(707) 963 3646 The restaurant and grill at **Meadowood** serve some of the best food in the Valley and certainly some of the best hotel food anywhere. Even the room service is exceptional. Executive chef Didier Lenders has the magic touch with wine-country cuisine as well as assembling a staff that executes it flawlessly. The restaurant features a menu that changes daily to incorporate fresh ingredients and the whims of the talented chef de cuisine, Steven Tevere, formerly of Boulevard. The grill is very country-clubby, with a view of the golf course and dishes like something your dad might order: roasted pork tenderloin, fried calamari, apple and caramel bread pudding. It's not staid or stuffy, and there is also an alluring spa menu with such tasty morsels as rock shrimp gazpacho and grilled salmon. The wine lists at both the restaurant and grill are diverse and well planned under the supervision of John Thoreen, the property's "wine tutor." (See the recipe for Stuffed Pasilla Chiles with Chorizo, Tomato, and Cotija on page 290.)

Miramonte

1327 Railroad Avenue, St. Helena
Sun–Thurs 11:30am–9pm, Fri–Sat 11:30am–10pm

(707) 963 1200

Most people either love or hate the waitstaff's fluorescent lime and blindingly bright orange shirts at **Miramonte.** And after a caparinha, a Brazilian elixir made with cachaça, a whole lime, and cane syrup, weighing in with your opinion can be unavoidable. The same bold hand that conceived the brilliant uniforms also designed Miramonte's stark dining rooms, upstairs and down, and filled them with pale wood chairs and white-linen-covered tables. The shirts stand out like bright flowers and are a reminder of the building's colorful history, which includes serving time as a cask factory as well as a brothel. Owner-chef Cindy Pawlcyn used the same deft strokes to paint her Americas' menu with color, imagination, and copious flavors. The ubiquitous Caesar salad—let's not forget it was invented in Tijuana—is flavored with a chile-spiced dressing. Her ceviche is taken over the top with coconut milk and whole pieces of coconut that rest on a wedge of coconut shell. The entrees have a Southern flair: Fried rabbit with corn cakes and mustard greens shares the table with macaroni and cheese with ham hocks and pasilla chiles. The wine list too promotes the Americas, with wines from Argentina, Chile, and even Mexico in addition to a list of well-liked local wines. All in all, Miramonte is a refreshing respite from the Mediterranean cuisine that dominates the Valley's menus.

Mustards Grill

7399 St. Helena Highway, Yountville
Mon–Thurs 11:30am–9pm, Fri–Sat 11am–10pm,
Sun 11am–9pm (summer hours extended 30 minutes)

(707) 944 2424

Dubbed a "deluxe truck stop," after a delivery truck blocked the parking lot in its early days, **Mustards** is anything but. In fact, it is often credited with bringing California cuisine to the Napa Valley and promoting an emerging California wine industry when it opened its doors in 1983. Practically a pioneer in the Napa Valley restaurant business, Cindy Pawlcyn, Mustards' owner and chef, moved to Napa Valley in 1980 to work at Meadowood. Since opening Mustards she has kept her place at the stove, continually turning out inventive dishes that have become as beloved as the whimsical sign out front and the no-nonsense décor inside. The Mongolian pork chops are one of her most popular dishes, the grilled liver pays homage to her homespun style, and the ahi tuna sandwich is one of those dishes you eat once and then want to order every time you return. For dessert, you must have the lemon-lime meringue pie. You must. (See the recipe for Mustards' Pork Satay Salad on page 284.)

Pasta Prego

3206 Jefferson Street, Napa
Lunch: Mon–Sat 11:30am–2pm; Dinner: daily 5–9pm

(707) 224 9011 **Pasta Prego** is the old standby for locals, nice enough to go to for a special occasion, casual enough to go on impulse. Hidden in an outdated strip mall, it is easy to overlook. There are only twelve white-cloth-covered tables inside, with a few more set out in the adjoining courtyard when the weather is warm. The pasta is delicious, especially their lasagna, which is made with ethereally tender sheets of handmade noodles. Their wine list is small but complete. This is a sure bet for a memorable meal at a site that is definitely off the radar of most visitors.

Piatti Restaurant

6480 Washington Street, Yountville
Sun–Thurs 11:30am–9pm, Fri–Sat 11:30am–10pm
(summer hours extended 1 hour)

(707) 944 2070 **Piatti** is a tried-and-true Italian restaurant that can easily accommodate a couple on a date or a family of four who want solid, familiar Italian dishes. Don't pass up their signature garlic bread: crisp bread topped with roasted garlic and baked in the wood oven. They have a pleasing assortment of antipasti, salads, pasta, pizzas, and main courses, including pork loin saltimbocca, risotto, and rotisserie chicken. They offer a daily chef's menu that showcases some of the season's freshest ingredients as well as wines by the glass.

Pinot Blanc

641 Main Street, St. Helena www.patinagroup.com
Lunch: Tues–Thurs, Sun 12–3pm, Fri–Sat 11:30am–3pm;
Dinner: Tues–Thurs, Sun 5:30–9pm, Fri–Sat 5:30–10pm

(707) 963 6191   Executive chef Sean Knight has consistently won critics' and diners' hearts with his cooking talent. **Pinot Blanc** is the work of Joachim Splichal, of Los Angeles's megasuccessful Patina Group. When he opened his Napa Valley spot, he not only brought the talented Sean, he also imported a certain chicness that is visible in every detail, from the perfectly executed seasonal menu to the cozy red leather bar stools. The dining room is a Provençal fantasy: Every surface is covered in green, gold, or rust, with stripes and plaids mingling in harmony and large banquettes offering a prime view of the room. The menu features the most decadent of foods, from succulent scallops and sea-fresh mussels to creamy risotto, tender duck, and melt-in-your-mouth short ribs. The appetizers and entrées will seduce you, but be sure to save room for dessert. The bread pudding, a breathtaking combination of croissants, bittersweet chocolate, and cream, is so delicious you'll crave it for months and even years to come.

Roux

1234 Main Street, St. Helena www.rouxrestaurant.com
Dinner: Tues–Sat 5:30–10pm

(707) 963 5330   It's all about the plate at **Roux.** The restaurant is no larger than a modest home dining room, with a small back patio and an even smaller bar, but you won't feel cramped. They have a keen sensibility that shines through in the small details, like the terra-cotta wall lined with white plates, the Laguiole knives, and the Riedel glassware. Chef Vincent Nattress spent his formative years cooking at wineries throughout the Valley before he and his wife, Tyla, opened Roux. He mans the kitchen, churning out such delicious plates as Seared Maine Day-Boat Scallops, Braised Short Ribs, and Butternut Squash Ravioli that, manners be damned, will have you lapping up the sauce with your bread, preventing you from licking the plate. Tyla oversees the dining room and buys the wines. The wine list is short and savvy. Every wine featured is produced in volumes smaller than one thousand cases. Roux is a tiny restaurant, but the enjoyment of dining there is enormous. (See the recipe for Roux's Baby Beets with Herbed Goat Cheese on page 257.)

Rutherford Grill

1180 Rutherford Road, Rutherford
Sun–Thurs 11:30am–9:30pm, Fri–Sat 11:30am–10:30pm

(707) 963 1792

This is the place to watch the movers and shakers of the wine business do lunch and after-work cocktails. Conveniently located in the center of the Valley, **Rutherford Grill** is the link in a national chain called Houston's, but they've been in Napa so long they are part of the landscape here. The large horseshoe-shaped dining room is lined with spacious booths that are convenient for people watching. The menu is straightforward: a couple of salads, ribs, big cuts of beef, and a few vegetable plates. The service is usually fast, so it's a terrific place to take kids. There are lots of fun side dishes to try and even one—Jake's Bone—to take home for your dog. The wine buyer's skill shows in the impressive wine list. Among the many labels they feature are Paradigm Merlot, Saddleback Zinfandel, Jade Mountain Syrah, Heitz Cabernet Sauvignon, Lewis Vin Gris, Mason Sauvignon Blanc, and Caymus Conundrum.

Terra Restaurant

1345 Railroad Avenue, St. Helena
Dinner: Wed–Mon 6–9pm and occasionally to 10pm

(707) 963 8931

Hiro Sone and Lissa Doumani opened **Terra** in 1988 after falling in love with the building: a turn-of-the-century fieldstone structure with arched floor-to-ceiling windows. The restaurant is divided into two rooms, both with fireplaces, soft lighting, and minimal décor, and tables that are arranged to invoke a sense of privacy no matter where you are seated. The couple's cooking credentials are just as impeccable. He's a Japanese-born chef who learned to cook from France's master chefs Pierre Troisgros, Joël Robuchon, and Paul Bocuse. She perfected her craft under the guidance of Nancy Silverton at Spago in West Hollywood, where she and Hiro met. After working in Tokyo and Los Angeles and traveling together, they wanted a quieter life and returned to Lissa's hometown to open Terra. Their experience and world travels shine through in their perfectly executed arrangements of ingredients. Everything is good, everything is well made, and everything is fresh. There are no bad choices. That being said, everyone raves about their signature appetizer, the rock shrimp salad, and you can't go wrong with either the sea bass or the salmon with Thai red curry.

Tra Vigne Restaurant

1050 Charter Oak Avenue, St. Helena
Open daily 11:30am–10pm

(707) 963 4444   Since the day it opened its doors, **Tra Vigne** has been a destination restaurant. Its main dining room is a warm, energetic space crowned by an open kitchen that features a wood-burning oven. The outdoor patio and courtyard are *the* place to spend a leisurely meal on a warm afternoon or evening. The food may not be as reliable as it once was, but this is still one of the prettiest restaurants in the Valley. The seasonal California-Italian menu does offer a few no-misses. Try the handmade mozzarella antipasti, the Caesar salad, or the rosemary flat bread. The pastas are a fairly sure bet, as is the roasted chicken. The wine list, which has as many Italian as California producers on it, also has some stellar Italian varietal wines grown in the Valley, such as Dalle Valle Sangiovese.

Triple S Ranch & Resort

Petrified Forest Road, Calistoga
April–Dec: Mon–Sat 5–9pm, Sun 4–9pm (closed on Mondays during football season)

(707) 942 6730   The restaurant at **Triple S Ranch** seems out of place in the Napa Valley until you take into account the large horse community in the Valley (maybe that's why Robert Redford, the Horse Whisperer, spends so much time here). Triple S Ranch is named for the Schellenger family that runs the joint—and it is a joint. In addition to the restaurant there is an inn and horse stables, but it is the restaurant that is absolutely captivating. A cowboy place to be sure, the forty-year-old establishment is decorated with moose heads, shotguns, and old Coke trays on the walls; a dark red plaid carpet on the floor; red-and-white checkered tablecloths with a steer-head-and-cowboy-hat motif on the tables; and red leather stools at the bar. The whole place was once the barn, and the bar, where country western music, of course, is played on the radio, was formerly the breezeway with stalls filled with farm animals. The menu isn't fancy; there are five categories of entrees: beef, chicken, pork, seafood, and pasta and vegetarian. Every dinner is served with soup or salad and—a relish plate! It all tastes homemade and wholesome—exactly what you'd want after a day of riding on the range.

Wappo Bar & Bistro

1226 Washington Street, Calistoga
Lunch: Wed–Mon 11:30am–2:30pm; Dinner: Wed–Mon 6–9:30pm

(707) 942 4712

A meal at **Wappo** is an opportunity to taste dazzling flavors gathered from around the world. Venturesome owners Aaron Bauman and Michelle Mutrux drew on their collective global experiences when they created their menu. Start with the Turkish meze or their famous Chiles Rellenos, chiles filled with savory ingredients and topped with a walnut-pomegranate sauce. At dinner, try their paella or the braised Sonoma rabbit. Their Brazilian chowder, made with a mixture of succulent fish, coconut milk, and toasted peanuts, is part soup, part stew, and wholly divine. Slake your thirst with their signature Wappo Water, flavored with cucumbers, lime, oranges, and lemons—a drink worthy of a town whose water was the foundation for its existence. Don't be alarmed if you show up on a summer evening and there doesn't appear to be a soul in the restaurant. Just walk through the long, narrow dining room and you'll find a contented-looking crowd sitting under the grape arbor outside.

Wine Spectator Greystone Restaurant

2555 Main Street, St. Helena
Sun–Thurs 11:15am–9pm, Fri–Sat 11:15am–10pm

(707) 967 1010

The sprawling dining room at the **Wine Spectator Greystone Restaurant** is built around three open kitchens. It is an ideal space for a large party, but a little noisy and cavernous for an intimate dinner. The menu is created by the very talented Pilar Sanchez, who was the chef de cuisine at Meadowood before taking some time away from the restaurant scene to appear on the Food Network. But now she's back and turning out a select menu of seasonal dishes, many of which use ingredients grown in the school's organic herb and vegetable garden. Pilar's culinary efforts are complemented by Frette napkins, Riedel stemware, sterling silver flatware, and an impressive wine list. It is to be expected that any restaurant with the words *Wine Spectator* in its name would of course wow oenophiles with its wine list. Greystone's thorough selection of vintages and varietals is presented in an unusual way: The list is divided into unique sections, such as Philanthropy, Premier, Intriguing Whites, and Narsai David's Collection, which consists of bottles donated by Narsai and his wife to raise funds for the school, a nonprofit organization. And the best part is that many of the wines are not only available by the glass, but also in flights that arrive at the table with accompanying descriptions.

Zuzu

829 Main Street, Napa
Lunch and dinner: Mon–Thurs 11:30am–10:30pm, Fri 11:30am–12midnight; Dinner: Sat 4pm–12midnight, Sun 4–10:30pm

(707) 224 8555

Zuzu screams urban hipness. From the pressed-tin ceiling to the iron lamps hanging above the handcrafted redwood bar, it oozes sophistication. The décor is city smart and the food is Napa chic: a fusion of Mediterranean, Latin, and California, presented in small portions ideal for sharing several at one time. There is little elbow room in the two-tiered dining room, but the person or persons sitting next to you will most likely be enjoying themselves as much as you are, making the whole experience festive. The owners, all young, energetic men, help set the tone with their welcoming attitude and friendly banter. The tapas-style menu and reasonable prices are ideal conditions for sampling lots of dishes. The excellent paella should be first on your list: perfectly seasoned al dente rice topped with a juicy oxtail and a dollop of garlicky aioli. The Moroccan lamb chops balance spice and tang, and the goat cheese baked in tomatoes is sublime in its simple preparation and complex flavors. The tuna and avocado salad with grapefruit is a tasty way to cleanse your palate between courses or before dessert. Be adventurous and order some of the wines from the regions representing the origins of the different dishes; they may not be Napa Valley nectar, but they are well chosen. (See the recipe for Zuzu's Sautéed Piquillo Peppers on page 302.)

CORKAGE Corkage refers to the practice of bringing your own bottle of wine to a restaurant as well as the fee charged for doing so. Little known outside the wine country, bringing your own wine is done when a desired wine isn't on a restaurant's list, either because it's an old vintage, a rare wine, or very special for another reason. Corkage may have started with vintners bringing their own labels to share during a meal. It may also have begun with wine-country visitors buying a bottle of wine while out touring and then wanting to drink it that night. Although corkage is readily accepted, there are many arguments against its use. Restaurants rely on the revenue from their wine sales, and corkage affects their bottom line and can ultimately jeopardize the wines they are able to offer. Also, the profits from wine sales support a restaurant's entire wine program, such as having a wine steward on staff, a choice of glassware and decanters, and a knowledgeable staff that knows how to serve wine properly. Benefits for the consumer too are lost with corkage, including exposure to a restaurant's wine list and the opportunity to try new wines. All that being said, there may be occasion to bring a bottle of wine to a restaurant. If you do so, call ahead as a courtesy and be prepared to pay a corkage fee and a tip for the waitstaff for service.

Napa Valley's finest soaps.

SKIN-CARE PRODUCTS

Living in a place of such unapologetic beauty tends to raise your standards on all counts. Why use a generic soap when you can bathe with a bar made from your neighbor's lavender? Why buy a mass-marketed skin-care product when you can use a scrub, mask, or oil handmade by a local artisan? Not only is the Napa Valley a garden for herbs, flowers, and other aromatic, beneficial ingredients, it is one of the only places where grape seeds, high in rejuvenating antioxidants, are widely available and put to use in a large range of unique products, from body oils to lotions.

Flora Napa Valley Fragrances

1466 Railroad Avenue, St. Helena
www.napavalleyfragrances.com

(707) 963 9381

It shouldn't be surprising that Susan Costner Kenward, the force behind **Flora Napa Valley Fragrances,** has a vivid culinary background. The art of creating balanced and elegant fragrances is not that different from the alchemy of blending the flavors and aromas of food. Cielo, the first fragrance Susan created, was inspired by the perfume of Napa Valley; it hints of grape leaves, fig leaves, and oak moss. Its captivating scent is sold in several forms, including a perfume, an eau de parfum, a lotion, a French milled soap, candles, and room spray, all of which are handsomely packaged. Susan's second fragrance, Bohème, is just as lush, with notes of herbs, warm woods, and roses. Flora Napa Valley Fragrance products are available at Earth and Vine, Meadowood, and St. Helena Olive Oil Company.

Napa Soap Company

P.O. Box 1062, Calistoga
www.napasoapcompany.com

(707) 942 1024

Napa Soap Company's Serious Chef's Soap finally solves the problem that plagues all cooks: how to remove food odors from your hands. Owner Sheila Rockwood's masterful combination of essential peppermint oil; grape, soybean, and olive oils; and coffee grounds—their scent is undetected and they have wonderful deodorizing properties—can remove all kinds of odors from your skin. I keep a bar in the kitchen and another next to the bathroom sink to remove the smell of garlic, onions, fish, as well as non-kitchen odors like bleach, swimming pool chlorine, and even gasoline. There are eight other types of soap, including Cabernet Soapignon, which is the essence of Napa Valley in bar form. Each is unique and luxurious, and all are packaged in homemade paper with leaves and petals in the weave that evoke the ingredients inside. Look for Napa Valley Soaps at the Culinary Institute of America Spice Islands Marketplace, the Napa Valley Car Wash, and Beau Fleurs.

Napa Valley au Naturel

hearmeroarherbal@aol.com

(707) 363 0571   Creator Anna Wingfield followed her passion to develop **Napa Valley au Naturel**'s richly aromatic skin-care products. All of her products are made with essential oils and local herbs and serve as reminders in a busy, overloaded world, to stop and smell the roses—rose geranium, that is, or any of the other sweet fragrances found in her elixirs.

Napa Valley Spa Products

421 Walnut Street, Suite 204, Napa

(707) 257 9808   You can't walk into a spa in Napa Valley without coming face to face with Jeanette O'Gallagher's **Napa Valley Spa Products,** a line of body treatments made from grape seeds. The seeds are collected from more than fifty Napa Valley wineries and milled in five different processes before being transformed into rejuvenating spa products. Among these are Devine Body Mud, a blend of French clay and grape seeds mixed with water to create a silky mask ideal for face or body—a little like making mud pies the way you did when you were a kid. Her Crush Body Scrub feels a bit like rubbing dirt all over yourself, but the results are dazzling: refreshed, luminous, exfoliated skin. The Napa Valley Spa Product line also includes Anti-Oxidant Grapeseed Bath Tea, Lavender Rose Bath Gel, Lavender Body Oil, and Lavender Body Lotion, all made with grape seeds and intended to provide priceless benefits to your skin.

Uvavita

P.O. Box 73, Rutherford
www.uvavita.com

(707) 967 8482   **Uvavita,** a name that means seed of life, has created an entire
(800) 963 3432   skin-care system that exploits the restorative properties of grapes. Their five primary products are Daytime Antioxidant Moisturizer, with a velvety texture and luscious subtle fragrance; Nighttime Antioxidant Moisturizer, creamy as custard; Exfoliating Dead Sea

Mud Mask, a silky, thick purée with just the right amount of grit and a refreshing citrus aroma; Exfoliating Body Scrub, which smells so much like chocolate, plums, and berries you'll want to eat it instead of slather it on; and Hydrating Body Lotion, a lightweight emollient with a rich texture. All five contain healthy doses of grapeseed polyphenols, a high-powered antioxidant that is meant to protect the body from free radicals and thus save your skin from aging brought on by sun exposure, pollution, and dietary imbalances. Using a collective and extensive knowledge about oenology, chemistry, viticulture, and skin care, the five principals who started the company have found a way to create a distinctive skin-care line using the by-products of the Valley's wine industry. In doing so, they've bottled the magic of the wine country in potions that will make your skin healthy and happy. Uvavita products are available at Niebaum-Coppola Estate Winery, Earth and Vine, The Spa at Silverado, and Rutherford Grove Winery.

NOTEWORTHY NEIGHBORS
Sumbody

118 North Main Street, Sebastopol
www.sumbody.com

(707) 823 4043   Tiramisù. Chocolate Smoothie. Lemon Meringue. Desserts or heavenly body-care products? Both. Since all of the products created by **Sumbody** owners Debra Burns and Kila Peterson are made from entirely natural products, they are literally edible. But don't eat them or you'll miss out on the sensational effects they have on your skin. Debra and Kila, body chefs as they refer to themselves, have developed masks, soaps, scrubs, bath salts, and more out of sumptuous, alluring ingredients such as chocolate, avocado, nuts, honey, and herbs. All are intended to pamper, refresh, and relax you as well as connect you to the earth. Sumbody products are used in treatments and are available at Mount View Spa and Auberge du Soleil.

The Indian Springs Spa in Calistoga.

SPAS AND RESORTS

There is no better place to be pampered and indulged than Napa Valley. Whether you want to spend a few days in the lap of luxury (Meadowood), a single day off (Villagio), or just an hour for a deep-cleansing facial (Greenhaus), there is a place here to fulfill your needs and desires. And the best part of Napa spas are the treatments that make use of local resources, such as herbs, lavender, grapes, mud, and natural hot springs.

Auberge du Soleil

180 Rutherford Hill Road, Rutherford
www.aubergedusoleil.com

(707) 967 3159

Standing in the center of **Auberge du Soleil**'s relatively new spa, it's possible to see every color of green in the surrounding flora. Built into the hill, as is the rest of the resort, the spa is horseshoe-shaped, with treatment rooms on both sides of a lovely courtyard filled with herbs, native plants, olive trees, and a fountain. The rooms are light and breezy, with inviting beds adorned with fresh herbs. The menu of treatments is broken into four categories: the Vineyard, treatments from grapes; the Garden, treatments from herbs and flowers; the Grove, treatments from olives; and the Valley, treatments from mud and minerals. Choose from among such tantalizing treatments as Garden Foot Therapy, which uses a locally made mint-salt scrub; Meyer Lemon Olive Oil Massage; or Warm Grapeseed Oil Hair and Scalp Treatment. Outdoor showers and Jacuzzis complete the whole spa experience. For relaxing, there is an infinity pool at the far end of the spa and lots of alcoves filled with comfy chaise longues that provide a sense of privacy wherever you decide to rest and rejuvenate. The only disappointment is that the spa is accessible only to guests of the hotel. But staying at the hotel is hardly a hardship. This stunning resort has rooms that feature their own patio and bird's-eye views of the Valley. The grounds contain extraordinary sculptures tucked into the foliage and arranged along the paths. And Auberge's restaurant is a destination in and of itself.

Health Spa Napa Valley

1030 Main Street, St. Helena
www.napavalleyspa.com

(707) 967 8800

The sister spa of Meadowood, **Health Spa Napa Valley** offers a day spa retreat in the heart of St. Helena. There is a modest pool with swimming lanes, an outdoor whirlpool, fitness facilities, and full amenities, including robes, slippers, and lockers. The treatments range from outdoor massages in one of the garden-accented rooms to a hand-and-foot sugar-honey scrub. There is also a full menu of body treatments, including Grapeseed Mud Wrap, Herbs of the Valley Wrap, and Sugar-Honey Glow, a gentle exfoliation of your entire epidermis.

Indian Springs

1712 Lincoln Avenue, Calistoga
www.indianspringscalistoga.com

(707) 942 4913

Indian Springs is where you go to "take the waters." Built in 1862, its appeal is timeless. With one of California's oldest and largest pools heated with mineral waters from one of their four geysers, it is an attractive location to spend the day or the weekend. Cute bungalows line the driveway that leads to the spa. White wicker furniture, flourishing plants, and a tinkling fountain complement the spa's California-style façade. Mud baths, mineral baths, and a bevy of body treatments are offered, and all use the resort's own line of restoratives. And for those "with child," Indian Springs offers massages by trained prenatal-massage therapists.

Meadowood Resort

900 Meadowood Lane, St. Helena
www.meadowood.com

(707) 963 3646

Meadowood is a fantasy camp for grownups. Well-appointed cabins with fireplaces, bathrooms the size of ballrooms, and fluffy down comforters are tucked away among the trees in the historic valley that belongs to Meadowood. The resort includes a wine center that expands the wine enthusiast's knowledge via tastings, winery visits, and lots of wine and food consumption. The grounds include a golf course, a croquet field, tennis courts, a challenging hiking route, two swimming pools, and the spa. The spa is hidden behind the locker rooms in the same building where a gym and aerobics room are housed. A warmly lit hallway leads to a few treatment rooms that exude tranquility and envelop you in serenity. The staff is professional and can put even the most stressed at ease instantly. Their signature treatment, the Chardonnay Rosehip Mud Wrap, is heavenly. It begins with an exfoliation of your skin using grape seeds. Just when you think there can't possibly be another inch of skin to rub, the therapist applies a warm mask made of grape seeds and rose hips that smells like a cross between melted chocolate and toasted nuts. Once completely covered, you are wrapped in warm towels and blankets so that the rich nutrients and antioxidants in the mask can do their work, and while you lie there more relaxed than you ever thought possible, the therapist begins to massage your face and scalp, hitting every pressure point.

When you feel tingly all over, the blankets are removed and you are guided to the shower to rinse. And then you return for the pièce de résistance, the delectable full-body application of grapeseed oil that makes your skin feel like the soft cheeks of a baby. You won't want to move for days, you'll be so rested. Want more or less? There is a complete menu of spa treatments, including gentlemen's facials, body bronzing, and massages administered by two therapists to work every muscle and pressure point. The bad news: The spa is available only to guests of the hotel, spa members, and their companions. The good news: Similar treatments are available at Meadowood's sister property, Health Spa Napa Valley.

Mount View Hotel

1457 Lincoln Avenue, Calistoga
www.mountviewhotel.com

(707) 942 6877
(800) 816 6877

The spa at the **Mount View Hotel** is the perfect place to kick back for a day of pampering. The hotel comes with credentials, as the Hoovers stayed there during his presidency. The staff is very friendly and accommodating. The treatment rooms are cheerful and light, with beautiful showers or tubs that are also used in the hydrotherapy treatments. And the treatments offered are a variety of classic massages, facials, and body treatments that make the most out of local grapeseed products. They also offer the mud bath that Calistoga spas are famous for. The best part is that you can spend the day at the spa and hang out at the pool in the back, the same spot where Mrs. Hoover once planted a rosebush.

Silverado Country Club and Resort

1600 Atlas Peak Road, Napa
www.silveradoresort.com

(707) 257 5555
(800) 918 4772

The **Silverado Country Club and Resort** is a Napa Valley institution. Built in the 1970s, it has attracted people from all over the world who want to golf or just relax. In 1999 they added a full spa, with body care, skin care, massage, fitness programs, and beauty services such as haircuts, manicures, and pedicures. Very modern, the spa is accessible for those wanting the convenience of a day spa and its amenities, including a pool, a Jacuzzi, and a bevy of treatments to choose from, including the ginger wrap, which resonates with the essence of cinnamon, almonds, and tangerine. The lavender sugar scrub invigorates and calms. And the lavender rose bath soothes and energizes. The spa technically is available only for guests and members of Silverado, but depending on the season and traffic flow, other arrangements can sometimes be made. It's worth checking out.

Villagio

6481 Washington Street, Yountville
www.villagio.com

(707) 948 5050

Villagio is paradise. Italian cypresses, olive trees, and palm trees line the property. Water, from a large fountain that crowns the separate spa pool to the tiled waterway that travels the distance between the lobby and spa, offers soothing background sounds. The spa has a decidedly Mediterranean feel to it, with rust- and lemon-colored walls, frescoes, and vineyard views from the pool, but the treatments are pure Napa Valley. Aveda products share the spotlight with Napa Valley Spa Products, and hot mineral pools have been created in the tradition of the area's natural springs. The hotel rooms are delightful and the amenities generous, but even if you don't stay at the hotel, spending the day at the spa should definitely be scheduled into a trip to Napa. Be warned: You may not want to leave.

A SMALL INDULGENCE Everyone deserves to be pampered, even those with limited time or funds. These two Napa spas cater to clients who want luxurious treatments without the full spa surroundings or the requirements of a hotel stay. **Glow,** a warm, cheery spa near Copia, is the province of sisters Jackie Serrano and Nancy Brace, who have garnered an impressive amount of collective experience at the Valley's most revered spas. They offer a range of treatments, from massages to facials and use a variety of local products including a Grapeseed Back Treatment that cares for your back the way you would if you could reach it. 1180B Silverado Trail, Napa; (707) 253 0883.

Sonja Akey opened the **Greenhaus** to provide European-style treatments for guests who wanted intensive skin care. Sonja's German training emphasizes the health of the skin as well as the therapeutic aspects of facials and body care, resulting in individualized treatments that soothe both body and soul. Try any of the facials offered at the spa, or indulge in a full-body treatment that uses lavender and grapeseed products for a strictly Napa experience. 1091 Fifth Street, Napa; (707) 257 8837.

An outdoor setting is the preferred location for many of Napa's special events.

SPECIAL EVENTS

Napa Valley knows how to throw a party. From elaborate fundraisers to small celebrations, we take our festivities seriously. Wine and food are always on the menu. The grander events often offer an array of dishes prepared by more than one chef and a bevy of wines from the Valley's finest vintners—a unique opportunity to get a broad taste of Napa Valley in one sitting. Another bonus is the opportunity to visit spectacular locations, mainly private wineries and homes, otherwise not available to the public.

American Harvest Workshop

Cakebread Cellars   8300 St. Helena Highway, Rutherford
www.cakebreadcellars.com
Held the second weekend in September

(707) 963 5221
(800) 588 0298

Imagine a handful of the nation's top chefs joining forces with prestigious members of the media at one of the most glorious locations in the world, and you will have a picture of this phenomenal culinary occasion. The **American Harvest Workshop** began as a forum for chefs and food producers to meet and discuss the state of the food union. It has since grown into an annual event at Cakebread Cellars. Each year the chefs change, as do the menus. Past chefs have included such culinary heavyweights as Charlie Trotter, Rocco DiSpirito, and Bradley Ogden. The chefs "shop" at an open market set up for the occasion, then on Monday and Tuesday night create extraordinary dishes fit for a king using products from local purveyors, from caviar to lobster, exotic mushrooms to goat cheese, and venison to quail. So if you are feeling noble, mark your calendar and make plans to attend.

Hands Across the Valley

Niebaum-Coppola Estate Winery
1991 St. Helena Highway, Rutherford
Early August

(707) 226 6136

What do you do if you want to raise dough for the Napa Food Bank? If you are Francis Coppola you do just that—literally. Every year in August, Francis hosts **Hands Across the Valley** at his winery. Restaurants and caterers cook up marvelous tidbits of both sweet and savory foods to sample in a walk-about fashion. To accompany Napa Valley's finest noshes, wineries pour some of their best wines, from Robert Craig's Cabernet Sauvignon to Stags' Leap Winery's Petite Sirah. A silent auction offers a variety of rare items, from music memorabilia (a letter from John Lennon to Yoko Ono was on sale one year) to rare wines. The event culminates in a celebrity pizza dough tossing MC'd by Francis, while celebrities like former 49er Steve Young, actor Michael Douglas, and comedian Rob Schneider take a turn throwing the dough around.

WINERIES JUST WANT TO HAVE FUN Throughout
the year there are dozens of events hosted by wineries to celebrate occasions
that run the gamut from Cinco de Mayo to harvest. If you want to keep up
with who's opening their doors and throwing a party, check out these two
Web sites: www.napavalley.com and www.localwineevents.com. From there, you
might just find yourself eating, drinking, and dancing at St. Supéry, Folie à Deux,
Carneros Creek, Franciscan Oakville Estate, Domaine Chandon, Peju Province
or Sequoia Grove.

Napa Valley Mustard Festival

P.O. Box 3603, Yountville
February and March

(707) 259 9020   The annual **Napa Valley Mustard Festival** has grown from a
simple quest to draw visitors to the Valley during winter into
a prosperous event that spans several weeks and incorporates
multiple wine- and food-centric events. It kicks off with a grand
opening, followed by a series of events held throughout the Valley
featuring wild mustard: a photo contest that culminates in an
awards dinner, tastings at various restaurants and gourmet food
shops, a recipe contest, and the signature marketplace. The marketplace showcases cooking demonstrations, wine tasting, food
sampling, and a myriad of entertainment events. Not a bad way to
spend a late-winter weekend.

Napa Valley Wine Auction

P.O. Box 141, St. Helena
www.nvvintners.com

(707) 963 3388 If you could come to Napa only once in your life and attend only one event, the **Napa Valley Wine Auction** should be it. It is simply like no other. It kicks off every year with a sensational barrel event. Guests gather on Thursday at the host winery for an afternoon of noshing, wine tasting, and previewing the auction lots. Bites of succulent grilled lamb, rich, creamy cheeses, and savory finger foods from local purveyors are washed down with lush wine stolen from the barrel with "wine thieves," while the auction goes on in the background. Each barrel, donated from over one hundred wineries in the Valley, is available for bidding on. Prices are written on a wooden placard, then slid into a long slot on giant boards. As new bids are added, the old placards fall to the floor with a loud boom. Like your lover's heartbeat, it is a reassuring sound that the auction is alive and well. The barrel auction runs through the whole weekend and is joined by silent auctions for art and private wine collections: Residents and friends donate bottles from their cellar for this part of the auction. Friday and Saturday, the bidding moves to Meadowood so that the banging of falling placards is never far from earshot. Thursday night and Friday daytime are every foodinista's dream. Celebrated chefs are brought in from around the country to cook extravagant meals paired with rare Napa Valley wines, all of which are served in settings rarely visited by non-wine cognoscenti. Guests feast on Thomas Keller's iconoclastic cuisine at Marston Family Vineyards, sail on Diamond Creek Vineyard's private lake, tour Harlan Estate's cellar, dine around the pool at the home of John and Barbara Shafer, and dress up in "cowboy black tie" at Long Meadow Ranch. The Big Dinner, a black-tie affair on Friday night, is the stuff of dreams: waiters greeting you with champagne as you descend the red carpet. Then there's dinner under the big tent with live entertainment by such popular performers as Patti La Belle and Lyle Lovett. The party reaches a frenzy on Saturday when everyone reassembles at Meadowood for a taste of Napa Valley. Nearly every chef in the valley offers one of his or her signature dishes for guests to dine on before the live auction begins. The air inside the tent is filled with electricity as the bidding begins, and as the day progresses, the charge gets stronger. When the last gavel goes down, a family-style dinner is served on Meadowood's great lawn, followed by dancing under the stars.

IF THE GLASS SLIPPER FITS, DRINK OUT OF IT

When my first invitation to the Napa Valley Wine Auction arrived a few years ago, I felt like Cinderella. The four-day event is a nonstop party that makes me proud to live in Napa. Every year in June, some two thousand people gather at Meadowood Resort to eat, drink, and make merry in style and to build a community. The Napa Valley Wine Auction is the largest charity wine auction in the world, and it raises spectacular amounts of money. It was conceived more than two decades ago as a humble event to develop a fund for transient residents—mostly seasonal vineyard and winery workers—in need of health care. It has grown into an extravaganza that supports health care, youth, housing, and special community organizations as well as a safety fund—essentially a savings account to cover emergencies should the auction proceeds ever fall short. In 2000, the $8.8 million that was raised included a phenomenal $500,000 spent on one bottle of wine, a double magnum of Screaming Eagle. That single bottle paid for after-school programs for five hundred kids in American Canyon, prenatal and support services for Napa's Healthy Moms and Babies, an upgraded emergency response system for Angwin's Community Ambulance, and an expanded fund for patient care for Hospice of Napa Valley. And that was less than 10 percent of the total money distributed. Each year, more than twenty-five organizations are the recipients of the event's funds. By the time the monies are distributed in the fall, the excitement of the auction weekend is as distant a memory as the warm weather. However, for the recipients who have been on the receiving end of the nearly $30 million dollars raised since 1981, those few hours of late autumn are the best part of the auction.

Sutter Home Build a Better Burger Contest

277 St. Helena Highway, St. Helena
www.sutterhome.com

(707) 963 3104   The **Build a Better Burger Contest** was conceived in 1990 as a promotional gimmick but has grown into a beloved event. Once a year, zealous burger makers from across the country are invited to put a spin on America's most popular food. Ten finalists are then gathered at Zinfandel Ranch, Sutter Home's winery in St. Helena, to grill up their concoction. A group of esteemed judges select the winners and distribute a hefty check for the best-tasting burger. Until a few years ago, the event was limited to just a few guests of the winery. Now, it's a party. Burger enthusiasts are invited to sample some of the past winner's creations, build their own burger, sample Sutter Home's wines, listen to live music, and win prizes in a raffle. And best of all, the fee for attending is contributed to a local charity to help feed those in need.

A GENTLE CRITIC L. Pierce Carson is the luckiest man in Napa Valley. For more than twenty years, Pierce has been the reporter on the food, wine, and arts beat for the *Napa Valley Register*. With notebook and pencil in hand, Pierce is present at every party, every performance, and every special event in the valley, taking it all in and then relaying it to readers with skillfully arranged words. A convivial man, he has made more friends than enemies during his tenure as the Valley's cultural aesthete, most likely due to his tendency to praise rather than criticize, or as Belle Rhodes once put it, "When we stub our toes, he lets us down easy." And for those who've always wondered, the L. is for Lyle.

❖

A stack of California-style sushi.

SUSHI

Napa has a relatively large Japanese population. Some work for the wine industry and others are in training for Japan Airlines. And Napa is home to Hakusan Sake, one of only half a dozen American sake manufacturers. Maybe because of this, or maybe just by coincidence, there are a few reputable sushi restaurants here.

Fujiya

921 Factory Stores Drive, Napa
Lunch: Tues–Sun 11:30am–2pm; Dinner: Tues–Sun 5–9:30pm

(707) 257 0639

At first glance, you may think that **Fujiya**'s location is a stroke of genius—what could be more ideal for a Japanese restaurant than an outlet mall heavily trafficked by Japanese shoppers? But Fujiya occupied this space long before the outlets invaded Napa Valley. Their sushi menu is jammed with a plethora of sushi rolls, nigiri, and hand rolls. Each features a healthy selection of fish, from the more common eel and ahi tuna to the more exotic surf clams and jellyfish. They offer both lunch and dinner specials consisting of teriyaki plates, tempura, and *gyoza*, a steamed Japanese dumpling. It has the added benefit of being the only place in Napa Valley where you can see women wearing kimonos and you can sit on a tatami mat to eat Japanese style.

Saketini, *see under* Cafés and Casual Restaurants.

Sushi Mambo

1015 Coombs Street, Napa
Lunch: Mon–Fri 11:45am–2pm; Dinner: Mon–Sat 5:30–9pm

(707) 257 6604

East meets west at **Sushi Mambo.** A serene ocean-blue floor borders brick walls. The lamps and shelf behind the bar are miniature displays of Japanese architecture, and the menu is an entertaining collection of authentic Japanese cuisine and so-very-California sushi concoctions. The Sunny California roll is the classic avocado and crab rolled up in rice, but this version is deep-fried—and you thought sushi was supposed to be healthy. The Rock and Roll is eel, cucumber, and more California avocados. The Batman is eel and cream cheese. The Caterpillar is cucumber layered with avocado and then sprinkled with sprouts. And my favorite, Green Eggs and Ham, is a nigiri-style sushi with quail eggs and spicy *tobiko*. On the other side of the menu there are more traditional dishes like udon noodles, *yosenabe*, and tempura. And of course lots of Hakusan sake. At lunch, the best deal is the bento-box special: a combination of miso soup, terikayki, rice, salad, and sushi or tempura.

St. Helena's premier tableware store Vanderbilt and Company.

TABLEWARE

The table is an important place. The plates, glasses, serving platters, linens, and accessories that adorn the table are as crucial as the food and drink that share the space with them. Fortunately, the Valley has some very talented tableware artists and some posh stores with exquisite pieces for sale that will render any table praiseworthy.

Calistoga Pottery

1001 Foothill Boulevard, Calistoga www.calistogapottery.com
Open daily 11am–5pm

(707) 942 0216   Sally and Jeff Manfredi, a husband-and-wife pot-throwing team, produce earthy, handsome stoneware. Her work as a painter and his former life as a chef have led to dinnerware and serving pieces that truly reflect a cook's style. Many of **Calistoga Pottery**'s utilitarian pieces are put to work at restaurants such as Tra Vigne and Cantinetta, and are available for purchase at the Manfredis' studio and through NapaStyle. All of their clever pieces, like their salt containers with a lid to keep out the dust and their richly colored bowls ideal for pasta or soup, are intended for use but are so attractive they could just as easily serve as art.

Josephine European Tableware

1407 Lincoln Avenue, Calistoga
Summer: Mon–Sat 10:30am–5pm, Sun 11am–4pm;
Winter: Thurs–Mon 10:30am–5pm

(707) 942 8683   No bigger than a wide hallway, **Josephine European Tableware** carries a mix of French and Italian ceramics, glass, and stunning linens for the dining room or garden table. Many of the serving platters and bowls are similar to what you'd find in Deruta or Provence; all would make a lovely gift for yourself or someone special.

The Napa Valley Collection

Sherman Nobleman   355 La Fata Street, St. Helena
Open by appointment only

(707) 967 8167   **The Napa Valley Collection** is the handiwork of Sherman Nobleman, who specializes in one-of-a-kind platters and plates with glass handles. His signature tile-shaped platters feature playful phrases, bold colors, and Napa-inspired images of wine bottles, grapevines, and olive branches. He also produces large serving platters and dinnerware plates with romantic floral prints that incorporate fruit, vegetable, and checkered patterns spilling over the edges. Shop for Sherman's handmade wares at Vanderbilt and Company, NapaStyle, and winery retail rooms.

Napa Valley College Potters Guild

2277 Napa-Vallejo Highway, Napa   www.plasm.com-ceramics
Call for hours

(707) 253 3205   Carolyn Broadwell began the ceramics program at **Napa Valley College** and shaped it on a Japanese philosophy that plates, bowls, and platters should accommodate particular food items and should not necessarily follow a traditional form. Carolyn's early influence and the demand for designs that showcase a chef's work motivate students into crafting pottery in a plethora of one-of-a-kind shapes and colors. Pieces from local potters and students are available for sale by visiting the college or at Cakebread Cellars' American Harvest Workshop. And if you don't want to buy any pottery, sign up for class and learn to make your own.

Vanderbilt and Company

1429 Main Street, St. Helena
Open daily 9:30am–5:30pm

(707) 963 1010   A visit to **Vanderbilt and Company** will inspire you to set the
(800) 799 1949   table with more enthusiasm than you've shown since you received your first allowance for doing so. With a focus on the table and a minor spotlight on the bed and bath, Vanderbilt has amassed a stunning collection of linens, glassware, dinnerware, accessories, and personal items that make a table gorgeous. Many of the store's goods, including Susan Kenward's Cielo fragrances and Michael Turrigiano's ceramic pears come from local artists. They also offer an extensive array of Vietri's imported Italian ceramics, such as intricately painted serving pieces and warm pastel bowls and plates shaped to please the eye. They also carry an impressive selection of Napa books, such as Charles O'Rear's *Napa Valley*.

La Luna's master burrito maker at work.

TAQUERIAS

Taquerias have a long history in Napa Valley if you count the tamale manufacturer that's listed in the 1928 town directory. By the size of the crowds that fill our taquerias, it would be easy to surmise that burritos fuel the Valley's workforce. Gathered around the counter on any given day, you are likely to find vineyard workers, shopkeepers, tasting-room staff, and office personnel. And yes, they are fueling up on burritos, tacos, and quesadillas. And why not, they are a flawless meal: hand-holdable, quick, cheap, and most importantly, absolutely unbeatable in taste.

La Luna Market Taqueria

1153 Rutherford Road, Rutherford
Open daily 8am–7pm

(707) 967 3497 "If it's not from the moon, it's not good," reads the printed menu above the taqueria in the back of the **La Luna** store. Everything is handmade, from the *carnitas* to the beef tongue, the tamales to the roasted chicken, the beans to the rice. Locals agree that La Luna makes a mighty burrito, and their tacos are big sellers, too. If you walk in during the lunch-hour rush, you'll most likely have a few minutes' wait. Watch and you'll see this: Two guys staring down an overflowing steam table. They take a glance at the ticket taped to the shelf above. For a burrito, they pull off a slice of foil, grab a tortilla from the towering stack, slap it down onto the foil, fill it with a spoonful of beans, rice, meat, a handful of onions and cilantro, and a douse of hot sauce. Then they gather both ends of the tortilla, fold it over the bulging contents, roll it up, and pass it off like quarterbacks with a football. For tacos, two corn tortillas are set on the foil, filled with meat, a scoop of onion and cilantro, and a splash of hot sauce. They repeat this hundreds of times a day. If you want an authentic Napa meal, this is the place to get it.

Villa Corona

[1]3614 Bel Aire Plaza, Napa *Tues–Fri 9am–9pm,*
Sat 8am–9pm, Sun 8am–8pm
[2]1138 Main Street, St. Helena *Tues–Sun 10am–8pm*

[1](707) 257 8685 All a Mexican-food enthusiast needs to know about **Villa Corona**
[2](707) 963 7812 is that they make their own corn and flour tortillas. They sell these tortillas as well as a thicker, smaller corn tortilla used for sopitos, an open-faced taco with the contents piled high. Their plates include enchiladas, chimichangas, and flautas. Their burritos are different from other taquerias in the area, more Mexican than American. The *adobada* is made from meat marinated in a traditional chile sauce. The *camarón* is a savory mixture of shrimp, pasilla chiles, and mushrooms. The vegetarian burrito includes mushrooms, grilled onions, and peppers. On weekends, the place is jammed with folks that go for the *birría* (barbecued goat), menudo (traditional tripe soup), and shrimp dishes. After dinner, try one of the traditional Mexican pastries baked there. (See the recipe for Mole Sopitos on page 300.)

A MOVEABLE FIESTA Don't be dissuaded by the RVs that serve as homes for our roving taquerias. The food is good and the wait nonexistent. Not only are these popular stops for a quick bite after work, but regular patrons—chefs and other foodinistas—rave about them. The three that are best are **Taqueria Guadalajara** in the parking lot of a gas station on Solano Street at Redwood Road (one block north of Highway 29), **Michoacán,** which usually sets up shop on the north side of Soscol Street at Pearl Street, and a few blocks north, my favorite, **Tacos La Playita,** also on Soscol Street. The tacos here are the best. Be sure to request the grilled onions: green onions lightly caramelized and tender on the outside, crisp on the inside. Slip the onions into your taco and enjoy.

The Robert Mondavi Winery in Oakville.

WINERY PROGRAMS

Vintners love to offer programs that educate, enhance, and generally expand an enthusiast's perspective on matters of the table. Programs range from the historical to the instructive, with lots of opportunities to taste both food and wine.

Clos Pegase

1060 Dunaweal Lane, Calistoga www.clospegase.com
Open daily 10:30am–5pm

(707) 942 4981

"Bawdy and stimulating" is how **Clos Pegase** describes their monthly presentation, *Bacchus the Rascal: A Bacchanalian History of Wine Seen through 4,000 Years of Art.* Owner Jan Schrem entertains visitors with this tale, shown in their cave theater every third Saturday of the month, February through November. For a scintillating and unique perspective on wine, consider planning your visit to Clos Pegase to coincide with this presentation. Or, attend one of the other events that Clos Pegase hosts throughout the year, from their New Year's Eve Dinner to their murder mystery dinners. Reservations aren't necessary for *Bacchus the Rascal.*

Domaine Chandon

California Drive, Yountville www.chandon.com
Open daily 10am–6pm

(707) 944 2280

Sparkling wines are the most accommodating beverage when pairing wine with food, yet they tend to be overlooked as a main-course choice. **Domaine Chandon**'s wine-and-food pairing seminars are designed to change that. A discussion of food-and-wine pairing precedes a tasting that includes Domaine Chandon sparklers as well as their smaller-production still wines. They also host vineyard programs for the gardening enthusiast. Advance reservations are required.

Franciscan Oakville Estates

1178 Galleron Road, Rutherford www.franciscan.com
Open daily 10am–5pm

(707) 963 7111
(800) 529 WINE

To truly appreciate the art of wine, you need to know the details of how it is made and best served. Riedel stemware is boasted to be the only vessel that really shows off every nuance of a wine, because every wine varietal has a glass designed to showcase that specific varietal. To test this for yourself, **Franciscan Oakville Estates** offers, among their visitor programs, a Riedel Vinum Glass Tasting. These glasses will truly change your vision—of wine,

WINE-TASTING TIPS Spending a day or two, or a week, in the wine country is heavenly. To make it as effortless and successful as possible, here are a few helpful tips.

- Call ahead. Many wineries require reservations for tours and even tastings. Calling beforehand will ensure that you get to visit the wineries you really want to.
- Allow at least one hour per winery. If you are visiting a winery simply to see it and or to sample wines, you'll want to make sure that you have enough time to really look around without feeling rushed. Plan to arrive at least 30 minutes before closing time.
- Consult a map and make a plan. The Valley is relatively small and easy to navigate, but you'll get more out of your visit if you create a manageable schedule and an efficient route.
- Spit. It seems like a shame to spit out something so delicious, but if you are going to taste several wines, you won't want to mar the experience by any mishaps. Spitting the wine into a provided container once you've rolled it around in your mouth to taste it, like the pros do, is the best defense.
- Don't leave wine in the car unprotected. In the summer, when temperatures outside hover in the eighties and nineties, most cars turn into ovens. If you buy wine and have to leave it in the car, place it in an ice cooler or be sure to keep it in the coolest part of the car and head for shade when parking. Otherwise, the heat can change the taste of your wine or push the cork out of the bottle and cause leaking, which can be harmless but messy.

that is. Franciscan also offers interactive tastings that explore such topics as mastering blending and pinot noir clone tasting. The winery hosts a bevy of events, from wine releases to book signings, that offer the opportunity to taste their wines paired with food being prepared by their resident chef, Morgan Robinson. Reservations are required. (See the recipe for Morgan Robinson's Pasta Primavera on page 265.)

Merryvale

1000 Main Street, St. Helena   www.merryvale.com
Open daily 10:30am–6pm

(707) 963 7777   Chardonnay and steak? Cabernet and halibut? These and other topics are covered at **Merryvale**'s Wine and Food in Balance seminar on the fourth Saturday of every month. The two-hour program begins with a tour of the winery, followed by a sit-down tasting of wine and food in the winery's dramatic cask room. The engaging and friendly guide quickly begins busting long-held myths about wine and food pairing. A description of food-flavor profiles and how they can affect the taste of wine leads to a hands-on lesson. A small plate filled with olives, grapes, lemon, and chocolate is tasted alongside two wines to demonstrate how sweet and sour tastes of food can change the perceived taste of wine. It is an interesting exercise, and the surroundings make it all the more memorable. Reservations are required.

Robert Mondavi Winery

7801 St. Helena Highway, Oakville   www.robertmondavi.com
Open daily 9am–5pm

(707) 968 2000   Robert Mondavi, often called America's wine ambassador, along
(800) RMONDAVI   with his wife Margrit and their large family, designed the visitors' programs at **Robert Mondavi Winery** to demonstrate the importance of wine and food as part of a lifestyle. Today, the winery offers an extensive selection of programs that showcase wine and food. The Vineyard and Winery Tour concludes with a tasting of wine and a sampling of an hors d'oeuvre chosen to complement a selected wine. The Winegrowing Tour and Tasting offers wine enthusiasts a more in-depth experience that focuses on the vineyards and wine making. A sit-down tasting follows, paired with an

assortment of cheese and fruit. Food lovers can also choose from four outstanding programs that showcase the glories of the Napa table. Picnic in the Vineyards is meant to provide a look at the vines with the reward of a stunning lunch. Wine and Food: A Balancing Act begins with a tour of the winery and then a sit-down with a chef who will illustrate the effects seasoning can have on both food and wine. The Appellation Tour and Lunch not only provides a thorough overview of Napa's distinct regions, you'll sample wines that reflect the *terroir* of selected areas, followed by lunch in the Vineyard Room, the winery's private dining room. The Art of Wine and Food celebrates the cultural significance of both. A tour of the winery and vineyard is followed by a presen-tation, which culminates in a three-course luncheon, prepared by the winery's chef and complemented by Napa Valley and district wines (single-appellation wines), in the Vineyard Room. Reserva-tions are recommended for the Vineyard and Winery Tour, which is given several times daily. The others are offered on various days of the week and require reservations. (See the recipe for Annie's Apricot and Cherry Tart on page 270.)

Robert Sinskey Vineyards

6320 Silverado Trail, Napa   www.robertsinskey.com
Open daily 10am–4:30pm

(707) 944 9090   There are three driving forces behind the emphasis on food and wine at **Robert Sinskey Vineyards.** The first is the founder Rob Sinskey's strong belief that the two belong together. The second is Rob's wife, Maria Helm, who is one of Northern California's most acclaimed chefs; and the third is the chef in residence, Scott Weidert, also known as the Director of Gluttony. Scott's role keeps him in the winery kitchen, often cooking dishes for guests to try, such as pizza from the wood-burning oven or his coveted herbed almonds. He also oversees their wine-and-cheese-tasting program. He keeps about six cheeses from top-notch American producers, with a few imports added for diversity, in a French cheese cave for formal tastings and for creating plates for customers who want to nosh while sipping. The winery also offers an exclusive opportu-nity to learn about local food growers via the dishes that Maria and Scott craft with selected producers and chefs at their artisan cooking classes. A series of six classes is offered every year, featuring a demonstration, a tour, and a four-course menu paired with Robert Sinskey wines. (See Scott's recipe for Herb-Flavored Almonds on page 297.)

MONDAVI U The first year I lived in Napa I was a struggling freelance writer. I needed a job to supplement my income—i.e. pay the rent. I landed at Opus One Winery for the summer in their guest-relations department. It was a luxury that afforded me the opportunity to learn about wine via the everyday goings-on at a winery, and it also offered an up-close view of what makes the Mondavi family so infinitely wonderful. Patriarch Robert and his wife, Margrit, have always had a vision that one day wine would flow as freely on American tables as on those in Europe. To achieve this goal they emphasize education, disseminating knowledge about the health benefits of wine, the history of wine, the process of growing and producing wine, the pleasures of consuming wine and food together, and the importance of wine's place in our cultural tableau. The message is clear: Wine is a significant part of the dining experience. But to truly appreciate wine, one must understand it, and to understand it one must be exposed to it. And therein lies the magic of the Mondavis' vast educational programs that are available to the public. At Robert Mondavi Winery, groups of interested individuals can partake of the many programs that explain every aspect of wine, from soil to savoring, guided by the winery's wine educators, many of whom are certified masters of wine and master sommeliers. Guests from all over the world are welcomed for a day of swirling, sniffing, and sipping, because this is how the Mondavis get the word out: one mouth at a time.

❖

Swanson Vineyards

1271 Manley Lane, Rutherford   www.swansonvineyards.com
Wed–Sun by appointment only

(707) 967 3500   "Decadence with a wink" is how the Salon, the tasting room at **Swanson Vineyards,** is described. The over-the-top décor of the room is amusing, inspiring a festive mood for the tasting, which includes a sampling of cheeses selected to express different characteristics of the wines. The final sip of wine is served with an Alexis bonbon, a truffle made with a wine-enhanced ganache and lightly dusted with a savory and surprising curry powder. And just when you think you're through, you're offered a glass of New Orleans coffee, a tonic that will have you smacking your lips as you leave through the oversized French doors.

ZD Wines

8383 Silverado Trail, Napa
Open daily 10am–4:30pm

(707) 963 5188   **ZD** offers a wine-and-cheese-pairing program once a day on
(800) 487 7757   Saturdays and Sundays. Guests are greeted by a knowledgeable
ext. 107   staff member, led on a tour of the winery, then guided through the tasting of four cheeses from American and European artisanal cheese makers, paired with four carefully selected wines. The tastings are held for small groups, and reservations must be made in advance.

WINE AND TOAST The piece of bread that pops out of the toaster every morning and that bottle of '94 cab you have squirreled away in the bottom of a closet have a lot in common. Both rely on a degree of toastiness—light, medium, and dark, to be specific—to stimulate your senses and please your palate. Just as bread develops a complex range of flavors when exposed to direct heat, so do wine barrels. French and American oak barrels are constructed here in Napa at several cooperages, and one, Seguin Moreau, offers daily tours for the public to watch the barrels being assembled and toasted—an experience that will make you think of Napa every time you smell caramel, butterscotch, or vanilla. Tours are offered three times a day, Monday through Friday. 151 Camino Dorado, Napa; (707) 252 3408.

Back Room Wines' inventory.

WINESHOPS

Visiting wineshops in Napa Valley can be a near-religious experience for the serious oenophile or collector. With their close proximity to the wineries, retailers here have the advantage of developing long-term relationships with vintners and can thus secure wines that are otherwise difficult to come by.

Back Room Wines

974 Franklin Street, Napa   www.backroomwines.com
Sun–Mon, Wed–Thurs 10am–6pm, Fri–Sat 10am–9pm

(707) 226 1378
(877) 322 2576

Owner Dan Dawson is the quintessential wine geek. He has worked in various roles in the wine business, including wine buyer and director at All Seasons Wine Shop, sommelier at the French Laundry, and wine merchant at Dean & Deluca, before pursuing his own business. Now, as the proprietor of **Back Room Wines,** he shares his vast experience and talents with customers who want to purchase fine wines, many from boutique wineries that Dan has forged a relationship with. He also offers intermittent wine-maker dinners, a small menu of wine-friendly snacks, and lively chatter about various wines and wineries. If you can't make it to his downtown wineshop, visit his Web site. (See the recipe for Dan's Antipasti on page 299.)

Bounty Hunter

101 South Coombs Street, Napa
Mon–Fri 9am–5pm, Sat 10am–4pm

(707) 255 0622
(800) 943 9463

The **Bounty Hunter** has the prettiest location in Napa. Set on the Napa River in a historic former tanning building, the retail room offers a superb view of the water. But wine lovers will be more interested at looking at what's on the shelves: an impressive selection of elite local and imported wines. The Bounty Hunter also carries accessories like wine safes and stemware. Big bottles and wine futures round out their inventory, some of which is available through their wine club and newsletter.

Brix, *see under* Restaurants.

The Cork and More

1106 First Street, Napa
Mon–Fri 11:30am–2pm and 5–9pm, Sat 4–9pm

(707) 253 9375   The ten-thousand-bottle inventory at **The Cork and More** is an eclectic collection of imported and domestic wines. Older, rare wines fill the racks, including lots of mid-eighties through mid-nineties vintages of Ridge Montebello, Clerc Milon, Château Margaux, Leoville Las Cases, Staglin, Stags' Leap Cask 23, Dominus, Shafer, and Far Niente. Take a peek, if only for the chance to see such rare bottles of wine.

Groezinger Wine Company

6528 Washington Avenue, Yountville
Mon–Sat 10am–5pm

(707) 944 2331   **Groezinger Wine Company** is the only Napa Valley wineshop with a disco ball. That in itself distinguishes it from other Valley wineshops, and so does this shop's outstanding collection of wines from small producers. Most of the rotating stock of one hundred labels are from wineries in California, with a few Oregon labels added into the mix. Few if any of the wineries produce more than one thousand cases. The owner, Rick Beard, and shopkeeper, Justin Rush, taste each of the wines in the rotating inventory and can offer solid buying advice based on any criteria you may have. Gottlieb Groezinger, one of Napa Valley's first vintners, for whom the store was named, might roll in his grave at the thought of Grateful Dead posters in the shop, but he'd be content with the selection of wines from such wineries as Cain Five, Barnett, Neal Family Vineyards, and Scott Paul.

Enoteca Wine Shop

1345 Lincoln Avenue, Calistoga
Open daily 12–5pm

(707) 942 1117   The museum quality to Margaux Singleton's **Enoteca Wine Shop** is due to the glass cases of antiques and other knickknacks as well as the precious labels she sells. In another life, Margaux worked for the University of Virginia and belonged to a wine-tasting group, where she was introduced to two wines that changed her path:

a Bordeaux and a Rhône. In 1997 she opened the doors of Enoteca (Italian for wineshop), and began selling wines from small artisanal producers across the country. She has a startling collection of local vintners like Behrens and Hitchcock mixed in with more esoteric wines like cabernet sauvignon from Virginia. Her hands-on approach is similar to the *négociants* of France: She develops a relationship with the vintner, tastes each wine before she buys it, and uses her motto, "The right wine for the right home," when helping her customers make a purchase.

JV Beverage Warehouse

426 First Street, Napa   www.jvwarehouse.com
Open daily 8am–9pm

(707) 253 2624
(877) 4MYWINE

Joe Vallergas opened his first grocery store on what is now the parking lot of **JV Warehouse.** Before that, Joe's family grew vegetables where Copia is and sold them to nearby residents. Less than ten years after opening his store, Joe built a new, larger, and at the time, very modern building that is now JV, the Valley's biggest wineshop. With a wide-ranging portfolio that spans from jug wines to Dom Pérignon, JV is the best place to shop for a party or to fill a cellar. The wine buyer, Jon Sevigny, brings in lots of great wines at great prices, like Joel Gott Zinfandel that debuts at a bargain but sells out in a minute, and Mason Sauvignon Blanc, a perennial good buy. With almost fifteen hundred wines in their inventory, there is something for every taste and every budget.

St. Helena Wine Center

1321 Main Street, St. Helena   www.shwc.com
Mon–Sat 10am–6pm, Sun 10am–5pm

(707) 963 1313
(800) 331 1313

St. Helena Wine Center has a civilized, almost clubby interior that feels like a posh wine cellar. Not a bad impression, since that is their business and has been for almost three decades. Large-format bottles, magnums and up, as well as older vintages are in decent supply. With a diverse selection that ranges from York Creek to Long Vineyards, buyers seeking hard-to-find and collectible wines from Napa Valley producers will be happy to find this shop. And with a catalog and wine club, shopping for those wines has never been easier.

St. Helena Wine Merchants

699 St. Helena Highway, St. Helena   www.shwinemerchants.com
Open daily 10am–6pm

(707) 963 7888
(800) SAY WINE

There isn't anything fancy about **St. Helena Wine Merchants.** The stacks of wine cases, lined up in rows on the floor, are all that's necessary. Wines that are hard to find outside of Napa fill the shop, including many small producers and cult wines, like T-Vine, Ancien, Summers, Buonchristiani, Melka, and Cedarville. If you are looking for reserve wines and older vintages, this is a good place to start. The staff is extremely knowledgeable, whether you are seeking a specific wine or just want a suggestion. And they are sometimes offered special wines from private collections for resale, making their services even more valuable.

GETTING YOUR WINE HOME One minute you have a single bottle that will stow nicely in the bottom of your suitcase, and next thing you know you're looking at a case of wine. What to do? The best solution is to ship your wine home. Although most wineries restrict their wine shipments to a few states, there are several places that will pack and ship wine for consumers. In St. Helena, try the **St. Helena Mailing Center,** 1241 Adams Street, (707) 963 2686. In Napa, try **Buffalo's Shipping Post,** 1247 Solano Avenue, (707) 226 7492 (it's located conveniently next to the Lincoln Avenue exit on the eastern side of Highway 29), or **Wrap It Transit** at 1325 Imola Avenue West, (707) 252 9367.

DAY TRIPPING Nestled into the Valley of the Moon, a name that is credited to its crescent shape, is the historic town of Sonoma. It should be a destination for anyone visiting the wine country. The town square, which is only twenty minutes by car from Napa, is an excellent place to walk around, visit the shops, and tour the mission, the last one on the El Camino Real. Spend the day. There are historic wineries to visit, including **Sebastiani,** a few blocks off the Square, and **Gundlach-Bundschu** on the eastern edge of town (founder Carl Bundschu was the wine maker at Inglenook). Shop at the fabulous **Sonoma Market.** Take a class or two from a celebrated chef at Ramekins. Plan to eat there. Either of the **Mary's Pizza Shack** restaurants is an excellent choice for pasta or pizza for lunch or dinner. Go to **Happy Dog** for a burger so tasty it would bring Wimpy to his knees. **Café La Haye** serves a superb brunch on Sunday and awesome dinners in a small space decorated with eclectic art from the gallery next door. Visit **Deuce** for an unforgettable meal. And **Juanita Juanita** is a must, a funky shack where the Mexican food is authentic, the beer is cold, and Jill, one of the owners and part-time waitresses, is fabulous.

RECIPES

A Taste of Napa Valley at Home

Dining in Napa Valley is magical no matter where you partake of a meal, and cooking and eating at home can be as exciting as being fed by one of our world-class chefs—sometimes it's even better.

Gatherings are usually kicked off with something small to snack on while enjoying a glass of wine. Casual dinners with friends might lead right into the main course, while more formal occasions might include a first course, the entrée, and a cheese course before dessert.

Wine is essential. A meal is usually preceded by sparkling wine or a fresh, crisp white wine, such as a pinot grigio or sauvignon blanc. The same wine often accompanies a simple dinner. For multiple-course meals, it isn't unusual to serve a different wine with each dish, progressing from white to red. Usually the more robust a wine is, the later it will appear in the meal. And because this is the wine country, dessert wines are always welcome on the table.

SPRING

Roux's Baby Beets with Herbed Goat Cheese

Vincent Nattress, chef and owner of Roux, knows a thing or two about hors d'oeuvres. The former caterer and chef in residence at Robert Sinskey Vineyards, he's prepared his fair share of finger food. These stuffed beets make a handsome and delicious hors d'oeuvre that is sublime with sauvignon blanc.

12 small (golf-ball-sized) baby beets, scrubbed and stems trimmed to ½ inch
5 ounces fresh white goat cheese at room temperature
3 tablespoons chopped fresh herbs, such as chives, tarragon, thyme, basil
1 teaspoon minced lemon zest
Kosher salt
Freshly ground pepper
Pea shoots, chervil, or flowering thyme sprigs for garnish

Bring a large saucepan of well-salted water (at least 8 cups or the water will cook away before the beets are cooked) to a boil over high heat. Prepare a bowl of ice water. Add the beets to the boiling water and cook until tender when pierced with a fork, 12 to 15 minutes. Transfer to a colander to drain. Immediately transfer to the ice-water bath to stop the cooking.

Stem and peel the beets by gently rubbing off the skin using your hands or a clean dish towel. Cut each in half lengthwise. Cut a very small sliver from the rounded side of each half so it will sit flat on a platter. Remove a bit of the center of each half with a very small melon baller. (At this point, the beets can be cooled to room temperature, covered, and refrigerated for up to 2 days.)

Mash the cheese with a fork in a small bowl to soften. Add the herbs and lemon zest and mix well. Transfer to a pastry bag fitted with a rosette tip. Sprinkle the beets with salt and pepper and arrange on a serving platter. Pipe a rosette of cheese into the center of each beet. Garnish each beet with a bit of the greens.

SERVES 4 TO 6 AS AN APPETIZER

Pavi Micheli's Baby Artichokes

Artichokes often get a bad rap as a vegetable that doesn't marry well with wine. This simple recipe proves that belief untrue. Pavi Micheli and her husband, Rob Lawson (he's the wine maker for the Napa Wine Company), make an exceptional pinot grigio, called Pavi, that we drank one evening when her mother prepared these artichokes. The combination of the salt on the artichokes and the fruity essence of the wine was a hit.

1 lemon, halved
2 pounds baby artichokes (about 10 to the pound)
3 tablespoons extra-virgin olive oil
2 teaspoons medium-coarse sea salt

Preheat the oven to 350°F. Fill a large bowl with water. Squeeze the lemon juice into the water and add the lemon halves.

Remove the outer layer of tough leaves (at least 3 or 4 layers) from the artichokes until only the tender leaves that are entirely edible remain. Trim away the woody exterior of the stem, leaving the length intact. Cut the artichokes in half lengthwise and add to the bowl of lemon water. Let sit for 15 minutes.

Drain the artichokes and pat dry with paper towels. Transfer to a baking sheet and pour the olive oil over the artichokes. Toss to coat evenly. Spread out into a single layer and bake until browned on all sides, 30 to 40 minutes, turning often to brown evenly. Remove from the oven and sprinkle with the salt.

SERVES 4 TO 6 AS AN APPETIZER

Herb Gougère

Gougères are a savory version of cream puffs without the filling. With the addition of herbs and cheese, the otherwise plain dough becomes a tasty morsel on its own and a delectable hors d'oeuvre to serve with sparkling wine. Try Mumm Cuvée Napa DVX or Mumm Cuvée Napa Blanc de Noirs.

---

1 cup water
½ cup (1 stick) unsalted butter
1 cup all-purpose flour
¼ cup chopped fresh chives
1 teaspoon chopped fresh thyme
1 teaspoon chopped fresh sage or tarragon
1 teaspoon coarsely ground pepper
1 cup grated Asiago or Jarlsberg cheese
4 eggs

Preheat the oven to 400°F. Line a baking sheet with parchment paper.

Bring the water and butter to a boil in a large, heavy saucepan over medium-high heat. Add the flour all at once and stir until the ingredients form a mass. Continue cooking and stirring for 1 to 2 minutes. Remove from heat and transfer to the bowl of a heavy-duty electric mixer fitted with the paddle attachment. Add the chives, tarragon, thyme, and pepper. Mix on low speed. While the mixer is running, add the cheese and mix to combine. Add the eggs, one at a time, until each is fully incorporated.

Transfer the dough to a pastry bag fitted with a 1-inch tip (you can also use a plastic bag with a corner cut off as a piping bag). Pipe golf-ball-sized mounds 1 inch apart on the prepared baking sheet. Bake until golden brown on the outside and dry on the inside, 35 to 40 minutes. Serve warm or at room temperature.

SERVES 6 TO 8 AS AN APPETIZER

Laura Chenel's Roasted Asparagus with Goat Cheese

Roasting asparagus intensifies its flavor. Laura's combination of lemon zest and goat cheese adds a bright acid component to the asparagus, making it a great match with a Carneros-district pinot noir wine, such as one made by Artesa, ZD, or Robert Sinskey.

---

2 tablespoons olive oil
1 large garlic clove, minced
½ teaspoon minced lemon zest
1½ teaspoons kosher salt
½ teaspoon freshly ground pepper
1¼ pounds asparagus, tough ends removed
1 large red bell pepper, roasted, peeled, and cut into ¼-inch-wide strips
3 ounces fresh goat cheese at room temperature (see Laura Chenel, page 55)
½ cup walnuts, toasted and coarsely chopped

Preheat the oven to 400°F. Whisk the olive oil, garlic, lemon zest, salt, and pepper together in a small bowl. Put the asparagus in a baking dish large enough to hold them in a single layer. Pour the olive oil mixture over the asparagus. Toss until well coated. Roast until the asparagus is tender when pierced with a fork but still firm, 15 to 20 minutes, depending on the thickness of the stalks. (Stalks larger than ½ inch may need to be cooked longer.) Be careful not to overcook.

Divide the asparagus among 4 plates. Arrange the roasted pepper strips over the top in a decorative fashion. Crumble the goat cheese into medium clumps over the peppers. Pour any remaining oil from the roasting pan over the vegetables. Top with the toasted nuts.

Serve warm or at room temperature. This is most delicious when still warm, as the heat from the asparagus softens and warms, but does not melt, the goat cheese.

SERVES 4 AS AN APPETIZER OR SIDE DISH

Baby Lamb Chops with Honey-Mustard Glaze

A few years ago I was sent by a local magazine to interview Don and Carolyn Watson of the Napa Valley Lamb Company. I became so enamored by their farming methods and their devotion to raising high-quality lambs that I wanted to write a whole cookbook about lamb. This is one of the recipes I devised to showcase the tender meat of a rack of lamb. The fusion of mint, mustard, and honey in the marinade is a classic combination, and using it on baby lamb chops really makes the flavors pop. Prepare the marinade up to 3 days in advance and refrigerate in a sealed container. Kent Rasmussen Carneros Pinot Noir will do this lamb justice.

½ cup dry white wine
2 tablespoons Dijon mustard
1 tablespoon honey
1 tablespoon minced fresh mint
1 large shallot, chopped
1 teaspoon kosher salt
½ teaspoon freshly ground pepper
16 lamb rib chops (about 2 ounces each), Frenched (see Note)
Chopped fresh flat-leaf parsley for garnish

Combine the wine, mustard, honey, mint, shallot, salt, and pepper in a blender. Purée until smooth. Transfer to a shallow bowl and add the lamb chops. Let sit for 30 minutes.

Preheat a gas grill to medium-high or light a fire in a charcoal grill. Grill the lamb chops for 2 to 3 minutes on each side for medium rare. Transfer to a serving dish and sprinkle with the parsley.

Note: Ask your butcher to "French" a rack of lamb (clean the bones and trim away any extra fat), and cut the rack into separate chops. You can also do it yourself if you're confident with your knife skills.

SERVES 2 AS A MAIN COURSE OR 4 AS AN APPETIZER

Napa Valley Lavender Company's Risotto with Lavender, Meyer Lemon, and Chicken Sausage

Risotto, which appears year-round on menus, is easily tailored to the season. This recipe from the Napa Valley Lavender Company is subtly flavored by lavender florets, which blend beautifully with sausages and Meyer lemon. The Provence and Grosso varieties of lavender are best to use if you grow your own. Otherwise, you can sometimes find lavender in the spice section. NapaStyle's Herbes de Napa and Morton & Basset's Herbes de Provence are both acceptable substitutes. Try this dish with Rudd Napa Valley Chardonnay.

---

1 pound chicken sausages
3 cups low-sodium vegetable stock
¼ cup olive oil
½ yellow onion, diced
2 garlic cloves, smashed
3 cups Arborio rice
3 cups dry white wine
¼ cup fresh lemon juice, preferably from Meyer lemons
1 teaspoon dried lavender florets
1¾ cups grated Gruyère cheese
2 tablespoons extra-virgin olive oil

Preheat a gas grill to medium-high, light a fire in a charcoal grill, or heat a cast-iron skillet over high heat. Grill the sausages, covered, until browned on all sides, 8 to 9 minutes, turning to cook evenly. Transfer to a cutting board and cut into bite-size pieces.

Heat the vegetable stock in a medium saucepan over medium-low heat to a low simmer. Heat the olive oil in a large, heavy saucepan over medium heat. Add the onion and garlic and sauté until the onion is translucent, about 5 minutes. Add the rice and sauté until the rice is opaque, 1 to 2 minutes. Add the wine and increase the heat to high. Bring to a boil, reduce heat to medium, and cook, stirring until the liquid is absorbed, about 6 minutes. Add the vegetable stock 1 cup at a time, stirring frequently and cooking until all the liquid is absorbed before adding the next cup. Cook until the rice is al dente, about 15 minutes. Add the lemon juice and lavender; stir until the liquid is absorbed, about 3 minutes. Add the sausages, cheese, and extra-virgin olive oil. Stir until the cheese melts and the sausage is mixed in. Spoon into warmed shallow bowls.

SERVES 4 AS A MAIN COURSE OR 6 AS A SIDE DISH

Pan-Roasted Salmon on Pasta with Chanterelles

In late winter, wild chanterelles begin to appear in the market. They are especially savory when added to a dish with wild salmon. A lovely, bright Carneros pinot noir partners well with both the salmon and the mushrooms. Try Schug or Saintsbury.

2 tablespoons all-purpose flour
1 teaspoon kosher salt
¼ teaspoon freshly ground pepper
Four 4-ounce wild salmon fillets, skinned
1 tablespoon grapeseed oil
½ cup (1 stick) unsalted butter, cut into pieces
1 large shallot, minced
8 ounces chanterelle mushrooms, thinly sliced
2 teaspoons fresh thyme leaves
½ cup dry white wine
8 ounces angel dried hair pasta
Juice of 1 lemon
2 tablespoons minced fresh chives

Combine the flour, salt, and pepper in a large bowl. Add the salmon, one piece at a time, and toss to coat lightly.

Heat the oil in a large nonstick skillet over high heat. Add the salmon and cook for 4 minutes on each side, or until browned on the outside and still slightly translucent in the center. Transfer to a plate. Wipe the skillet out with a paper towel. Add one-third of the butter and melt over medium-high heat. Add the shallot and cook for 30 seconds. Add the mushrooms and thyme and sauté until the mushrooms begin to turn crisp, about 5 minutes. Add the wine and cook until nearly evaporated, about 5 minutes. Reduce heat to low and add the remaining butter a little at a time, swirling the pan until incorporated. Remove from heat. Cover and keep warm.

Cook the pasta according to the package directions until al dente, about 3 minutes. Drain. Add to the mushrooms and toss to combine. Increase heat to high and cook 1 to 2 minutes. Divide among 4 plates. Return the skillet to high heat. Add the salmon and drizzle the lemon juice over it. Cook for 1 minute. Place a fillet on each serving of pasta and sprinkle with the chives.

SERVES 4 AS A MAIN COURSE

Morgan Robinson's Pasta Primavera

Fava beans are the harbinger of spring. Truth be told, they are a hassle to cook because they have to be shelled and peeled, but the effort is quickly forgotten with one bite. Puréed and added to pasta, the beans gently flavor every bite. Morgan was inspired by Franciscan's Cuvée Sauvage, a chardonnay made with wild yeast, when he chose the ingredients for this dish.

3 pounds fava beans, shelled
4 small garlic cloves, minced
½ cup freshly grated Parmigiano-Reggiano cheese
Kosher salt
Freshly ground pepper
8 ounces dried orecchiette pasta
2 tablespoons olive oil
1 pound bay scallops
6 large fresh basil leaves, stacked, rolled, and cut into fine shreds
1 tablespoon unsalted butter
Stripped zest of 1 lemon
Lemon olive oil for drizzling

Bring a large pot of salted water to a boil over high heat. Cook the fava beans until tender, 30 seconds to 1 minute. Drain. Pinch the skin of each bean and pop out the bean. Set aside a small handful of beans for garnish. Combine the remaining beans, three-fourths of the garlic, and the cheese in a food processor. Pulse until finely chopped but not puréed. Add a generous pinch of salt and pepper. Pulse to combine.

Bring a large pot of salted water to a boil over high heat. Cook the pasta and until not quite al dente, 1 to 2 minutes less than package directions. Transfer to a colander to drain, reserving about 1 cup of the cooking water.

Heat the olive oil in a large nonstick skillet over medium heat. Add the scallops, the remaining garlic, the basil, and a few grinds of pepper. Stir until the scallops begin to release their liquid. Add the fava bean mixture, 2 to 3 tablespoons of the pasta water, and the pasta. Cook until al dente, 2 to 3 minutes. If dry, add more water. Add the butter and stir until melted. Divide among 6 plates. Arrange the zest and reserved beans over each serving. Drizzle a small amount of the lemon oil around the pasta by holding your thumb over the top of the bottle and releasing a thin stream onto the edge of the plate.

SERVES 4 AS A MAIN COURSE OR 6 AS A SIDE DISH

Duck Roulade with Cauliflower Purée

Jim Reichardt of Sonoma Poultry says that he likes to roll an entire duck breast into a cylinder and cook it just until the fat is rendered off. I thought it seemed too easy until I tried it and realized what an ingenius idea it is. It's like having a built-in timer. This dish is especially agreeable with cabernet sauvignon. Try Cakebread Cellars or Turnbull.

---

1 whole boneless duck breast (about 1½ pounds)
Kosher salt
Freshly ground pepper
2 tablespoons chopped fresh flat-leaf parsley, plus more for garnish
1 garlic clove, minced
1 teaspoon minced lemon zest
1½ pounds cauliflower, cut into florets
½ cup heavy cream
3 tablespoons unsalted butter

Trim the excess skin away from the meat. Put the scraps into a small saucepan and cover with 1 cup of water. Bring to a boil over medium-low heat. Cook the scraps until very brown and crisp, about 50 minutes, being careful not to let them burn once the water has cooked away. Transfer to paper towels with a slotted spoon. Chop into small pieces. Set aside.

Place the breast on a flat surface, meat-side up, and season with salt and pepper. Combine the parsley, garlic, and lemon zest in a small bowl. Spread over the duck, roll into a cylinder, and secure with twine. Heat a heavy, nonstick skillet over medium heat. Add the duck and cook until the fat is completely rendered and the outside begins to brown, 30 to 35 minutes, turning occasionally to cook all sides evenly. Transfer to a cutting board and let sit at least 5 minutes.

While the duck is cooking, bring a saucepan of salted water to a boil over high heat. Add the cauliflower and cook until tender, about 20 minutes. Drain. Set a food mill over a saucepan and purée the cauliflower. Return to low heat. Whisk in the cream and butter. Taste and season with salt and pepper. Keep warm.

Divide the cauliflower purée among the serving plates. Remove the twine, cut the duck into thin slices, and arrange over the cauliflower. Sprinkle with the cracklings and parsley.

SERVES 2 TO 4 AS A MAIN COURSE

Tangerine Meringue Tartlets

Early spring, when tangerines are at their sweetest, is the best time to prepare this dessert. This is one dessert that shouldn't share the spotlight with a wine. It should be consumed all by itself.

---

1 cup sugar
8 eggs, separated
¾ cup fresh tangerine juice (about 2 tangerines)
Stripped zest of 1 lemon
¼ cup fresh lemon juice
½ cup (1 stick) unsalted butter, cut into pieces
4 egg whites
¼ teaspoon salt
½ teaspoon orange oil or pure orange extract

Whisk ½ cup of the sugar, the egg yolks, tangerine juice, lemon zest, and juice together in a heavy saucepan over medium heat. Add the butter and stir constantly with a wooden spoon until the mixture coats the back of the spoon, 6 to 7 minutes. Remove from heat and strain through a fine-meshed sieve. Cover with plastic wrap and refrigerate for up to 2 days.

Preheat the oven to 200°F. Line a baking sheet with parchment paper.

Beat the 4 egg whites and salt with an electric mixer on high speed until soft peaks form, about 2 minutes. Gradually add the remaining ½ cup sugar and beat until stiff peaks form, about 5 minutes. Add the orange oil and beat on high speed until shiny, about 5 minutes. Scrape into a pastry bag fitted with a plain ½-inch tip. Pipe onto the prepared baking sheet in concentric circles to make a 3-inch-diameter round. Pipe one circle on top of the outer ring to make a rim. Repeat to make 6 rounds. Smooth out the centers with a spoon. Bake until dry, about 1½ hours. If the meringues begin to brown before they are dry, turn off the oven and let them sit in the oven until dry, 30 minutes to 1 hour. Let cool on the baking sheet for 5 to 10 minutes. Transfer to a wire rack for 5 to 10 minutes. Use immediately, or place in an airtight container for up to 2 days.

Place the meringues on 6 dessert plates. Spoon some curd into each meringue and serve.

SERVES 6 AS A DESSERT

Individual Chocolate Soufflés

Napa Valley should be awash in soufflés, given that cream of tartar, or tartaric acid, is a by-product of the wine-making process. There was a cream of tartar works here, from 1880 to 1906, when the San Francisco earthquake caused a fire that burnt it to the ground. Today, most cream of tartar sold for cooking is imported from Europe.

When there's extra red wine in the bottle after dinner, serve it with this chocolate dessert. The raspberry purée and the balsamic in the soufflé preserve the fruit taste of the wine.

---

2 tablespoons unsalted butter, melted
4 tablespoons sugar
One 8-ounce package frozen unsweetened raspberries, partially thawed
¼ cup fresh tangerine or orange juice
1 tablespoon Grand Marnier
3 ounces bittersweet chocolate, chopped
3 tablespoons unsalted butter
1 tablespoon blackberry-flavored balsamic vinegar or regular balsamic
3 egg yolks at room temperature, beaten
5 egg whites at room temperature
Pinch of cream of tartar

Preheat the oven to 425°F. Brush the bottom and sides of four 8-ounce ramekins or custard dishes with the melted butter. Coat each with 1 tablespoon of sugar. Set on a heavy baking dish.

Purée the raspberries, juice, and Grand Marnier in a blender. Strain through a fine-meshed sieve. Set aside.

Heat the chocolate and butter together in a large heavy saucepan over low heat until they start to melt. Remove from heat and stir until completely melted. Whisk in the balsamic vinegar and the egg yolks.

Beat the egg whites and cream of tartar together with in an electric mixer on high speed until soft peaks form, about 2 minutes. Stir some of the egg whites into the chocolate mixture, then fold back into the egg whites. Pour into the prepared dishes and bake for 15 minutes.

Remove from the oven and insert a teaspoon into the center of each soufflé. Pour a small amount of the raspberry purée into the hole and serve immediately.

SERVES 4 AS A DESSERT

Annie Robert's Auction Apricot and Cherry Tart

In 2001, Annie Roberts, executive chef of Robert Mondavi Winery, was the culinary chairperson of the Napa Valley Wine Auction. She prepared this tart for the last night of the auction, when everyone gathered on the great lawn for a family-style meal and dancing. She captured the best of the season with the apricots and cherries, which are at their peak in early June. Serve with a glass of Robert Mondavi Winery Moscato d'Oro.

Pastry
1 cup all-purpose flour
1 tablespoon sugar
⅛ teaspoon salt
6 tablespoons unsalted butter, cut into small pieces
½ cup ice water

Almond Filling
½ cup (1 stick) unsalted butter at room temperature
½ cup almond paste
1 tablespoon granulated sugar
2 teaspoons flour
1 egg, beaten

Fruit Topping
2 pounds small apricots, halved and pitted
8 ounces sweet cherries, halved and pitted
2 tablespoons granulated sugar
1 tablespoon unsalted butter, melted
1 tablespoon raw sugar

To make the pastry: Combine the flour, sugar, and salt in the bowl of a food processor. Process to blend. Add the butter and pulse until the mixture is crumbly. Add the ice water while pulsing, until the dough comes together, being careful not to overmix. Transfer to a lightly floured board and shape the dough into a disk. Cover tightly with plastic wrap and refrigerate for 30 minutes. Roll out the dough into a round ¼ inch thick. Transfer to parchment paper–lined baking sheet. Refrigerate while making the filling.

To make the filling: Combine the butter and almond paste in the bowl of an electric mixer. Beat until light and fluffy. Add the sugar and flour and mix until thoroughly combined. Add the egg and mix until blended.

Preheat the oven to 400°F. Remove the dough from the refrigerator and spread the filling evenly over it, leaving a 1-inch border.

To make the fruit topping: Arrange the apricots, cut-side down, over the filling. Place the cherries, cut-side down, between the apricots. Sprinkle with the granulated sugar. Fold the 1-inch border over the fruit and brush it with the melted butter. Sprinkle the raw sugar over the crust. Bake until the crust is golden, about 30 minutes.

SERVES 8 AS A DESSERT

NapaStyle's Crazy Strawberries

Less is often more—much of Italy's cuisine is built on this maxim. And Michael
Chiarello, the founder of NapaStyle, follows it in this recipe for ripe, juicy strawberries combined with his marinade, Pazzo, crazy. Almost any dessert wine will
pair well with the marriage of sweet and sour in this recipe.

NapaStyle Pazzo Marinade (or to purchase, see NapaStyle, page 161)
6 tablespoons balsamic vinegar
½ cup superfine sugar
Finely ground grey salt
Freshly ground pepper

2 cups fresh ripe strawberries, hulled and quartered
6 biscotti
½ cup mascarpone cheese at room temperature, stirred until smooth

---

To make the marinade: Combine the vinegar and sugar in a small bowl. Stir
until the sugar dissolves. Add a pinch of the salt and pepper and stir to mix well.
Let sit for 15 minutes.

Put the strawberries in a bowl. Stir the marinade and pour over the berries.
Toss gently to coat. Crush the biscotti and divide among 4 serving bowls. Divide
the strawberries among the bowls. Top each serving with a dollop of the mascarpone cheese. Pour any remaining marinade over the top and serve immediately.

Or, for an elegant presentation, place the biscotti upright in martini glasses.
Spoon the marinated berries into the glasses and top with mascarpone.

SERVES 4 AS A DESSERT

SUMMER

Grilled Pita Pizzas

Wood-burning ovens are as ubiquitous in Napa Valley restaurants as good wine lists. And the single most popular food that emerges from them is pizzas. These grilled pizzas capture some of the wood and smoke flavor of those ovens, and they are extremely easy to prepare. An assortment of toppings makes them perfect party fare. Big, fruity zinfandels and petite sirahs, such as Red, White, and Green Zinfandel and Elyse Petite Sirah, are fun wines to serve out by the grill.

1 tablespoon olive oil
2 teaspoons balsamic vinegar
1 garlic clove, chopped
1 teaspoon Italian seasoning
1 large onion, cut into ½-inch-thick slices
4 tablespoons sun-dried tomato pesto
4 pita breads, uncut
8 ounces Teleme cheese, sliced

Preheat a gas grill to low or light a fire in a charcoal grill.

Combine the olive oil, vinegar, garlic, and Italian seasoning in a small bowl. Put the onion slices in a shallow dish and cover with the olive oil mixture. Let sit for 15 minutes.

Spread 1 tablespoon sun-dried tomato pesto over each pita bread and set aside. Grill the onion slices until tender, about 3 minutes on each side. Separate the onion rings and arrange on the pita breads. Top with equal amounts of cheese. Place on the grill over indirect heat. Cover the grill and cook until the cheese melts, about 5 minutes. Cut the pizzas into quarters and serve hot.

Variations: Substitute sliced zucchini or portobello mushrooms for the onion. Use a basil pesto in place of the sun-dried tomato pesto. Top with Gorgonzola or feta cheese instead of the Teleme.

SERVES 4 TO 8 AS AN APPETIZER

Garlic Croutons with Eggplant and Roasted Pepper Spread Topped with Grilled Shrimp

Grilled eggplant and roasted red peppers are prominent ingredients in many of the Mediterranean-inspired dishes found in this area, most likely because the two vegetables grow so well in our climate. Here they are married with chipotle chiles and garlic for a spicy purée that can be used as a dip for vegetables, a spread for sandwiches, or a sauce for grilled meats. A chilled crisp rosé is a superb wine to serve with this hors d'oeuvre.

---

2 small round eggplants (about 8 ounces each), cut into ½-inch-thick slices
2 teaspoons kosher salt, plus more for seasoning
8 ounces (about 12) medium shrimp, peeled
4 large garlic cloves, 3 whole, 1 chopped
½ teaspoon chopped serrano or jalapeño chile
5 tablespoons olive oil
Juice of ½ lemon
1 large red bell pepper
Twenty-four ½-inch-thick baguette slices, cut on the diagonal
Freshly ground pepper
1 to 2 chipotle chiles (taste for heat and add adjust amount accordingly)
Juice of 1 lime
Chopped fresh flat-leaf parsley for garnish

Preheat a gas grill to medium or light a fire in a charcoal grill.

Arrange the eggplant slices on a paper towel–lined baking sheet. Sprinkle with 1 teaspoon of the salt. Let sit to extract any excess moisture while preparing the shrimp.

Put the shrimp in a large bowl. Add the chopped garlic, serrano chile, 1 tablespoon of the olive oil, and the lemon juice. Stir to combine and set aside.

Combine the remaining 4 tablespoons olive oil and the whole garlic cloves in a small saucepan. Cook over low heat until the oil reaches a boil, about 3 minutes. Remove from heat.

Put the bell pepper on the grill directly over the hottest part of the fire. Cook until blackened on all sides, about 4 minutes per side. Transfer to a plastic bag and seal.

Arrange the bread slices on a baking sheet and brush the tops with some of the garlic olive oil. Place the bread on the grill and cook until golden brown, about 30 seconds on each side. (Typically, by the time all of the bread slices are set on the grill, it's time to begin turning the bread. Once they are all turned, begin removing them in the same order.) Transfer to a serving bowl or basket.

Arrange the eggplant on the grill, cover, and cook until tender, about 3 minutes on each side. Transfer to a cutting board.

Place the shrimp on the grill and sprinkle with salt and pepper. Cook 1 to 2 minutes on each side, or until bright orange. Transfer to a cutting board and cut in half lengthwise.

Peel and chop the eggplant. Peel the skin off the bell pepper. Combine the eggplant, bell pepper, the remaining garlic oil with the whole garlic cloves, the chipotles, and the lime juice in a food processor. Purée until smooth. Season with salt and pepper.

Spread each garlic crouton with 1 to 2 teaspoons of the purée and top with a shrimp half. Sprinkle with the parsley and serve.

SERVES 6 TO 8 AS AN APPETIZER

BREAKING THE RULES To think or not to think. Nearly everyone has a philosophy on combining wine and food. Some are simple and some convoluted, and nearly all of them work, but not every time. I believe that wine and food are to be enjoyed, not worried over. So, forget about everything you've been told about pairing wine and food. Forget about flavors, color, weight, contrasting, complementing, and bridging and concentrate on what you like to drink and eat. It's as simple as that. Your favorite combinations don't have to follow anyone's rules but your own.

Heirloom Tomato Salad with Capers and Golden Balsamic Vinegar

The climate in Napa is ideal for cultivating tomatoes, and nearly everyone with a garden or a farm grows them. Growers like Long Meadow Ranch, Living Water Farm, and Big Ranch Farms specialize in heirloom tomatoes, which make magnificent salads because the range of tastes and textures of these varied beauties run the gamut from tart to sweet, meaty to delicate. In this recipe I like the intense flavors from salt-cured capers. If you can't find them, use vinegar-cured capers.

---

2 pounds assorted heirloom tomatoes, cut into ¼-inch-thick slices
1 small garlic clove, sliced
1 teaspoon grey sea salt (see Sea Star Sea Salt, page 163)
1 tablespoon salt-cured capers, rinsed
2 tablespoons golden balsamic vinegar (see Sparrow Lane, page 147)
1 tablespoon extra-virgin olive oil
1 tablespoon fresh thyme leaves
Freshly ground pepper

Arrange the tomatoes on a large plate or small platter. Put the garlic on a cutting board, pour the salt over the garlic, and chop into very small pieces and until the salt begins to dissolve slightly. Put the capers in a small bowl and mash lightly with a fork. Add the garlic mixture and stir together. Add the vinegar and olive oil and mix well. Pour over the tomatoes. Sprinkle with the thyme and pepper.

SERVES 4 TO 6 AS A FIRST COURSE

Classic Caesar Salad with Garlic Croutons

Caesar salad was invented in Tijuana in the 1920s, by chef Caesar Cardini. In Napa it appears on every menu at every restaurant, which provokes many conversations about which is the best and whether or not you can judge a restaurant by their Caesar. This recipe is inspired by the many wonderful Caesars I've tasted in the Valley.

Croutons
2 cups crustless 1-inch cubes sourdough bread
2 tablespoons olive oil
1 garlic clove, minced
½ teaspoon herbes de Provence (see Herbs of the Napa Valley, page 105)

2 anchovy fillets, or 1 tablespoon anchovy paste
2 garlic cloves
½ teaspoon kosher salt
½ teaspoon freshly ground pepper, plus more for seasoning
2 tablespoons red wine vinegar
1 tablespoon fresh lemon juice
1 teaspoon Dijon mustard
½ teaspoon Worcestershire sauce
⅓ cup extra-virgin olive oil
½ cup freshly grated Parmigiano-Reggiano cheese
6 hearts of romaine lettuce, leaves separated

To make the croutons: Preheat the oven to 350°F. Put the bread cubes in a bowl and add the olive oil, garlic, and herbs. Toss to coat. Spread on a baking sheet and bake until the cubes are crisp but not hard, about 7 minutes.

Put the anchovies and garlic cloves on a cutting board and chop together until coarse. Pour the salt and the ½ teaspoon pepper over the mixture and continue chopping until a thick paste forms. Transfer to a small bowl and add the vinegar, lemon juice, mustard, and Worcestershire sauce. Whisk together and begin adding the olive oil in a thin stream, whisking constantly. Stir in half of the cheese.

Put one-sixth of the lettuce leaves in a medium bowl and add a spoonful of the vinaigrette. Toss to coat evenly. Arrange on a serving plate and sprinkle with cheese, a grind of fresh pepper, and some croutons. Repeat for each serving.

SERVES 6 AS A FIRST COURSE

Feta-Stuffed Gems

Big Ranch Farms grows a dark-green squash called a Gem that is the size and shape of a baseball. The seeds that Big Ranch Farms used to start its crop were gifts from expatriate Afrikaners who missed the vegetable, which was part of their diet at home. The squash are fairly firm and take a long time to bake, but the end result is an attractive vegetable dish that is great for making ahead and serving to guests. Another round squash that is easy to find is Ronde de Nice, which is slightly less dense and cooks faster. The flavors of this dish make it compatible with a lot of wines, from a big red wine like Franciscan Oakville Estate's Magnificat méritage blend, to a an elegant white like Chateau Montelena Chardonnay.

4 baseball-sized globe squash (Gem or Ronde de Nice)
3 tablespoons olive oil
2 large shallots, minced
½ cup panko (Japanese bread crumbs)
½ cup crumbled feta cheese
¼ cup freshly grated hard cheese, such as an aged goat cheese, dry jack, or Asiago
¼ cup dry white wine
2 teaspoons fresh thyme leaves
½ teaspoon kosher salt
¼ teaspoon Hungarian sweet paprika

Preheat the oven to 400°F. Cut the tops off the squash and scoop out the pulp to make a hollow container. If using long zucchini, cut in half lengthwise and scoop out the center to create a canoelike container. Chop the pulp into a coarse mixture and set aside.

Heat 1 tablespoon of the olive oil in a large skillet over medium heat. Add the pulp and cook until tender, 2 to 3 minutes. Transfer to a bowl. Return the skillet to medium heat and add the remaining 2 tablespoons olive oil. Add the shallots and sauté until translucent, 2 to 3 minutes. Add the bread crumbs and cook until golden brown, 3 to 5 minutes. Transfer to the bowl with the pulp and add the feta, hard cheese, wine, thyme, salt, and paprika.

Divide the filling among the squash. Arrange in a small baking dish and bake until the squash is tender, 45 to 50 minutes for Gem squash, about 30 minutes for Ronde de Nice or zucchini. Let sit for about 5 minutes before serving.

SERVES 4 AS A SIDE DISH

California Ceviche

A few years ago I joined a wine-tasting group that is as serious about food as it is wine (it is made up almost entirely of vintners and other wine-industry professionals). Once our tastings conclude we pour a glass of our favorite from the tasting or from one of the other bottles that magically appear, and then we belly up to a potluck buffet. This ceviche was inspired by one that was served after a California chardonnay tasting on a hot summer night in Anne Moses and James Hall's backyard. I can't recall the specific wines, but I can remember every ingredient that made its way into that salad. Although ceviche is usually uncooked, relying on the acid to "cook" the seafood, I like to slightly parboil the fish just past the raw stage before marinating it. And, yes, a chardonnay, such as one made by Patz and Hall, is an excellent choice to drink with it.

1 pound red snapper, cut into 2-inch cubes
8 ounces sea scallops, halved
8 ounces medium shrimp, peeled and deveined
2 ripe tomatoes, diced
1 bunch green onions, thinly sliced on the diagonal
1 small yellow bell pepper, diced
1 carrot, peeled and grated
½ cup chopped fresh cilantro
2 tablespoons chopped fresh mint
1 small jalapeño chile, seeded and minced
1 garlic clove, minced
½ cup red verjus (see Note)
Juice of 1 lime
Juice of ½ lemon
1 tablespoon extra-virgin olive oil or lemon olive oil
2 avocados, diced
Kosher salt
Freshly ground pepper
8 small butter lettuce leaves

Bring a large saucepan of water to a boil. Gently lower the snapper and scallops into the water, and then immediately transfer them to an ice bath with a slotted spoon. Transfer with the slotted spoon to a colander to drain. Add more ice to the water, if needed, to ready the ice bath for the shrimp. Return the water in the saucepan to a boil and add the shrimp. Remove from heat and let sit for

2 minutes. Transfer to the ice bath. Drain and cut the shrimp in half lengthwise. Add to the colander with the other fish.

Mix the tomatoes, green onions, bell pepper, carrot, cilantro, mint, jalapeño chile, and garlic together. Add the snapper, scallops, shrimp, verjus, lime juice, lemon juice, and olive oil. Stir to mix well. Gently stir in the avocado and refrigerate for at least 2 hours before serving. Taste and season with salt and pepper.

Stack 2 lettuce leaves on top of each other to form a cup and spoon in one-fourth of the ceviche. Repeat to make 4 servings.

Note: Red verjus is made from green, unripe grapes and a small percentage of red grapes (see page 164). For this recipe, you can substitute unsweetened grape juice or double the quantity of lemon and lime juices.

SERVES 4 AS A MAIN COURSE

Mustards' Pork Satay Salad

Cindy Pawlcyn introduced fusion cuisine to Napa Valley when she opened Mustards in the early eighties. This dish is very easy to make, and most of the ingredients can be found in a well-stocked grocery store or supermarket. Kaffir limes are more difficult to find, but Dean & DeLuca sells them frozen. If you can't find them, you can leave them out. A suitable companion with this dish is a sparkling wine with some residual sugar like Schramsberg Crémant Demi-Sec.

Marinade
2 tablespoons Asian fish sauce
1 tablespoon fresh lime juice
2 tablespoons sugar
4 garlic cloves, chopped
3 lemongrass stalks, thinly sliced
7 kaffir lime leaves, cut into fine shreds
2-inch piece fresh ginger, peeled and finely grated
1 small fresh red hot chile, minced

1½ pounds pork tenderloin, cut into 1-inch cubes
16 long bamboo skewers

Dipping Sauce
6 tablespoons Asian fish sauce
2 tablespoons fresh lime juice
2 teaspoons sugar
2 small fresh hot red chiles, thinly sliced
2 green onions, thinly sliced on the diagonal

8 ounces rice noodles
12 lettuce leaves such as red leaf or iceberg
1 large carrot, peeled and shredded
½ cup fresh mint leaves
½ cup fresh basil leaves
¼ cup fresh cilantro leaves

To make the marinade: Combine the fish sauce, lime juice, and sugar in a large bowl. Stir until the sugar dissolves. Add the garlic, lemongrass, kaffir lime leaves, ginger, and chile. Add the pork and let sit for 20 to 30 minutes. Meanwhile, soak the bamboo skewers in water for at least 30 minutes.

To make the dipping sauce: Combine the fish sauce, lime juice, and sugar in a small bowl. Stir until the sugar is dissolved. Add the chiles and green onions. Divide among 6 small bowls.

Preheat a gas grill to medium-high heat or light a fire in a charcoal grill. Thread the skewers with the pork pieces. Trim any exposed skewer to prevent it from burning. Discard the marinade.

Cook the rice noodles according to the package directions. Drain and rinse well. Arrange the lettuce leaves on 6 plates. Divide the noodles among the plates and top each with equal amounts of carrot, mint, basil, and cilantro.

Put the pork on the grill, cover, and cook for 3 minutes on each side. Arrange 2 to 3 skewers on top of each salad and serve with the dipping sauce.

SERVES 6 AS A MAIN COURSE

Spice-Rubbed Grilled Salmon with Cucumber Salad

Holly Peterson Mondavi wowed the guests of the 2000 Napa Valley Auction when she built an open fire twenty feet long and grilled salmon tied to planks directly over the flames. Alas, the presentation might be less impressive on your backyard grill, but the taste will be just as great. A fruit-forward red wine like merlot will taste luscious with the salmon. If you want to be more conservative, sip a chardonnay.

2 cups alder and/or cedar wood chips
2 tablespoons lightly packed light brown sugar
2 tablespoons plus ½ teaspoon grey sea salt
2 tablespoons dry mustard
Eight 8-ounce salmon fillets
¼ cup vegetable oil
1 English (hothouse) cucumber
¼ cup extra-virgin olive oil
1 tablespoon fresh lemon juice
2 tablespoons chopped fresh dill
¼ teaspoon freshly ground pepper

Soak the wood chips in water for at least 1 hour prior to lighting the grill.

Combine the brown sugar, 2 tablespoons of the salt, and the mustard in a small bowl. Rub the salmon with the oil and sprinkle the spice mixture evenly over it.

Score the peel of the cucumber using a channel knife or zester. Cut the cucumber into paper-thin slices using a mandoline or sharp knife. Transfer to a medium bowl. Whisk the olive oil and lemon juice together in a small bowl. Add the dill, the remaining ½ teaspoon salt, and the pepper. Pour over the cucumbers and toss to mix well.

Preheat a gas grill to medium or light a fire in a charcoal grill. Drain the wood chips and sprinkle over the hot coals. (If using a gas grill, set the chips in a smoke box or an aluminum foil pan set in the corner.) Place the salmon on the grill, skin-side down, cover, and cook until browned on the outside but still slightly translucent in the center, about 6 minutes on each side. Spread the cucumber salad on a serving platter and top with the salmon.

SERVES 8 AS A MAIN COURSE

Tri-Tip with Fennel and Peppercorn Crust and Grilled Potatoes

Year-round grilling is common in Napa Valley because the area is graced with such agreeable weather. Tri-tip is a great cut of meat, as it is both tender and flavorful. My friend Hilary and her sister Leslie swear that flank steak is just as good if you can't find a tri-tip. It is best to cook the meat no more than medium rare because the rub becomes a crispy crust that soaks up the juices of the meat when it is sliced, and the longer the meat cooks the less juice it will release. Try a hearty red wine, such as Stonegate Winery's Merlot, or be adventurous and serve a fruity, dry rosé.

---

2 tablespoons fennel seeds
1 tablespoon chopped fresh rosemary
1 tablespoon dark-roasted coffee beans, or 1 teaspoon finely ground
  dark coffee beans
2 teaspoons whole peppercorns
1½ teaspoons grey sea salt
½ cup olive oil
1½- to 2-pound tri-tip or flank steak
1 pound red potatoes
2 garlic cloves, minced
1 teaspoon Dijon mustard
2 teaspoons chopped fresh tarragon
Kosher salt
Freshly ground pepper

Toast the fennel seeds in a small saucepan over medium-high heat until fragrant, about 5 minutes. Remove from heat and transfer to a spice grinder or mortar. Add the rosemary, coffee beans (if using), peppercorns, and salt. Grind to a medium-fine mixture. Transfer to a small bowl and add ¼ cup of the olive oil (if using ground coffee, add it now). Stir to combine. Rub over the steak to coat completely. Let sit for 30 minutes.

Preheat a gas grill to medium-high or light a fire in a charcoal grill. While the grill is preheating, put the potatoes in a large saucepan and cover with water. Add a pinch of salt and bring to a boil over high heat. Cook until just barely tender when pierced with a fork, 10 to 15 minutes. (It is better to undercook than overcook them.) Drain and let cool. Cut into quarters and place in a bowl. Whisk the remaining ¼ cup olive oil, the garlic, and mustard together in a small bowl. Pour over the potatoes. Toss to coat evenly.

Carefully place the potatoes on the grill, cut-side down. (Do not wash out the bowl.) Cook until grill marks appear, about 2 minutes on each side. Return to the same bowl. Add the tarragon. Gently mix. Taste and season with a generous amount of salt and pepper.

Add the steak to the grill and cook until medium rare, 8 to 10 minutes on each side for a 3-inch-thick piece of meat. Transfer to a cutting board and let rest for at least 5 minutes. Cut the steak into thin slices, arrange on a platter, and pour the juices over the steak. If using flank steak, cut it crosswise into sharply diagonal slices. Arrange the potatoes around the edge of the platter and serve.

SERVES 4 TO 6 AS A MAIN COURSE

Stuffed Pasilla Chiles with Chorizo, Tomato, and Cotija

Alejandro Ayala, Meadowood banquet chef, and Javier Guzman, Meadowood sous-chef, are Napa Valley Wine Auction veterans. Both have been on board since the eighties and have probably clocked more man hours cooking for the event than anyone else. In 2002 they were selected as guest chefs, and their stuffed chiles have a pizzazz that clearly demonstrates their passion for cooking. Schramsberg's North Coast Mirabelle is the perfect sparkling wine for this dish.

---

12 large poblano chiles (see Note)

¼ cup olive oil

2 pounds Mexican chorizo sausage, removed from casing

2 onions, diced

6 cloves garlic, chopped

2 bunches cilantro, 1 bunch chopped, 1 bunch intact for garnish

1¼ cups (6 ounces) crumbled cotija cheese

Kosher salt

Freshly ground pepper

½ cup crème fraîche

Juice of 1 lemon

1 teaspoon Hungarian sweet paprika

Place the chiles directly over the gas flame of a stove or under a preheated broiler until all the sides are charred, about 3 minutes per side. (Be careful not to overcook the chiles or they will tear when being filled.) Put in a bowl, cover with plastic wrap, and let sit for 30 minutes, but no longer.

Preheat the oven to 325°F. Heat the olive oil in a large skillet over medium heat. Add the chorizo, onions, and garlic. Cook until the sausage is cooked through and all of the liquid has evaporated, about 10 minutes. Remove from heat. Stir in the chopped cilantro and cheese. Mix thoroughly. Taste and season with the salt and pepper.

Gently peel, stem, and seed the chiles. Stuff each chile with the sausage mixture, being careful not to rip the chile. If one tears, simply pull the sides together and secure with a toothpick. Place stuffed chiles on a baking sheet and bake for 10 minutes.

Mix the crème fraîche, lemon juice, and paprika together in a small bowl. Arrange the chiles on a large platter. Drizzle the crème fraîche mixture over each one. Put remaining cilantro sprigs in the middle of the platter and serve.

Note: Poblano chiles are fresh, dark-green triangular-shaped chiles, sometimes called pasillas in California.

SERVES 6 TO 8 AS A MAIN COURSE

Upside-Down Plum Sour Cream Cake

Bera Ranch is one of the regular purveyors at both the Napa and St. Helena Farmers' Markets. While plums are in season, Bera Ranch carries a substantial variety. The folks who sell the fruit know just about everything about each kind, which is very helpful in selecting different plums for different uses. I like both Santa Rosa and Black Amber for this recipe. This cake isn't too sweet, making it a perfect complement to a fruity dessert wine.

1¾ cups cake flour
½ cup slivered almonds, ground
1 teaspoon baking soda
1 teaspoon baking powder
½ teaspoon salt
1 cup sugar
½ cup (1 stick) unsalted butter at room temperature
3 large eggs
1 cup sour cream
1 teaspoon vanilla extract
1½ pounds ripe, firm plums, pitted, peeled, and cut into ¼-inch-thick slices
1 tablespoon lightly packed brown sugar
Crème fraîche for garnish

Preheat the oven to 350°F. Generously butter a 9-inch square or round baking dish.

Stir the flour, ground almonds, baking soda, baking powder, and salt together in a medium bowl. Set aside. Beat the sugar and butter together until light and fluffy. Beat in the eggs, then add the sour cream and vanilla. Beat until smooth and creamy. Stir in the dry ingredients until well blended.

Combine the plums and brown sugar in a medium bowl. Stir well. Spread the plums in the baking dish. Gently pour the batter over the fruit, smoothing it with a spatula and pressing the fruit into the bottom as necessary. Bake until a skewer inserted in the center comes out clean, about 50 minutes. Let rest for 5 to 10 minutes, then unmold onto a plate. (Do not let sit too long, or the fruit will stick to the bottom of the dish.) Cut into serving pieces and top with a dollop of crème fraîche.

SERVES 6 TO 8 AS A DESSERT

Jan Janek's Blackberry Ice Cream

Blackberries are one of the most aggressive plants in the world and almost impossible to get rid of. For the first five years I lived in Napa, I fought a battle with the waist-high brambles that constantly threatened to take over my entire yard. Finally, I gave up and just let them be, and I was rewarded with big, luscious berries. My friend Jan, a pastry chef extraordinaire who spent her externship at Spago, suggested we make ice cream. This is the recipe she developed to show-case those wild berries. Serve it with shortbread cookies or fresh whole berries.

2 cups heavy cream
1 cup whole milk
1 vanilla bean, split lengthwise
5 egg yolks
¾ cup sugar
3 cups (about 3 small baskets) fresh blackberries
½ cup chocolate nibs (see Scharffen Berger, page 166)

Prepare an ice cream maker.

Combine the cream and milk in a heavy saucepan. Scrape the seeds from the vanilla pod into the saucepan and add the pod. Heat over medium heat until small bubbles form around the edges of the pan, about 5 minutes. Remove from heat.

Whisk the yolks in a medium bowl until pale in color. Gradually whisk in the sugar until the mixture is thickened. Whisk about one-fourth of the warm cream mixture into the yolks. Add the remaining cream mixture and cook over medium heat, stirring constantly, until the mixture coats the back of a spoon. Strain through a fine-meshed sieve into a bowl. Place the bowl in an ice-water bath to cool the mixture, stirring occasionally.

Purée the berries in a food processor. Strain through a sieve, pressing on the solids with the back of a large spoon. Stir into the cooled custard. Cover and refrigerate for 1 hour. Add the nibs and stir to combine. Freeze in an ice cream maker according to the manufacturer's instructions.

SERVES 4 TO 6 AS A DESSERT

AUTUMN

Scott Weidert's Herb-Flavored Almonds

Robert Sinskey Vineyards is one of several wineries in the Valley that emphasize the important relationship between food and wine. To that end, they have a
full-time chef, Scott Weidert, who cooks for special events, runs a cheese-and-
wine-pairing program, and prepares an array of savory treats for winery visitors
to sample while tasting wine. One of his signature nibbles is almonds cooked in
olive oil and finished with herbs and salt in traditional Spanish style. They are
easy to prepare and make terrific finger food for casual entertaining or a snack
before dinner. Although they taste delicious with just about any wine, they are
especially tasty with Robert Sinskey Vineyards Pinot Blanc, a crisp, fruity wine
with bright acid.

½ cup olive oil

2 cups blanched whole almonds

½ cup fresh herb leaves, such as sage, thyme, tarragon,
   washed and patted completely dry

1 teaspoon coarse sea salt

Heat the oil in a medium, high-sided sauté pan or skillet over medium heat for
about 3 minutes, or until the surface shimmers. Add the almonds and increase
heat to medium high. Cook, stirring constantly, until the almonds begin to brown,
about 3 minutes. Add the herbs (make sure they are completely dry, or the oil
will splatter) and reduce heat to medium low. Cook until the herbs are crisp, 1 to
2 minutes. Transfer the almonds and herbs with a slotted spoon to a fine-meshed
sieve set over a bowl to drain completely. Save the oil for another use, if desired.
Transfer the almonds and herbs to paper towels to absorb any extra oil. Sprinkle
with the salt and let cool. Serve in decorative bowls, or store in an airtight container for up to 2 weeks.

SERVES 4 TO 6 AS AN APPETIZER

Dry Jack and Red Pepper Biscuits

Vella Cheese Company in the town of Sonoma has reached acclaim through the production of their dry jack cheeses. The dry Monterey jack and the Special Selection cheeses are shaped into round molds, brushed with oil, then coated with ground black pepper and cocoa powder. The former is typically aged less than a year and the latter for closer to a year. Both grate easily and blend well with the red pepper flakes in this biscuit. I make a few batches at a time and store the dough in the freezer so that I always have something on hand to serve with a glass of wine. Mason Sauvignon Blanc or Domaine Chandon Étoile are both sure bets as an aperitif, and both are agreeable with this crunchy biscuit.

½ cup all-purpose flour
½ cup semolina flour
1 teaspoon kosher salt
¼ teaspoon red pepper flakes
6 tablespoons cold unsalted butter, cut into small pieces
1 cup finely grated dry jack cheese
2 to 4 tablespoons sour cream

Combine the all-purpose flour, semolina, salt, and red pepper flakes in a food processor. Process to blend. Add the butter and pulse until the mixture becomes crumbly, 10 to 20 seconds. Add the cheese and pulse until combined. Add 2 tablespoons of the sour cream and pulse until the dough forms a ball, adding 1 or 2 more tablespoons of sour cream if necessary.

Transfer the dough to the center of a large piece of plastic wrap. Shape into a log 1 inch in diameter and wrap in the plastic. Refrigerate for at least 2 hours or freeze for up to 1 month.

Preheat the oven to 325°F. Cut the dough into ¼-inch-thick slices and place on a baking sheet. Bake until golden, 25 to 30 minutes.

SERVES 6 TO 8 AS AN APPETIZER

Back Room Wines Antipasti

In the spirit of an Italian *enoteca,* or wine bar, Back Room Wines owner Dan Dawson suggests these open-faced sandwiches for a light meal with wine. Bresaola is salted and air-dried beef that is a specialty of Lombardy in northern Italy. It is usually easy to find at most upscale delis and Italian markets. Montbriac cheese is a soft, blue cheese from the center of France. Dan suggests Spelletich Cellars 1999 Bodog Red, a Napa Valley blend of zinfandel, cabernet sauvignon, and merlot, as a wine to serve with the bresaola and Montbriac. This spicy, full-bodied red wine is a perfect foil for the strong flavors on the plate.

---

10 slices bresaola
3 ounces Montbriac cheese, cut into thin slices
1 cup arugula or watercress sprigs
½ lemon, cut into wedges
4 to 6 thick (about ½ inch) slices artisan-baked French or sourdough bread
Extra-virgin olive oil for drizzling
Kosher salt or fine sea salt
Freshly ground pepper

On a large plate or small platter, arrange the bresaola, cheese, greens, and lemon. Drizzle a slice of bread with the olive oil. Stack a slice of bresaola, some greens, and a piece of cheese on top and give it a squirt of lemon juice. Sprinkle with salt and pepper and enjoy. Or, mix and match the ingredients any way you see fit.

SERVES 2 AS AN APPETIZER

Mole Sopitos

Traditional Mexican mole is a complex sauce made with a blend of roasted chiles, nuts, dried fruit, and spices that can take hours to prepare. This version is just as rich, but daring in its simplicity and relatively quick to prepare. It is hot, so you may want to adjust the amount of chipotle by adding it gradually to the sauce and tasting after each addition. I like to use pork for this dish because you can cook it in the sauce, but you can also use chicken. Just poach it first and tear it into shreds, then add it to the mole sauce at the end. The mole also makes a delicious sauce for enchiladas.

Mole

6 unpeeled large garlic cloves

¼ cup sesame seeds

1 tablespoon bacon grease or olive oil

1 small onion, diced

3 cups chicken broth

½ cup canned chipotle chiles in adobo sauce

½ cup crunchy peanut butter

½ cup raisins

½ cup crushed tortilla chips

¼ cup unsweetened cocoa powder

1 teaspoon dried oregano

½ teaspoon ground cumin

Dash of ground cinnamon

Kosher salt

2 pounds pork butt, trimmed of fat and sinew and cut into 2-inch cubes

1 cup finely shredded napa or savoy cabbage

¼ cup whole flat-leaf parsley leaves

2 tablespoons red wine vinegar

1 tablespoon olive oil

Kosher salt

12 sopitos or 24 regular corn tortillas (see Note)

¼ cup crumbled cotija cheese

To make the mole: Heat a large nonstick skillet over medium-high heat. Add the garlic and cook, stirring frequently, until the skin begins to turn brown and peels off easily, about 15 minutes. Transfer the garlic to a plate to cool. Add the sesame seeds to the skillet and toast, stirring frequently, over medium heat until browned, about 3 minutes, stirring frequently. Transfer to a bowl. Add the bacon grease to the skillet and heat. Add the onion and cook until tender, 5 minutes. Transfer the onions to a blender. Add the chicken broth, chipotle chiles, peanut butter, raisins, tortilla chips, cocoa, oregano, cumin, and cinnamon to the blender. Peel the garlic and add to the blender. Add the sesame seeds and blend on medium speed until smooth. Taste and season with salt.

Transfer to a medium saucepan and add the pork. Bring to a boil over medium heat. Reduce heat to as low as possible. Cover and simmer until the pork is tender enough to pull apart, 1 to 1½ hours. Transfer the pork with a slotted spoon to a plate and let cool to the touch. Tear the pork into shreds and return to the sauce.

Combine the cabbage and parsley in a small bowl. Add the vinegar, olive oil, and a healthy pinch of salt. Toss to coat evenly. Set aside.

Heat a large cast-iron skillet over medium-high heat. Put the sopitos or tortillas in the skillet and cook until heated through, 1 to 2 minutes on each side. Arrange on a serving platter or large wooden board and top with a spoonful of the mole mixture. Place a small amount of the cabbage over the meat and sprinkle with the cheese.

Note: A sopito is a small, thick disk of tortilla dough. Villa Corona (see page 235) produces and sells them at their stores. If you can't get them, use 2 corn tortillas for each sopito.

SERVES 6 AS A MAIN COURSE OR 8 AS AN APPETIZER

Zuzu's Sautéed Piquillo Peppers

Because of their Spanish origins, piquillo peppers aren't as well known in Napa as ingredients from south of the border, but they fit right into Zuzu's menu of Spanish-inspired tapas. These mild peppers taste similar to roasted bell peppers and are wonderful eaten straight off the plate or placed on top of bread. They can be purchased from Tienda on their Web site, Tienda.com, or by calling them at (888) 472 1022.

⅓ cup extra-virgin olive oil, plus more for drizzling
2 large garlic cloves, minced
One 10-ounce jar roasted piquillo peppers, drained
¼ cup balsamic vinegar
Sea salt
Freshly ground pepper
6 large fresh basil leaves, stacked, rolled, and cut into fine shreds

Heat the ⅓ cup olive oil in a small pan over medium heat. Add the garlic and cook until fragrant, 1 to 2 minutes. Add the peppers and increase the heat to medium-high. Cook until the peppers are heated through, 2 to 3 minutes. Add the balsamic vinegar and cook for 1 minute. Season with salt and pepper. Transfer to a serving dish and top with the basil. Drizzle with additional olive oil.

SERVES 2 AS A MAIN COURSE OR 4 AS AN APPETIZER

Bistro Jeanty's Tomato Soup

This soup is a showstopper. The taste depends heavily on the ripeness and potency of the tomatoes, so if your tomatoes taste mild, adjust the flavor by using a smaller amount of cream and increasing the amount of tomato paste. Applying the puff pastry takes a little practice, but even if it doesn't look perfect, it will still taste perfect. Enjoy it with a glass of Rhône-style wine such as Joseph Phelps Mistral.

½ cup (1 stick) plus 2 tablespoons unsalted butter
2 yellow onions, thinly sliced
2½ pounds ripe red tomatoes, cored and quartered
¼ cup tomato paste
6 garlic cloves
2 teaspoons black peppercorns
1 teaspoon fresh thyme leaves
1 bay leaf
2 cups heavy cream
Kosher salt
½ teaspoon freshly ground white pepper
1 pound thawed frozen puff pastry
1 egg beaten with 1 tablespoon water

Melt the ½ cup butter in a stockpot over medium heat. Add the onions. Cover and cook until tender, about 5 minutes. Add the tomatoes, tomato paste, garlic, peppercorns, thyme, and bay leaf. If the mixture seems dry, add up to 1 cup of water. Bring to a boil, reduce heat to low, and cook at a low simmer, uncovered, until the onions and tomatoes are tender, 30 to 40 minutes. Transfer to a blender and purée. Strain through a fine-meshed sieve set over a large saucepan. Whisk in the cream and the remaining 2 tablespoons butter. Taste and season with salt and white pepper. Let cool completely.

Preheat the oven to 450°F. Divide the soup among 6 ovenproof bowls. Roll the puff pastry out on a lightly floured surface to a ¼-inch thickness. Cut into 6 rounds about 1 inch larger than the top of the bowls, using an inverted bowl as a template. Brush the tops of each round with the egg mixture and place, egg-side down, over the top of each bowl, pulling lightly on the sides to create a snug fit. Press the pastry against the sides of the bowl. Brush the tops with the egg mixture and set the bowls in a baking dish. Bake until the dough has risen and is golden brown, 10 to 15 minutes. (Be careful not to open the door in the first few minutes, or the pastry won't rise.) Serve immediately.

SERVES 6 AS A FIRST COURSE

La Toque's Foie Gras with Fuji Apple and Mango

Fresh foie gras is divine. Over the last few years, it has become more accessible for the home cook, and Ken Frank's recipe provides thorough instructions for preparing it in your kitchen. One word of caution: Be careful not to overcook it. If you do, it will lose its silken texture and taste like ordinary liver. Both Hudson Valley Foie Gras and Sonoma Foie Gras are domestic growers that offer mail-order sales via their Web sites. This dish calls for a French sauternes, but a late-harvest riesling could also be a suitable match, such as the one made by Navarro Vineyards in nearby Anderson Valley.

---

1 Valencia orange
½ cup water
1½ tablespoons sugar
1 cardamom pod, or ¼ teaspoon ground cardamom
2 cloves
½ star anise pod
¼ teaspoon ground ginger
1 cup apple juice
1 tablespoon unsalted butter
½ large Fuji apple, peeled, cored, and cut into ½-inch dice
½ mango, peeled, pitted, and cut into ½-inch dice
Eight 1-ounce Sonoma Muscovy duck foie gras medallions
Kosher salt
Freshly ground pepper

Remove half the zest from the orange with a vegetable peeler. (Save the remaining orange and zest for another use.) Bring a small saucepan of water to a boil over high heat. Add the orange zest and cook for 30 seconds. Drain and repeat the process. Drain again. Combine the ½ cup water and the sugar in the saucepan and bring to a low boil over medium-high heat. Add the orange zest. Cook, stirring occasionally, until tender, about 10 minutes. Drain well and dry overnight. (Alternatively, put the orange zest on a wire rack and bake in a preheated 250°F oven until brittle, about 3 hours. Let cool completely before using.)

Combine the cardamom, cloves, and star anise in a small skillet and heat over medium heat until fragrant, about 5 minutes. Transfer to a spice grinder and grind to a fine powder. Transfer to a small bowl. Grind the orange zest in the spice grinder to a fine powder. Add it to the toasted spices. Add the ginger.

Combine the apple juice and ½ teaspoon of the spice mixture in a small saucepan. Bring to a low boil over medium heat. Reduce heat to low and cook on a low simmer, skimming off any foam, until only a few spoonfuls of syrup remain, about 1 hour. Set aside.

Melt the butter in a small sauté pan or skillet over medium heat. Add the apple and sauté for 2 minutes. Add the mango and sauté for 1 minute. Place one-fourth of the mixture in the center of each of 4 small plates. Set aside.

Generously season the foie gras with salt and pepper. Heat a large cast-iron skillet over high heat. Add the foie gras and sear for 20 seconds on one side and 10 to 15 seconds on the other. It should be rare in the center. Immediately remove the medallions from the pan and blot with paper towels to absorb any excess fat.

To assemble, place 2 medallions on top of each serving of the apple mixture. Drizzle with the apple syrup and sprinkle the foie gras and the rim of the plate with a little of the remaining spice mixture. Serve immediately.

SERVES 4 AS AN APPETIZER

Jamie Purviance's Smoked Pacific Rim Pork Tenderloin

Jamie Purviance, author of *Weber's Big Book of Grilling* and *The Art of the Grill*, spends a lot of time cooking with fire. Wood chips added to the fire add intriguing complexity to his recipe for pork tenderloin flavored with a slightly sweet soy-based marinade. Living in the wine country, Jamie is surrounded by vineyards, so occasionally he likes to break dried grapevine branches into small pieces and throw them on the fire instead of wood chips. He says he can't guarantee that the smoke will smell like wine, but it does cast a magical quality.

1 cup soy sauce
¼ cup cider vinegar
2 tablespoons lightly packed dark brown sugar
½ cup finely chopped yellow onion
2 tablespoons minced garlic
½ teaspoon cayenne pepper
½ teaspoon freshly ground pepper
2 pork tenderloins (about 12 ounces each), trimmed
2 teaspoons Asian sesame oil
1 large handful mesquite, hickory, or apple wood chips, soaked in water
    for at least 30 minutes, or grapevine branches

Whisk the soy sauce and vinegar together in a medium bowl. Add the sugar and stir until it dissolves. Add the onion, garlic, cayenne, and pepper. Put the tenderloins in a large self-sealing plastic bag. Pour the marinade into the bag. Press the air out of the bag and seal tightly. Place the bag in a bowl and refrigerate for 2 to 3 hours.

Preheat a gas grill to medium heat or light a fire in a charcoal grill. Remove the tenderloins from the bag, discard the marinade, and pat the meat dry with paper towels. Lightly brush the tenderloins all over with the sesame oil. Place on the grill, cover, and cook, turning every 5 minutes, until the tenderloins are browned on all sides, 15 to 20 minutes. Before the last turn, drain the wood chips and sprinkle them over the coals, or lay the grapevine branches over the coals. They should smoke for only about 5 minutes.

Transfer the tenderloins to a cutting board. Let rest for about 5 minutes. Slice and serve warm.

SERVES 4 TO 6 AS A MAIN COURSE

Chicken Ragout with Potatoes, Peppers, and Olives

During harvest, the Valley is buzzing with activity. Trucks overflowing with grapes fill the roads, tractors slide along the edge of vineyards, and grape pickers move among the vines. Lunches and dinners are made with the last fruits and vegetables of the summer garden. This autumn dish is almost a stew, a reminder that winter isn't far off. Enjoy it in the company of good friends and with a sturdy red wine, like a syrah.

2 tablespoons all-purpose flour
1 tablespoon chopped fresh rosemary
2 teaspoons chopped fresh thyme
1 teaspoon kosher salt
½ teaspoon freshly ground pepper
1½ pounds boneless, skinless chicken thighs
2 tablespoons butter
2 tablespoons olive oil
1 large onion, cut into 8 wedges
1 red bell pepper, cut into thin strips
4 garlic cloves, sliced
6 Yukon Gold potatoes, quartered
2 cups chicken stock
1 cup dry white wine
½ cup chopped olive salad such as Genova Muffaletta (page 80)
    or Jimtown Olive Spread (page 165), or tapenade

Combine the flour, rosemary, thyme, salt, and pepper in a medium bowl. Stir to blend. Add the chicken and mix to evenly coat. Melt the butter with 1 tablespoon of the olive oil in a heavy 4-quart saucepan or a Dutch oven over medium-high heat. Add the chicken and cook, turning often, until browned, 8 to 10 minutes. Transfer to a plate.

Add the remaining 1 tablespoon olive oil to the pan and heat over medium-low heat. Add the onion, pepper, and garlic. Cook until softened, 5 to 7 minutes. Return the chicken to the pan and add the potatoes, stock, and wine. Increase heat to high and bring to a boil. Reduce heat and cook at a medium simmer, uncovered, until the potatoes are tender, 30 to 40 minutes. Stir in the olive salad and serve in a large bowl.

SERVES 4 TO 6 AS A MAIN COURSE

Spiced Fruit Biscotti

Dessert wines are almost de rigueur at the end of a meal in Napa Valley. These crunchy cookies are perfect for dipping in a glass of sweet wine. The walnuts and spice will complement the raisin flavors in most late-harvest wines. Far Niente Dolce may be a little extravagant, but it would make the end of any meal memorable.

2¼ cups all-purpose flour
1 teaspoon baking powder
½ teaspoon salt
½ teaspoon ground cinnamon
¼ teaspoon ground nutmeg
3 eggs
¾ cup sugar
1 teaspoon vanilla extract
½ cup pine nuts, toasted
½ cup dried currants
¼ cup chopped candied ginger

Preheat the oven to 350°F. Butter a large baking sheet.

Stir the flour, baking powder, salt, cinnamon, and nutmeg together in a medium bowl. Set aside.

Beat the eggs and sugar together in a medium bowl until thick. Add the vanilla and stir to blend. Add the pine nuts, currants, and ginger. Stir to blend. Stir in the dry ingredients until blended.

On a work surface, divide the dough into 3 equal portions. Shape each portion into a 10-inch log using wet hands. Place the logs an equal distance apart on the prepared baking sheet. Bake for 30 minutes. Remove from the oven and carefully transfer the logs to a cutting board. Cut each into ½-inch-thick slices using a sharp knife. Arrange the slices on the baking sheet in a standing position and bake until crisp, 10 to 15 minutes.

MAKES ABOUT 3 DOZEN COOKIES

Apple Galette

The crust for this rustic galette is foolproof. The semolina helps to keep it crisp, and if it doesn't roll out into a perfect circle you can just tell everyone it's meant to be shaped like a rectangle. Botrytised, or late-harvest, wines are dessert wines made with grapes affected by "noble rot." They are a striking complement to the flavors of baked apples, cranberries, and allspice in this galette. Try Merryvale's Antiqua for a special occasion.

Pastry
¾ cup all-purpose flour
¼ cup semolina flour
2 teaspoons sugar
½ teaspoon kosher salt
6 tablespoons cold unsalted butter, cut into small pieces
2 tablespoons crème fraîche
2 to 4 tablespoons ice water

Filling
1½ pounds sweet-tart apples, peeled, halved, cored, and cut into ⅛-inch-thick
    lengthwise slices
2 tablespoons fresh lemon juice
2 tablespoons sugar
1 teaspoon freshly ground allspice
½ teaspoon freshly ground cinnamon
½ cup dried cranberries
2 tablespoons butter, melted
1 tablespoon raw sugar

To make the pastry: Combine the all-purpose flour, semolina, sugar, and salt in a food processor. Pulse to mix. Add the butter and pulse to form a mixture that looks like small peas. Add the crème fraîche and pulse to combine. Add the ice water, 1 tablespoon at a time, while pulsing, just until the dough sticks together, being careful not to overmix (to test, remove the top of the processor and gather the dough in your fingers. If it sticks together without crumbling, it's ready). Transfer to a lightly floured board and shape the dough into a disk. Cover tightly with plastic wrap and refrigerate for 30 minutes. Roll out the dough into a round ¼ inch thick. Transfer to parchment paper–lined baking sheet. Refrigerate for 30 minutes longer.

Preheat the oven to 400°F.

To make the filling: Combine the apples, lemon juice, sugar, allspice, and cinnamon in a large bowl. Toss to coat. Remove the dough from the refrigerator and pile the apple slices into the center of the pastry, leaving a 2-inch border. Add the cranberries to the bowl containing the juice from the apples. Toss to coat evenly. Distribute the cranberries evenly over the top of the apples, reserving the juice.

Fold the edge of the pastry over the apples, pleating the dough as you go. Pour the juice from the bowl over the fruit. Brush the edges of the dough and the top of the fruit with the melted butter. Sprinkle the raw sugar over the pastry and fruit and bake until the crust is golden brown and the apples are tender, about 45 minutes. Let cool slightly before serving.

SERVES 4 TO 6 AS A DESSERT

WINTER

Crostini with Pecorino Pepato, Honey, and Orange Zest

Italy's aged cheeses inspired this humble hors d'oeuvre. It is exceptionally delicious with Bellwether Farms pecorino pepato and Napa honey. Its simple combination of sweet, salty, and spicy makes this a classic partner for a wine like Robert Mondavi Winery's Moscato d'Oro, a slightly effervescent dessert wine that can be served at brunch or before dinner.

½ small baguette (about 4 ounces), cut into ¼-inch-thick slices
1 tablespoon olive oil
4 ounces pecorino pepato cheese
2 tablespoons orange blossom honey
Stripped zest of one orange
Freshly ground pepper

Preheat the oven to 400°F.

Brush the bread on one side with the olive oil. Arrange on a baking sheet and bake until crisp, about 7 minutes.

Cut the pecorino into thin shavings using a cheese knife or vegetable peeler. Arrange 1 slice on each piece of bread. Drizzle a small amount of honey over the cheese. Top with 1 to 2 strips zest and sprinkle with the pepper.

SERVES 4 AS AN APPETIZER OR CHEESE COURSE

Bistro Don Giovanni's Roasted Beet, Fennel, and Haricots Verts Salad with Roquefort Vinaigrette

Donna Scala is a splendid cook. Everything that emerges from her kitchen is delicious because she always uses the freshest seasonal ingredients. This salad is best in late winter or early spring, when fennel and beets are at their peak and haricots verts begin to appear in the market. If you have extra dressing, drizzle it over a wedge of iceberg lettuce for a simple salad at another time. It can be stored in a sealed container in the refrigerator for up to 1 week. This salad hollers for a pinot grigio from Luna or La Famiglia di Robert Mondavi.

Beets

2 pounds golden and/or Chioggia beets, greens trimmed to ½ inch
¼ cup plus 1 tablespoon golden balsamic vinegar (see Sparrow Lane, page 147)
2 tablespoons olive oil
2 teaspoons sugar
1 teaspoon kosher salt

Vinaigrette

1 cup (5 ounces) crumbled Roquefort cheese
¼ cup champagne vinegar
¾ cup olive oil
Kosher salt
Pinch of freshly ground pepper

1 fennel bulb, cut into ⅛-inch-thick slices
1 pound haricots verts, blanched
Leaves from ¼ head radicchio, julienned
1 avocado, ripe but not too soft, cut into ½-inch dice
1 bunch chives, chopped

Preheat the oven to 375°F.

To make the beets: Toss the beets with ¼ cup of the balsamic vinegar and the olive oil in a large bowl. Transfer to a baking dish and cover with aluminum foil. Bake until tender when pierced with a fork, about 1 hour. Let cool.

When cool enough to handle, trim and peel the beets. Cut into large dice. Transfer to a large bowl and sprinkle with the remaining 1 tablespoon balsamic vinegar, the sugar, and salt.

To make the vinaigrette: Combine half of the Roquefort with the champagne vinegar in a large bowl. Gradually whisk in the olive oil until well blended. Taste and season with the salt and pepper.

To make the salad: Add the fennel, haricots verts, and radicchio to the beets. Add half of the vinaigrette and toss to coat. Taste and add more dressing if needed. Divide the salad among 6 plates and top with equal amounts of avocado and the remaining Roquefort. Sprinkle with chives and serve.

SERVES 6 AS A FIRST COURSE OR SIDE DISH

Napa Valley Grapeseed Oil's Warm Winter Pear Salad

Salads in winter need more substance. This one, from the Pestoni family of Rutherford Grove Winery and Napa Valley Grapeseed Oil, relies on the taste of juicy ripe pears. Their sweet essence and tender texture is a peerless counterpoint to the slightly salty taste and crisp texture of the pancetta. And the balsamic brings all the flavors forward with just the right amount of acid. This salad makes a strong argument for red wines with a first course. Try Rutherford Grove Sangiovese or a merlot.

---

5 cups mixed baby salad greens
1 ripe pear, peeled, cored, quartered, and cut into thin slices
¼ cup pine nuts, toasted
2 teaspoons fresh thyme leaves
Kosher salt
Freshly ground pepper
¼ cup grapeseed oil (see Napa Valley Grapeseed Oil, page 143)
Five ¼-inch-thick slices pancetta, finely diced
2 tablespoons golden balsamic vinegar (see Sparrow Lane, page 147)

Combine the greens, pear slices, pine nuts, and thyme in a large serving bowl. Sprinkle lightly with salt and pepper.

Heat the grapeseed oil in a small skillet over medium-high heat. Add the pancetta and cook until browned and crisp, 7 to 10 minutes. Remove from heat and let cool 1 minute.

Pour the vinegar over the salad greens. Pour the pancetta and grapeseed oil over the greens and toss to coat evenly. Serve immediately.

SERVES 4 TO 6 AS AN APPETIZER

Roasted Brussels Sprouts with Olio Nuovo

The sweetest Brussels sprouts arrive on the coldest days of winter. This recipe enhances their flavor and nicely balances them with the peppery, intense *olio nuovo*, "new olive oil." If you don't have *olio nuovo* on hand, you can use a high-quality extra-virgin olive oil.

---

1 pound Brussels sprouts, halved
2 tablespoons olive oil
1 teaspoon kosher salt
½ teaspoon freshly ground pepper
2 tablespoons *olio nuovo* (see page 151), **or extra-virgin olive oil**
Fine sea salt

Preheat the oven to 400°F.

Put the Brussels sprouts in a baking dish just large enough to hold them in a single layer. Add the olive oil, kosher salt, and pepper and toss to coat evenly. Spread the sprouts out and bake until they begin to turn brown, about 30 minutes. Remove from the oven and drizzle with the *olio nuovo*. Sprinkle with the sea salt and serve.

SERVES 4 AS A SIDE DISH

Crab Cakes with Roasted Red Pepper Purée

Dungeness crab season begins in late November in Northern California. Crab cakes are one of the most popular uses for the succulent meat, but this recipe is so forgiving even frozen crabmeat can be used. William Hill Napa Valley Chardonnay is a great companion for these crab cakes.

Crab Cakes
8 ounces fresh lump crabmeat, picked over for shells
½ cup fresh sourdough bread crumbs
¼ cup mayonnaise
3 green onions, whites and greens parts, chopped
2 tablespoons chopped cilantro
2 teaspoons fresh lemon juice
½ teaspoon dry mustard
¼ teaspoon kosher salt, plus more for sprinkling
¼ teaspoon cayenne pepper
1 egg, beaten

Red Pepper Purée
2 small roasted red bell peppers, peeled, seeded, and diced
1 tablespoon lemon juice
1 tablespoon olive oil
Kosher salt
Freshly ground pepper

5 ounces microgreens, or 1 cup chopped frisee
2 tablespoons olive oil
2 teaspoons champagne vinegar
Freshly ground pepper
¼ cup chopped chives

To make the crab cakes: Combine the crab, bread crumbs, mayonnaise, green onions, cilantro, lemon juice, mustard, the ¼ teaspoon salt, and the cayenne in a medium bowl. Mix well. Stir in the egg. Shape into 6 patties. Refrigerate until firm, 30 minutes to 1 hour.

To make the red pepper purée: Combine the red peppers, lemon juice, and olive oil in a blender. Purée. Season with salt and pepper. Set aside.

Put the greens in a medium bowl. Add 1 tablespoon of the olive oil and the vinegar. Sprinkle with salt and pepper and toss to coat evenly. Set aside

Heat 1 tablespoon of the olive oil in large nonstick skillet over medium heat. Add the crab cakes and cook until golden brown, 2 to 3 minutes on each side.

Spoon a small amount of the red pepper purée into the center of 4 to 6 plates. Arrange a crab cake in the center and top with a small bunch of the greens. Sprinkle with the chives.

SERVES 4 TO 6 AS A FIRST COURSE

Café Kinyon's Beef Tenderloin with a Farci Crust

Caterer Kinyon Gordon is always looking for a new way to present fillet of beef, his most-requested main course. This recipe for tenderloin with a crust of Italian sausage and ground veal is an updated version of an unforgettable entrée he first enjoyed twenty-five years ago at the restaurant of Bay Area food personality Narsai David. Go for the traditional big cab with it. You can't go wrong with Shafer, Robert Mondavi, or Caymus.

---

1 pound sweet Italian sausage, casing removed
1 pound ground veal
½ cup chopped onion
2 teaspoons crushed garlic
½ cup heavy cream
4 egg yolks
1 teaspoon Worcestershire sauce
1 tablespoon dried tarragon
1½ teaspoons kosher salt
½ teaspoon freshly ground pepper
1 beef tenderloin (1½ pounds)
Olive oil for brushing

Place the sausage, veal, onion, and garlic in the bowl of a food processor and purée. Add the cream, egg yolks, Worcestershire sauce, tarragon, salt, and pepper. Pulse until thoroughly combined and the mixture is nearly smooth. Cover and refrigerate for 1 hour.

Preheat the oven to 375°F. Cut 2 sheets of waxed paper slightly longer than the beef tenderloin. Brush one side of each with olive oil. Spread the sausage mixture all over the first sheet of waxed paper. Cover with the second sheet and press the mixture into an even layer. Remove the top sheet. Place the tenderloin lengthwise on the long side of the sausage mixture. Carefully roll the mixture around the tenderloin to completely cover it, pressing the edges together to seal. Remove the wax paper, transfer to a roasting pan, and bake until browned on the outside and rare on the inside, about 60 minutes. Remove from the oven and let sit 5 to 10 minutes before slicing.

SERVES 6 TO 8 AS A MAIN COURSE

Brian Streeter's Orange-Braised Chicken with Broccoli Rabe

Brian Streeter is so talented that he makes everything he cooks look effortless. This dish is simple to prepare and bursting with bright flavors. It is delectable when enjoyed with Cakebread Cellars Sauvignon Blanc.

2 tablespoons olive oil
One 3- to 4-pound fryer chicken, cut into 8 pieces
Kosher salt
Freshly ground pepper
1 cup fresh orange juice (about 4 large Valencia oranges)
¼ cup dry white wine
2 bay leaves
3 small dried red chiles
1 pound broccoli rabe, cut into 3-inch pieces

Heat the olive oil in a heavy stainless-steel sauté pan or skillet over high heat. Season the chicken with salt and pepper. Sear until browned, about 3 minutes on each side. Transfer the breast pieces to a plate. Push the remaining chicken pieces to one side of the pan and pour out any oil. Add the orange juice and wine to the pan and reduce heat to low. Tuck the bay leaves and chiles in between the chicken pieces. Partially cover the pan. Cook on a low simmer for 15 minutes.

Return the breasts to the pan. Cover and cook 10 minutes.

While the chicken is cooking, bring a large saucepan of salted water to a boil. Add the broccoli rabe and cook until al dente, about 2 minutes. Drain and set aside.

Transfer the chicken to a serving dish and increase the heat to high under the pan. Cook until the liquid becomes thick and syrupy, about 5 minutes. Add the broccoli rabe and toss to mix. Arrange next to the chicken on the serving dish.

SERVES 4 AS A MAIN COURSE

Shannon O'Shaughnessy's Osso Buco with White Bean Purée

Howell Mountain was one of the first areas in Napa Valley planted to Bordeaux varietals, so it makes perfect sense that the O'Shaughnessys are producing a cabernet sauvignon there. Shannon O'Shaughnessy Ryan learned to cook this dish from her mother, Betty, who ran an informal cooking school in Minnesota before starting their winery. Osso buco begs to be accompanied with a glass of the O'Shaughnessy's wine or another of its stature.

Six 1-pound veal shanks, each 2 inches thick and 2½ inches in diameter
1 cup dry red wine
2 cups veal demi-glace (see Note)
3 tablespoons sun-dried tomato paste or regular tomato paste
10 garlic cloves
1 carrot, peeled and chopped
4 slices bacon, cooked and crumbled
3 tablespoons julienned fresh basil leaves
3 Turkish bay leaves or 1 California bay leaf (see Morton & Bassett, page 166)
1 teaspoon fresh thyme leaves
Chopped zest of 1 orange
Kosher salt
Freshly ground pepper

White Bean Purée
1 cup dried Great Northern beans, soaked overnight and drained
4 cups water
3 garlic cloves
2 teaspoons minced fresh sage
1½ teaspoons kosher salt
Freshly ground pepper

Preheat the oven to 350°F.

Heat a Dutch oven large enough to hold all six shanks in a single layer over high heat. Add the veal and cook, turning as needed, until browned on all sides, about 10 minutes. Transfer to a plate. Add the red wine to the pan and stir to scrape up the browned bits from the bottom of the pan. Bring to a boil and cook until reduced by half, about 5 minutes, stirring frequently. Add the demi-glace or stock and bring to a boil. Stir in the tomato paste. Return the veal to the pan and add the garlic, carrot, bacon, basil, bay leaves, thyme, and orange zest. Cover and bake in oven until the meat begins to fall from the bones, about 2 hours.

While the meat is cooking, make the beans. Put the beans in a large saucepan. Add the water, garlic, and sage. Bring to a boil over medium-high heat. Reduce heat to low, cover, and cook at a low simmer for 30 minutes. Taste for tenderness. Season with salt and pepper. Continue cooking until the beans are completely tender, about 30 more minutes. Drain the beans in a colander set over a bowl to capture the cooking liquid. Transfer the beans to a food processor and purée, adding the reserved cooking liquid ½ cup at a time as needed to make a smooth mixture. Taste and add salt and pepper if needed. Transfer to a clean saucepan with a lid. Set aside.

Transfer the veal to a plate, cover, and keep warm. Transfer the remaining contents of the Dutch oven to a food mill set over a bowl and purée. Return to the pan. Bring to a boil over medium-high heat and cook until reduced, 10 to 15 minutes. Season with salt and pepper to taste. Reheat the bean purée. Divide the purée among 6 plates and set a shank on top. Spoon the sauce over the top of the meat or around the edge of the plate.

Note: Demi-glace is an ultra-reduced brown stock with an intense flavor. For this recipe you can purchase demi-glace or substitute brown stock (page 332) in its place. The best commercial demi-glace is Demi-Glace Gold, a national brand sold in the soup aisle of most grocery stores.

SERVES 6 AS A MAIN COURSE

Zinfandel-Braised Lamb with Crème Fraîche Mashed Potatoes

It is not surprising that cooking with wine is nearly as common as drinking wine in the Napa Valley. This dish relies on red wine to add flavor and help tenderize the meat. Use a high-quality zinfandel, which can be easily found and will not be too expensive. Two cups is approximately half a bottle, so if you plan on serving the same wine with dinner, you may want to have another bottle on hand.

---

2 tablespoons all-purpose flour
2 tablespoons chopped fresh rosemary
1 teaspoon kosher salt
½ teaspoon freshly ground pepper
2 pounds cubed leg of lamb meat
6 garlic cloves
3 shallots, halved
½ cup olive oil
1 onion, cut into 1-inch dice
1 fennel bulb, quartered and sliced
2 large carrots, peeled and cut into 1-inch-thick slices
1 large celery root, peeled and cut into 1-inch cubes
1 large parsnip, peeled and cut into 1-inch cubes
2 cups zinfandel
2 cups chicken or brown stock (pages 332–333)

Crème Fraîche Mashed Potatoes
1½ pounds Yukon Gold potatoes, peeled and quartered
1½ teaspoons kosher salt
4 tablespoons butter
½ cup crème fraîche
¼ teaspoon freshly ground pepper

¼ cup chopped fresh flat-leaf parsley

Combine the flour, rosemary, salt, and pepper in a plastic bag or large bowl. Stir to mix well. Add the lamb and toss to coat evenly. Set aside.

Heat the garlic and shallots in a large sauté pan or skillet over medium heat until translucent, about 3 minutes. Increase heat to medium-high and add ¼ cup of the olive oil and the onion; cook for 5 minutes. Add the fennel, carrots, celery root, and parsnip and cook for 5 minutes. Transfer to a bowl with a slotted spoon. Add the remaining ¼ cup olive oil and heat over medium-high heat.

Add the lamb and flour mixture and cook, turning as needed, until the lamb is evenly browned, 5 to 7 minutes. Add the wine and stock. Bring to a boil. Return the vegetables to the pan, return to a boil, reduce heat to low, cover, and cook for 1 hour. Remove the lid and cook at a medium simmer until the lamb is tender and the liquid is thickened, 30 minutes to 1 hour.

To make the potatoes: Put the potatoes in a large saucepan and cover with water. Add 1 teaspoon of the salt and bring to a boil over medium-high heat. Cook until tender when pierced with a fork, 10 to 15 minutes. Drain. Return the pot to low heat and press the potatoes through a potato ricer into the pot. Add the butter and crème fraîche, stirring to combine thoroughly. Cook until the butter is melted, about 2 minutes. Add the remaining ½ teaspoon salt and the pepper.

Divide the potatoes among the plates. Spoon the lamb and vegetables over the potatoes and sprinkle with the parsley.

SERVES 4 TO 6 AS A MAIN COURSE

Banana-Walnut-Chocolate Tart

Walnuts were once a highly prized crop in Napa Valley, so much so that John Hartley entered his 1915 harvest and won first place at the Panama-Pacific Expo. There are still a few orchards around, but the commercial harvest is very small. Napa Nuts carries some walnuts grown in the Valley, but any high-quality walnuts will do in this recipe created by my friend Ann Martin. This dessert is great for winter when bananas are the most abundant fresh fruit. Serve this with a port or a late-harvest zinfandel.

---

1 ½ cups (6 ounces) walnut halves
2 tablespoons all-purpose flour
2 tablespoons lightly packed brown sugar
1 tablespoon butter at room temperature
½ cup heavy cream
1 tablespoon maple syrup
6 ounces semisweet chocolate, chopped
3 bananas, peeled and sliced

Preheat the oven to 375°F.

Spread the walnuts out on a baking sheet and bake until lightly toasted and fragrant, about 5 minutes. Remove from the oven and transfer 1 cup of the walnuts to a food processor. Add the flour and brown sugar and pulse until a fine mixture is achieved. Add the butter and pulse for 5 seconds to make a crumbly mixture. Press evenly into the bottom and sides of an 8-inch tart pan with a removable bottom. Bake until slightly firm, about 8 minutes. Remove from the oven and let cool completely.

Combine the cream and maple syrup in a small saucepan. Bring to a low boil over medium heat. Remove from heat, add the chocolate, and stir until smooth. Line the tart shell with the banana slices. Pour the chocolate mixture over the bananas. Arrange the remaining walnut halves around the edge of the tart. Refrigerate until chilled, 1 to 2 hours. Serve cold.

SERVES 6 AS A DESSERT

Faux Brûlée

Crème brûlée is pudding for grownups. Many pastry chefs add their own touch, as in Bistro Jeanty's crème brûlée with chocolate and Celadon's espresso-flavored version. The classic version is flavored simply with vanilla and topped with caramelized sugar.

1 cup heavy cream
1 cup half-and-half
1 vanilla bean, split lengthwise
3 egg yolks
5 tablespoons sugar

Preheat the oven to 300°F. Combine the cream and half-and-half in a small saucepan. With the tip of a knife, scrape the seeds from the vanilla pod into the saucepan. Add the pod and heat over medium heat until bubbles form around the edge of the pan, about 5 minutes. Set aside for 5 to 10 minutes to steep.

Beat the egg yolks and 1 tablespoon of the sugar together in a medium bowl until pale in color. Gradually whisk in the cream mixture in a steady stream. Return to the saucepan and cook, stirring constantly, over low heat until the mixture becomes thick enough to coat the back of the spoon, about 5 minutes.

Remove the vanilla bean pod and pour the custard into four 1-cup ramekins or custard dishes. Place in a baking pan with high sides and add hot water to the pan to reach halfway up the sides of the ramekins. Bake until set but still a little jiggly in the center, about 35 minutes. Remove from the oven and let cool. Refrigerate until chilled through, at least 2 hours.

At least 1 hour before serving, pour the remaining 4 tablespoons sugar into a small, heavy saucepan and heat over medium-low heat. Cook until all of the sugar is melted and begins to turn a golden brown, swirling the pan to melt the sugar evenly. (Be careful not to touch the sugar; it is very hot.) Spoon a very small amount of the sugar over each custard, spreading it out into as thin a layer as possible. Refrigerate for at least 1 hour.

SERVES 4 AS A DESSERT

Jim Neal's Dried Fruit Compote with Corn Bread Financiers

This dessert is a masterful solution for winter's scarcity of fresh fruits. It's crucial that really flavorful dried fruit from a reliable source is used. Financiers are traditionally made with almonds, but cornmeal makes a crunchy, satisfying cake as well. Almost any dessert wine would do this dish justice.

Dried Fruit Compote
½ vanilla bean, split lengthwise
1 cup red verjus (see Fusion Foods, page 164)
½ cup dried apricots
½ cup dried cherries
½ cup golden raisins
1 small stick cinnamon
½ teaspoon black peppercorns
2 cloves

Cornbread Financiers
½ cup (1 stick) unsalted butter
6 tablespoons plus ¼ cup granulated sugar
1 cup medium-grind cornmeal
½ cup confectioners' sugar
¼ cup cake flour
Pinch of kosher salt
¼ cup buttermilk
4 egg whites
Pinch of cream of tartar

To make the compote: With the tip of a knife, scrape the seeds from the vanilla pod into a medium saucepan. Add the pod, verjus, apricots, cherries, raisins, cinnamon, peppercorns, and cloves. Bring to a boil over medium heat. Cook until the liquid is completely absorbed, about 10 minutes. Remove the vanilla bean, cinnamon stick, peppercorns, and cloves. Let cool to room temperature.

Preheat the oven to 400°F.

To make the financiers: Melt the butter in a small saucepan over low heat. Remove from heat. Brush six ½-cup rectangular pastry tins with a little of the butter. Coat each with 1 tablespoon of the granulated sugar. Set the tins in the freezer to solidify the butter. Let the remaining butter cool.

Combine the cornmeal, confectioners' sugar, the ¼ cup granulated sugar, the flour, and salt in a medium bowl. Stir to blend. Stir in the buttermilk and remaining melted butter until blended.

Whip the egg whites and cream of tartar together with an electric mixer on high speed until soft peaks form, about 1 minute. Fold the cornmeal mixture into the egg whites. Divide among the prepared tins. Place on a baking sheet and bake until a skewer inserted in the center comes out clean, about 15 minutes. Remove from the oven and let cool for 5 minutes.

Unmold the financiers onto a cutting board and cut into ½-inch-thick slices, keeping the rectangles intact. Arrange on a serving platter and spoon the compote around the edge of the platter.

SERVES 6 AS A DESSERT

Brown Stock

Stock is the most important ingredient in any recipe that calls for it. This recipe for brown stock is made with a mixture of beef and veal bones, which are easy to get from any butcher. Making stock is simple but time consuming, so I suggest making it in large quantities and freezing it in 1- and 2-cup measures in plastic bags or containers for easy access. You can cook it for less time, but longer is better.

---

4 pounds veal bones
2 pounds beef bones
4 cups dry red wine
6 quarts water
2 onions, chopped
2 large carrots, peeled and chopped
4 celery stalks, chopped
One 4-ounce can tomato paste
2 teaspoons black peppercorns

Preheat the oven to 400°F.

Spread the veal and beef bones out in a single layer in a heavy roasting pan. Roast until browned, about 1 hour.

Transfer the bones to a large stockpot. Pour the fat out of the roasting pan and place the pan over medium-high heat. Add the wine and cook until reduced by half, about 5 minutes, stirring to scrape up the browned bits from the bottom of the pan. Add to the stockpot with the bones. Add the water, onion, carrots, celery, tomato paste, and peppercorns. Bring to a boil over medium heat. Reduce heat to the lowest temperature possible to keep the mixture at a low simmer. Cook, uncovered, until reduced by half, 12 to 18 hours (I usually start stock in the evening and let it cook overnight). Strain through a colander into a bowl. Strain through a fine-meshed sieve into a narrow container. Refrigerate until the fat solidifies on the top. Remove the congealed fat with a spoon or plastic spatula. Divide the stock among smaller containers and refrigerate for up to 3 days or freeze for up to 2 months.

MAKES 8 TO 12 CUPS

Chicken Stock

Chicken stock is a crucial ingredient that can really make an impact in the final taste of a dish. I prefer to only use homemade, but if you prefer to use a store-bought version, I recommend the stock that is sold in the box, not the can. Use the recipe below for a light stock, double the quantity called for and cook to reduce it for a rich stock.

---

5 pounds chicken scraps or necks and backs
4 quarts water
1 onion, chopped
2 large carrots, chopped
2 celery stalks, chopped
2 teaspoons black peppercorns
4 thyme sprigs

Preheat the oven to 400°F.

Spread the chicken pieces out in a single layer in a heavy roasting pan. Roast for 1 hour. Transfer to a large stockpot. Add the water, onion, carrots, celery, peppercorns, and thyme. Bring to a boil over medium heat. Reduce heat to the lowest temperature possible to keep the mixture at a low simmer. Cook, uncovered, until reduced by half, about 12 hours (I usually start stock in the evening and let it cook overnight). Strain through a colander into a bowl. Strain through a fine-meshed sieve into a narrow container. Refrigerate until the fat solidifies on the top. Remove the congealed fat with a spoon or plastic spatula. Divide the stock into smaller containers and store in self-sealing plastic bags or other containers and refrigerate for up to 3 days or freeze for up to 2 months.

MAKES 6 TO 8 CUPS

Restaurant Directory

This at-a-glance directory lists restaurants by the average price of a meal for two people. Following the restaurant name is the town where it is located and, when available, outdoor seating is noted.

The following values have been calculated based on dinner prices, and includes two starters, two main courses, and two desserts. Prices do not include beverages or tax.

GOOD VALUE

Café Kinyon; Yountville
Café Sarafornia; Calistoga
Cantinetta Wine Bar; St. Helena; OUTDOOR SEATING
Gordon's (Breakfast and Lunch); Yountville; OUTDOOR SEATING
Soscol Café; Napa

MODERATE

All Seasons; Calistoga
Bouchon; Yountville; OUTDOOR SEATING
Café Lucy; Napa
Compadres Mexican Bar & Grill; Yountville; OUTDOOR SEATING
Flat Iron Grill; Calistoga
Foothill Café; Napa
Fujiya Restaurant; Napa
Green Valley Cafe; St. Helena
La Boucane; Napa
Mary's Pizza Shack; Napa
Moore's Landing; Napa; OUTDOOR SEATING
Pacific Blues Café; Yountville; OUTDOOR SEATING
Pasta Prego; Napa; SEASONAL OUTDOOR SEATING
Pearl; Napa; OUTDOOR SEATING
Red Hen Cantina; Napa; OUTDOOR SEATING
Rutherford Grill; Rutherford
Saketini; Napa
Sushi Mambo; Napa
The Grill at Meadowood; St. Helena
Uva Trattoria; Napa
Zuzu; Napa

```
GOOD VALUE = $30 OR LESS
MODERATE = $31 TO $65
EXPENSIVE = $66 TO $100
VERY EXPENSIVE = $100 AND ABOVE
```

EXPENSIVE

Bistro Don Giovanni; Napa; OUTDOOR SEATING
Bistro Jeanty; Yountville
Brannan's Grill; Calistoga
Brix Restaurant; Yountville; OUTDOOR SEATING
Catahoula Restaurant & Saloon; Calistoga
Celadon; Napa; OUTDOOR SEATING
Cole's Chop House; Napa
Julia's Kitchen at Copia; Napa
Martini House; St. Helena, OUTDOOR SEATING
Miramonte Restaurant; St. Helena; OUTDOOR SEATING
Mustards Grill; Yountville
Piatti Restaurant; Yountville; OUTDOOR SEATING
Pinot Blanc; St. Helena; OUTDOOR SEATING
Roux; St. Helena
Terra Restaurant; St. Helena
Tra Vigne Restuarant; St. Helena; OUTDOOR SEATING
Triple S Ranch; Calistoga
Wappo Bar & Bistro; Calistoga; OUTDOOR SEATING
Wine Spectator at Greystone; St. Helena

VERY EXPENSIVE

Auberge du Soleil; Rutherford; OUTDOOR SEATING
Domaine Chandon; Yountville
La Toque Restaurant; Rutherford; OUTDOOR SEATING
The Restaurant at Meadowood; St. Helena
The French Laundry; Yountville

Index

Table of Equivalents

The exact equivalents in the following tables have been rounded for convenience.

LIQUID/DRY MEASURES

U.S.	Metric
¼ teaspoon	1.25 milliliters
½ teaspoon	2.5 milliliters
1 teaspoon	5 milliliters
1 tablespoon (3 teaspoons)	15 milliliters
1 fluid ounce (2 tablespoons)	30 milliliters
¼ cup	60 milliliters
⅓ cup	80 milliliters
½ cup	120 milliliters
1 cup	240 milliliters
1 pint (2 cups)	480 milliliters
1 quart (4 cups; 32 ounces)	960 milliliters
1 gallon (4 quarts)	3.84 liters
1 ounce (by weight)	28 grams
1 pound	454 grams
2.2 pounds	1 kilogram

LENGTH

U.S.	Metric
⅛ inch	3 millimeters
¼ inch	6 millimeters
½ inch	12 millimeters
1 inch	2.5 centimeters

OVEN TEMPERATURE

Fahrenheit	Celsius	Gas
250	120	½
275	140	1
300	150	2
325	160	3
350	180	4
375	190	5
400	200	6
425	220	7
450	230	8
475	240	9
500	260	10